CW00470187

PARADISE
REVEALED

PARADISE REVEALED

*Natural History
in nineteenth-century
Australia*

Colin Finney

Museum of Victoria
Melbourne

First published 1993 by the
Museum of Victoria
328 Swanston Street
Melbourne 3000

National Library of Australia
Cataloguing-in-Publication data:

Finney, C. M. (Colin Michael), 1950–
    Paradise revealed.

    Bibliography.
    Includes index.
    ISBN 0 7306 2494 3.

    1. Natural history — Australia — History. I. Museum of Victoria.
    II. Title.

508.94

This book has been phototypeset in 10½/12 pt
Bembo, and produced in an edition of
one thousand copies.

Cover and text designed by Peter Yates
Typeset by Abb-typesetting Pty Ltd, 126 Oxford Street, Collingwood, Vic 3066
Printed by Brown Prior Anderson, 5 Evans Street, Burwood, Vic 3125

To my parents:
Jayne King Finney
Clement Seymour Finney

CONTENTS

LIST OF ILLUSTRATIONS

19 'Punch's Illustrations of Natural History: Cynocephalus papio, or common baboon', *Melbourne Punch* 4 October 1866.

20 'Green Tree Snake: Dendrophis punctulata' by Gerard Krefft, from *The Snakes of Australia*, 1869.

21 'Australian Vegetation: Ficus Macrophylla (Moreton Bay Fig) in foreground', the frontispiece of W. R. Guilfoyle's *Australian Botany: specially designed for the use of schools*, second edition, 1884.

22 'The Sooty Opossum' from Gerard Krefft's *The Mammals of Australia*, 1871.

23 'Brush-tailed Phascogale [Tuan] *Phascogale*' by John Cotton.

24 An excursion of the Linnean Society of New South Wales on the Nepean River 29 September 1888. From left to right *standing* Professor J. W. Stephens, Messrs Skuse, Merick de Merick, J. J. Fletcher MA; *sitting* Messrs Henry Deane FLS, McBetchie, J. H. Maiden FLS, J. Brazier FLS, Dr J. C. Cot FLS, Sir William Macleay FLS. From the John Brazier Papers *by courtesy of the Mitchell Library, State Library of New South Wales.*

FOREWORD

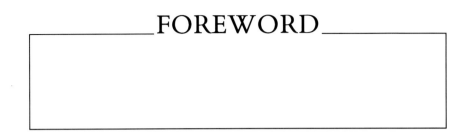

The early generations of European visitors to Australia found themselves surrounded by a flora and fauna entirely different from anything they had seen before. For naturalists, this land in which 'all things were queer and opposite' was a cornucopia, and from Joseph Banks onwards they avidly collected the novelties that abounded in order to classify and name them according to the principles of order established by Linnaeus or his successors. Short-term visitors carried away vast numbers of specimens to fill the drawing rooms and museum cabinets of Europe. Some of those who came and stayed made money by becoming professional collectors to supply the popular market 'at home'. Others, less commercially inclined, sought out new species for the purpose of serious scientific study, either by themselves or, as was almost always the case in the early years, by patrons in the upper echelons of European science.

As the settler population grew, so too did the number of residents who took a systematic interest in Australia's unusual natural forms. This made feasible the formation of scientific societies where like-minded people could seek support and encouragement, and exchange information and ideas. Colin Finney in his new book explores how this worked out in practice, from the coming together of the tiny but ambitiously titled Philosophical Society of Australasia, founded in Sydney in 1821, to the formation of the Australasian Association for the Advancement of Science (forerunner of ANZAAS), established in 1888 with very different objectives and embodying a rather different view of what the scientific investigation of nature amounted to. He offers us, in short, a social history of natural history in Australia during the nineteenth century.

In the early days, Finney shows, when the population of the various colonies remained small, any scientific society that was formed depended for its strength and legitimacy upon gaining the support of the local governor. Scientific societies flourished under scientifically inclined governors such as Sir Thomas Brisbane in New South Wales, 1821–25, or Sir John Franklin in Van Diemen's Land, 1837–43, but otherwise they languished. Yet in a small community, their depending so closely on gubernatorial support also meant that such societies quickly became involved in the factionalism and political in-fighting that invariably surrounded the governor's office, and rarely survived for very long.

The rapid rise in population during the gold-rush years and the granting of responsible government to the various southeastern colonies in the 1850s created a very different atmosphere for scientific work and for the formation of scientific societies.

Especially in the now separate colony of Victoria, a series of new scientific appointments provided a nucleus of professional scientists around whom strong central institutions could form. Finney describes how personal rivalries on a scale that had proved fatal to earlier scientific societies were here overridden by the interests of the larger group who wanted their institutions to survive, but how the group's early optimism was then seared by the disasters of the exploring expedition they sponsored under the leadership of Burke and Wills.

Finney goes on to discuss the impact of Darwinian theory on Australian natural history and the controversies it engendered, and also the emergence of natural history as a popular activity for the middle classes in the latter decades of the nineteenth century. In this context, he considers both the gradual introduction of systematic science teaching in some schools in the different colonies during this period, and the establishment of various field naturalists' clubs to cater for the enhanced public interest. Finally, he describes the rise of biology as a new, experimentally oriented and professionally based life science during the final decades of the century, the relegation of the old-style natural history to the status of an amateur pursuit, and the uneasy tension that developed between the two approaches, which persists to the present day.

The story Finney tells is an important one that brings new insights into how earlier generations of immigrant Australians went about studying nature's astonishing productions in the island continent that they had made their home. Natural history like any other science is an essentially social activity, the successful prosecution of which requires appropriate supporting institutions. Finney's work demonstrates this anew, and in the process tells us as much about the evolution of Australian society as it does about the history of Australian science.

R. W. Home
Department of History and Philosophy of Science
University of Melbourne

PREFACE

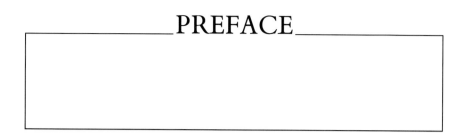

The recent upsurge of interest in all things historical means that a book about the social history of Australian science can no longer commence with a *tabula rasa*. In particular, two studies provided the stimulus for the present work. The first, David Allen's *The Naturalist in Britain; A Social History*, broadened my appreciation of the interactions between natural history and society. The second work, Michael Hoare's unpublished doctoral dissertation 'Science and Scientific Associations in Eastern Australia, 1820–1890' (Australian National University, 1974), not only provided the chronological framework for my study but also reference to many of the primary sources. Hoare's thesis outlines a temporal progression of scientific activity and the creation of scientific or philosophical societies in the Australian colonies: New South Wales in the early 1820s; Van Diemen's Land (Tasmania) from the late 1820s to 1850; Victoria from the 1850s to 1860; and on to intercolonial science during the 1880s.

While accepting Hoare's chronological framework, I have concentrated on examining scientific societies from a social, rather than a scientific or technical, standpoint. My work is therefore concerned with the social milieu in which science was conducted. The difference in Hoare's and my perspective has led to different interpretations of the historical record.

That a social history of natural history deals with groups of individuals is self-evident. For those who feel that Queensland, Western Australia and South Australia have not been given due consideration in this study, my rationale for concentrating on south-eastern Australia is that a social history of natural history requires a community of individuals who are interested in science. These groups did not develop in Queensland, Western Australia, and to a lesser extent South Australia, until much later than the south-eastern colonies.

If science were completely objective, a social history would perhaps be interesting but largely irrelevant. However, despite the much-claimed objectivity of science it is not and cannot be divorced from its practitioners. Changing social conditions affect scientific enquiry, and have a far greater influence on science than is commonly supposed. The agent of this influence is the scientist–naturalist, from the humblest amateur entomologist to the academic molecular geneticist. The concept of the facts and theories of science being in part socially determined may not be universally accepted, but science does not develop in a vacuum and its social environment can be readily shown to affect both the rate of scientific change and its direction. Such influences may be subtle, or as direct as the decisions made by politicians (often with little or no scientific background) as to which disciplines receive government funding. The interaction of science and society is not unidirectional. Just as the social climate may affect an individual scientist, science and scientists influence society. If one disregards the obvious example of nuclear weapons and looks at natural history, the growth of the conservation movement provides a ready example.

The present study, then, concentrates on the practitioners of natural history and the interaction between natural history and society rather than on the technical progress of natural history in Australia. The work is concerned not so much with scientific knowledge, but with scientific activity, and particularly with the social relations of naturalists: relationships between one naturalist and another, between naturalists and the prevailing power structures, and between naturalists and society as a whole. Consequently, there is a focus on groups of naturalists, in most cases on scientific societies, ranging from formal scientific and philosophical societies to groups of individuals with a specific interest in science (such as occasionally occurred in mechanics' institutes prior to the 1850s) and to the connections that existed only in the correspondence of isolated naturalists. In particular, the conditions under which scientific societies arose and the environment, both political and social, that ensured the success or failure of these societies, have been examined. Once societies existed for a few years they tended to settle into a mould, shaken only by the influx of members determined to take the society in a novel direction. But at their outset, societies often articulated the views and the ideology of a particular group of individuals. I have therefore concentrated on the conditions affecting the birth and initial growth of various coteries of individuals and societies. Focusing on social groups of naturalists provides a window through which the evolution of natural history in Australia may be discerned. This study, however, attempts complete coverage neither of all individuals nor all disciplines traditionally considered within the purview of natural history, and while my discussion includes some broad-based societies, the focus is primarily on events and individuals concerned with natural history.

C. M. Finney
Bath
United Kingdom
February 1993

ACKNOWLEDGEMENTS

In a synthesis such as attempted in this volume, one is necessarily dependent on previous research and discussion with colleagues. Although many people facilitated the present work, I can, of necessity, only mention the major contributors.

Firstly, I wish to acknowledge the Science and Humanities Committee of the Museum of Victoria. Under the chairmanship of Norman Wettenhall, the Committee's support for me as the Thomas Ramsay Science and Humanities Scholar for 1985–86 allowed the preparation of this history.

Librarians of various institutions were invariably patient and helpful. I thank in particular Julianne New, librarian of the Museum of Victoria, Tony Marshall and Nicola Foxlee of the manuscript section of the La Trobe Library, and Patricia Jackson, Janice Robertson and Linda West of the Mitchell Library. Other librarians at the Mitchell Library, Sydney; the La Trobe Library, Melbourne; the Tasmanian State Library; the Baillieu Library, University of Melbourne; the Library of the Royal Society of Victoria; and the Library of the Royal Society of Tasmania, were unstinting in their assistance.

Individuals who generously shared their knowledge with me include Barry Butcher, Tom Darragh, Linden Gillbank, Rod Home, Monica MacCallum, Allan McEvey, Roy MacLeod and David Miller. Clement Finney, Rod Home and Monica MacCallum read the entire manuscript. Monica MacCallum contributed substantially to Chapter One; Barry Butcher read Chapter Five and generously shared both primary sources and his ideas on the reception of evolutionary thought in Australia with me; David Miller read Chapters Two and Three; and Roy MacLeod read Chapters One, Five, Six and Seven. Each corrected some of my lapses but none of the aforementioned individuals should be considered to share my interpretation of the historical record. All errors of fact and interpretation remain my responsibility.

The illustrations were photographed by Rodney Start, Museum of Victoria, and Kate Lowe, Australian Museum. Permission to reproduce illustrations was granted by the La Trobe Library, Museum of Victoria, and Jane McGowan.

Finally, this study would never have been completed without the help and support of Denise Rennis.

CHAPTER ONE

the heroic age of natural history

ENGLAND AND AUSTRALIA, 1790–1860

Whatever the convicts' thoughts on being sentenced to transportation to Botany Bay, the European colonization of Australia occurred at an auspicious time in the development of natural history. The exploration and establishment of colonies in Australia coincided with the heyday of natural history in England. Five years prior to James Cook's embarkation on his globe-girdling voyage in HMS *Endeavour*, the English journal, *Critical Review*, declared that the pursuit of natural history had become a national pastime.[1] Although this was an exaggeration of the popularity of natural history, there is little doubt that an interest in the kingdoms—animal, mineral and vegetable—had become widespread. The scientific complement of the *Endeavour*, the inclusion of which established a precedent for future naval expeditions, was both accompanied and funded by young socialite Joseph Banks. Throughout the greater part of the nineteenth century it was European interest in natural history which provided the driving force to the development of natural history in Australia.

Inevitably, during the early years of the European colonization of Australia naturalists worked alone, often isolated for years from contemporaries. Away from the enthusiasm of like-minded colleagues, lacking all but the most elementary texts, their correspondence with other naturalists subject to the vagaries of time, distance, and the affairs of men, the lone naturalist required a single-minded devotion to the subject in order to carry on. It was the heroic age of the naturalist–explorer.[2] Many had only the crudest scientific equipment: a rude plant press for which they invariably lacked paper, a prized magnifying glass not easily replaced if lost or broken, and a receptacle for carrying specimens. The latter might be a vasculum for the better equipped, while the less fortunate often resorted to stripping off their shirts to carry home prize specimens. Whatever their equipment, the major requirement for early naturalists was enthusiasm, and self-education was almost always the only route to expertise.

Under these circumstances early naturalists in Australia were collectors and identifiers, not evaluators. Crates and barrels of specimens were regularly despatched to Europe, where they might be studied by individuals working in a private capacity or by the fortunate few employed in museums. Often the specimens were left to gather dust in ostentatious display, or stored in forgotten closets. Publication of the results of any investigation of the specimens was in distant European journals. A crude simplification of this early period is that natural history in Australia was the physical collection of specimens, and the labels classifying them.

Although this heroic age was to linger on in the unexplored, unsettled outlands of Australia, by the 1820s natural history had reached a secondary stage in New South

Wales and Van Diemen's Land. The number of resident naturalists increased, and formerly isolated naturalists began to make more frequent contact with each other. Natural history had become a social pursuit.[3] At this point a social history of natural history can commence.

Before the middle of the nineteenth century, the study of natural history in the Australian colonies involved little more than acting as a collecting outpost for European science. Australia was at both the physical and intellectual periphery of metropolitan science. One of those active in natural history during the early period, Thomas Parmeter, was somewhat premature in declaring scientific independence in 1829 and in announcing that the despatch of scientific specimens to Europe for evaluation insulted the scientifically literate of the colonies.[4] Although rudimentary institutions such as the Sydney Botanic Gardens and the Australian Museum existed, their potential to become centres of colonial science was limited. During the 1840s, when Ludwig Leichhardt contended that Australian specimens should be preserved in the colonies, the infrastructure of natural history was still lacking. By the 1860s, however, when the call was repeated by Frederick McCoy, there was sufficient local expertise to substantiate the proposal. The more obvious manifestations of European scientific colonialism had begun to break down in the 1850s. Europe was still regarded as the centre of natural history and Australia as peripheral to it, but this perception, for two reasons, was not as clear cut as in earlier years. First, some colonial naturalists, although European-trained, were prepared to dispute their subordinate and inferior role that had allowed European naturalists to dictate and define natural history. Naturalists in the colonies were ready to question, if not the central theories of metropolitan science, then at least isolated facts. Although Australia was far from achieving scientific independence at this time, it had begun the move towards it.[5] A second shift in the centre–periphery relationship occurred when the centre became a relative location. In 1821, whether one lived in Sydney or in the Wellington Valley, the scientific centre was Europe. By the 1860s and 1870s, individuals in towns such as Ballarat perceived Melbourne as the metropolis because of the number and quality of scientists who resided there. Those in Melbourne or Sydney, however, continued to locate themselves at the periphery with regard to Europe. Melbourne botanist Ferdinand Mueller might have had an Australia-wide network which supplied him with specimens, but in turn he was only part of Englishman George Bentham's globe-spanning network of collectors.

The terms 'naturalist', 'amateur', and 'professional' changed, not only over the course of the nineteenth century, but with individual use. It would be foolhardy to adopt precise definitions, but some definition of the terms is necessary to avoid misinterpretation. The word 'naturalist' is applied in this book to individuals working in the three traditional kingdoms of natural history: botany, zoology and geology, the latter generally in the more restricted category of mineralogy. Throughout much of the 1800s, the term 'naturalist' carried a certain ambiguity which was only clarified by the increasing use of the word 'biologist' late in the century. Before 1850, 'naturalist' included both those who earned their living in some other occupation and turned to natural history as an intellectual recreation, and those who derived at least some of their income from natural history, generally as specimen collectors or paid lecturers at mechanics' institutes. These two strands, the individual seeking intellectual amusement and the paid collector, evolved into what were later to be stereotyped by the terms 'amateur' and 'professional'.[6]

The dichotomy of amateur and professional naturalist existed in Australia from almost the first years of colonization, although the distinction was generally masked by social division. John White, surgeon-general of the colony, and Denis Considen, assistant surgeon on the transport *Scarborough*, began natural history observations and collections upon their arrival with the First Fleet in 1788. Three years later the first paid natural history collector, David Burton, began collections for Joseph Banks in the Port Jackson area. Burton can be considered at least a part-time professional, for although employed as a superintendent of convicts, he was paid the considerable sum of £20 per annum to collect for Banks. Burton's career was brief, for within six months of his arrival he died from an accidental, self-inflicted gunshot wound.

In the following years a number of naturalists took up residency in the colonies of New South Wales and Van Diemen's Land: William Paterson, John Lewin, George Caley, Adolarius Humphrey, George Bass, George Suttor, Allan Cunningham, Charles Fraser, and Robert Townson among them. With few exceptions these individuals can be divided into two categories: colonial officers, either military or civil, represented by White, Considen, Paterson and Bass (with the exception of Paterson all were surgeons); and paid collectors such as Burton, Humphrey, Lewin, Caley, Fraser and Cunningham. Despite their generally superior education and training, the officer naturalists upheld the tradition of the gentleman amateur. Natural history, for these men, was generally taken up as a pastime to enliven the tedium of service in the uncivilized regions of the empire. It had the added benefit that exotic specimens could be forwarded to superior officers or powers in the Colonial Office to curry favour. That some, such as William Paterson, seemed to devote more of their energy to this pastime than to their official duties, reflects their commitment to natural history, but does not alter their amateur status.

Several of the professional collectors, Burton and Lewin in particular, held civil posts yet still derived much of their income from collecting or illustrating specimens. More typical of the collectors were Caley, Fraser and Cunningham who obtained their income solely through natural history endeavours. Schooled in the traditional fashion of the Banksian botanical empire, through employment at one of the English botanic gardens, they lacked the formal training of the surgeon naturalist and often had trouble with the theoretical framework of their discipline. George Caley would complain to Joseph Banks of his difficulties with the taxonomic complexities of the Linnaean botanical classification, 'I have tried of late to use the language of Linnaeus in making descriptions, but I have to lament that this is above my reach, and I am afraid it will not be so easily understood . . .'.[7]

The greatest distinction between the amateur officer naturalist and the professional collector during the early years of Australian natural history was that of the individual's social position. Civil and military officers, whatever their background in England, formed the social élite of the colonies. The collectors, even those as talented as Allan Cunningham, never achieved the status necessary to enter this social circle. While often on friendly terms with the genteel military and civil servants, paid collectors were always junior partners rather than equals. Echoing a distinction rife in Victorian England, the remuneration collectors received, for what amateur naturalists did for love alone, lowered their social acceptability. However, none of the amateurs ever showed the dedication to natural history that men such as Caley, Fraser and Cunningham exhibited.

Around 1850, in Australia as in the rest of the Western world, the tension created by applying 'naturalist' to both paid collectors and amateurs led to increased usage of the qualifiers 'amateur' and 'professional'. The term 'professional' began to assume its present meaning of one with an income derived from scientific activity, a career structure, systematic knowledge, advanced training, high status, and membership of societies. In contrast, 'amateur' came to be defined negatively, encompassing all that was not professional. In retrospect a more positive definition is possible: an amateur did not necessarily work outside the knowledge base of the professional, but he or she neither aspired to nor adhered to the criteria set by the professional. The distinction between amateur and professional was bound up in the emergence of science as a career in Australia in the last quarter of the nineteenth century, and the concomitant attempt by scientists to achieve a measure of social justification for science. Much of the exaggerated distinction between amateur and professional was in fact no more than rhetoric employed by scientists as part of their claim for society's resources.

The change in terminology reflected a further shift which became obvious in Australia towards the end of the century and in Europe somewhat earlier: the separation of natural history from the scientific mainstream. Biology replaced natural history. The term 'biology' had been introduced in the early years of the nineteenth century but its popular use dates from the writings of the French philosopher, Auguste Comte, in the 1830s and 1840s. With its emphasis on physiology, biology tended to direct science away from the description and classification that were at the very heart of natural history. This re-orientation of science was a slow process and not achieved until the final third of the century. Natural history, which arose out of an amateur tradition, was captured by professional science for a limited period (approximately 1780 to 1870) and then returned exclusively to amateurs. Although natural history contributed to the way of doing science and helped to lay the foundations for biology, it failed to keep abreast of conceptual and methodological advances, and ignored conventions that were established for the presentation of science. Such has been the decline in standing of natural history that the very term is used pejoratively to describe non-rigorous efforts. Dictionaries now declare natural history to be the study of natural objects, plants, animals and rocks, 'especially as set forth for popular use'.[8] In spite of attempts to reconcile biology and natural history, and the fact that some individuals have bridged the gap, the separation has continued. The intellectual attractiveness of reductionism and specialization still hold sway for most biologists.

During the nineteenth century natural history was impelled by a variety of factors: technical, conceptual and social. Technical advances ranged from the invention of the Wardian case and its later developments, the aquarium and vivarium, to advances in microscopy, such as the correction of spherical aberration of lenses. Conceptual advances provided intermittent impetus. These included the development of natural, rather than artificial, classification systems early in the century; the triumph of geological gradualism in the 1830s, and the advance of evolutionary theory post-1859. Underlying these intellectual developments was a transformation in the way of doing science. Although by no means unknown before the nineteenth century, the concept of science as a way of thinking about the natural world, particularly as a way of asking specific questions about nature, rather than simply gathering large quantities of data for later analysis, was institutionalized towards the end of the century.

Less attention has been paid to the effect of social factors on the development of science than to technical advances. The connections between the colonial governments and naturalists, the rise of a middle class schooled in the ideology of rational amusement, the change in the relationship of science to society, and the status of scientific practitioners, are a few of the social factors that became important during the century.

Natural history in Australia was always driven by its connection with Europe. Major European ideas not only contributed to the century's fascination with science, but were also integral to the social and intellectual climate in which science and, in particular, natural history developed. Transferred to Australia these concepts shaped the intellectual milieu of the colonies. These influential ideas and concepts were mostly introduced into the Australian colonies via Britain, and it is the British interpretation of these ideas that affected natural history in Australia.

Conceptual Frameworks

Natural theology

At the dawn of the nineteenth century the underlying broad philosophical framework of natural history in Britain was the doctrine of natural theology. The rhetorical antagonism between theology and science that characterized much of the second half of the century and most of the twentieth century, was almost non-existent in the early 1800s.[9] Science, if it was considered to have any relationship with theology at all, was subsumed by natural theology, the religious doctrine that sought evidence from nature as proof of the existence of God. Natural theologians held that nature was God's word writ large in the book of the material universe. The study of nature was, therefore, the study of God's work and necessarily led to an admiration of that work. This belief, that nature was a clear manifestation of divine will, was a ready justification for the clergy's traditional interest in natural history.

One of the major attractions of natural theology was that it advanced an argument which, although not necessarily simplifying the bewildering complexity of the natural world, at least gave a reason for that complexity. The answer of the natural theologians to the seemingly unceasing discovery of unknown plant and animal species was that the complexity of the natural world was a signpost left by God to document his existence, for such intricacy would not be necessary to an omnipotent God. The labyrinthine nature of the physical world was testimony to God's existence—the myriad diverse elements of the world could not function together any other way. As a practical demonstration of this argument the Reverend William Paley proposed the example of a watch found on a heath. Despite its physical location in the natural world, the complicated mechanism of the watch immediately indicated its human origin. Paley noted, 'There cannot be design without a designer; contrivance without a contriver . . .'.[10] Just as the intricate mechanism of the watch indicated human intervention, so too did the immensely more complicated interactions of the material world indicate that it had been constructed by the ultimate designer.

The tenets of natural theology were all well-rehearsed before William Paley published his *Natural Theology; or, Evidences of the Existence and Attributes of the Deity collected from the Appearances of Nature* in 1802.[11] Paley, however, presented the argument in cogent terms and supplied practical illustrations (although many of these, including the archetypal watch on the heath, were recycled from previous writers).

Natural theology remained as the framework of natural history throughout the first decades of the nineteenth century and continued as a theological argument for much longer. The physical sciences, with their basic principles firmly grounded in mathematical and observational arguments, had removed God one step by the beginning of the nineteenth century. Natural philosophers continued to include God as the first cause in their world view, but confined their science to secondary causes. The uncoupling of natural theology from natural history had started by the 1820s, and was in part attributable to the concerted attempts of cleric geologists to use geological evidence to reinforce Biblical revelation. To link geology to a strict interpretation of the Mosaic record required that natural theologians support the 'catastrophe' view of geological development, instead of the gradualist thesis which held that geological changes occurred gradually. The Reverend William Buckland's *Vindiciae Geologicae; or, the Connexion of Geology with Religion Explained* (1820), *Reliquiae diluvianae* (1823) and *Geology and Mineralogy considered with reference to Natural Theology* (1836) linked geology to theology, although many contemporary observers felt it did so to the detriment of both. When geological gradualism gained supremacy over catastrophism in the 1830s, the close connection of catastrophism with natural theology tarnished some of the gloss of natural theology.

Emigrants and visitors arriving in the colonies brought the tenets of natural theology to Australian shores. One such individual was the Reverend Charles Wilton, fellow of both the Cambridge Philosophical Society and the Ashmolean Society of Oxford, who arrived in New South Wales in 1827. In publishing his *Australian Quarterly Journal of Theology, Literature and Science* (1828–29), Wilton championed the gospel of natural theology.

> The Botanist, in investigating the different orders and qualities of the various plants, which meet his researches, may have his mind directed to that Omnipotent Being . . . The Astronomer, while he surveys the brilliant luminaries of the skies . . . penetrates into the inner vail, even into the Heaven of Heavens—the abode of everlasting light and glory. The Mineralogist . . . may view the mighty wonders of that hand, which out of nothing formed the earth and all things . . . The Geologist . . . beholds the exact accomplishment of Scripture and is enabled, by adducing the strongest evidence of a universal Deluge, to put to silence the Infidel and the sceptic.[12]

Wilton also advocated natural theology in the pulpit and, in a sermon in 1827, he commenced with a passionate rendition of the design argument.[13]

Rational amusement

The ethical overtones of natural theology, and its explicit use of the natural world both to illustrate and justify a moral code, were absorbed into the diverse set of ideas that comprised rational amusement (also called 'rational entertainment'). Natural theology had its basis in theological dogma whereas the origins of rational amusement were deeply rooted in the social life of Victorian England. Rational amusement achieved wide influence because it not only acted as an organizing principle for the intellectual life of several economic classes, but was also seen by those in power as an instrument to maintain their position.

The concept of rational amusement was a reaction to the restrictive moral framework of the nineteenth century; it met the need of individuals to justify activities that otherwise could be criticized as frivolous entertainment. To qualify as rational amusement an activity had to be at least mentally instructive, but preferably morally instructive as well. As naturalists' clubs were always quick to point out, the pursuit of natural history had obvious intellectual, social, moral and physical merits. The study of natural history was eulogized as a panacea: intellectually, it helped train the mind; socially, it offered congenial company; physically, it rejuvenated the body by fresh air and exercise; and morally, it diverted men's thoughts from the burden and strife of everyday existence. The moral argument for rational amusement was always of greatest importance, and one of the most often repeated justifications for the pursuit of natural history during the nineteenth century was that it was opposed to materialism, the dreaded disease of the Victorian intellect.

Mechanics' institutes

The most obvious manifestation of rational amusement was the mechanics' institute movement. Mechanics' institutes originated in Britain during the first decades of the nineteenth century, and found a notable advocate in George Birkbeck. Birkbeck, appointed professor of natural philosophy at Anderson's University in Glasgow, offered lectures to mechanics and operatives from 1800 to 1804 and, subsequent to his arrival in London in 1809, was instrumental in the establishment of the London Institute for the Diffusion of Science, Medicine and Art.

During the early 1820s, prototype mechanics' institutes opened in both Britain (Edinburgh School of Arts, 1821; Glasgow Mechanics' Institute, 1823; London Mechanics' Institute, 1823, the last under Birkbeck's stewardship) and the United States (New York Mechanical and Scientific Institution, 1822). The Glasgow Mechanics' Institute, with a programme that included lectures, a library and a museum, provided a model for future institutes. By 1825 almost seventy mechanics' institutes had been established in Britain and during the late 1820s and 1830s the movement spread worldwide, including the Australian colonies.

The originators of the mechanics' institutes movement had two primary goals in mind: disseminating rational (scientific) knowledge among the working classes, and moral elevation through intellectual amusement.[14] Ostensibly, such institutes aimed to impart to ordinary workmen a sound basic knowledge of scientific theory relevant to their labours. A factory worker would be taught the mechanical principles upon which the operation of his machinery depended; a worker in the dye industry could study the chemistry of dyestuffs, and so on. There was also an ideological element in the idea of the institutes. The reason a worker should be taught the scientific principles of his employment was to make him a better and more productive employee. The quest for economic efficiency was hidden in the guise of education. Just as important were the social aspects of institutes. The possibility and desirability of educating the working masses was an accepted part of the mechanics' institutes' ethic. Tied to this was the idea that increased knowledge was an antidote to social unrest, and that by educating mechanics the latter would have a vested interest in maintaining the status quo.

The idea of, and arguments for, rational amusement arose in England. Transplanted to Australia the concept found fertile ground, first in mechanics' institutes and later in field naturalists' clubs. In 1825 the Reverend Thomas Scott brought a commission from England to establish mechanics' institutes in New South Wales. Subsequently an advertisement appeared in the *Sydney Gazette* heralding the formation of mechanics' institutes in Sydney, Parramatta, Liverpool and Windsor, under the authority of the Church and School Corporation.[15] Despite the advertisement, nothing eventuated in New South Wales until 1833.

In the first half of the century mechanics' institutes were established in the major towns of the Australian colonies, Hobart (1827), Sydney (1833), Newcastle (1835), Adelaide (1838), Melbourne (1839) and Launceston (1842). The rapid spread of the movement is evident from the inauguration of a Hobart institute within four years of the founding of the Glasgow and London models. The heyday of the institute in Australia, however, only really began in the 1850s and during the following two decades they became a feature of many smaller towns. However, when the popularity of the institutes was greatest, the institutes' active participation in science had declined. In Australia, the science presented at mechanics' institutes was superficial and best exemplified by the 'wonders of nature' approach. The extent of the moral content of rational amusement is apparent in the programme of the Prahran Mechanics' Institute, established in 1854 in what was then an outer suburb of Melbourne. The Institute was established for 'the mental and moral improvement of members, and providing rational amusement by means of lectures, library, etc.'[16] The first year's lecture series, which often took the form of a debate, included topics such as 'Has the introduction of machinery been a benefit to the working class?' (the meeting voted for benefit), 'Has the pen of the novelist been a benefit or injury to the mind?' (injury), 'Which has the more evil tendency, novel reading or music?' (music), and 'Whether the writings of Byron have moral or immoral tendencies' (immoral). When the Prahran Town Hall with its lending library opened in 1861, it took over many of the functions of the Prahran Mechanics' Institute and the Institute declined.

Clerics or strongly religious figures found a natural home in mechanics' institutes, taking the lead in both establishing institutes and organizing institute activities. Among the strong clerical contingent involved in early institutes were Henry Carmichael (Sydney Mechanics' School of Arts), John West and Charles Price (Launceston), John Lillie (Hobart), and William Moss (Prahran).

Particularly after the 1850s, rational amusement in Australia took on a special emphasis. The discovery of gold, which so changed the history of Australia, placed those of sterling moral rectitude in an uncomfortable position. One of the major worries for these moral arbitrators of society was the preoccupation of the lower and middle classes with the pursuit of money.[17] The arch-apologist for the aristocracy, de Tocqueville, in his four-volume study *Democracy in America* (1835–40), had warned of the almost universal passion of Americans for accumulating money. Australians seemed similarly acquisitive. This was of particular concern to the moral guardians, for the pursuit of money was seen as detrimental to moral development. This uneasiness had been voiced before the 1850s, but after the discovery of gold a continuous chorus of newspaper pundits decried the preoccupation of Australians with money-making and outdoor sports (horse racing and cricket featuring prominently).[18] Typical was the *Sydney Morning Herald*: 'It is often said of these communities by way of reproach, that they take little interest in anything beyond money-grubbing or in practical pursuits which lead to material advantage . . .'.[19]

The idea that material wealth led to a preoccupation with sensual pleasure and therefore moral degeneracy was constantly reiterated to Australian society. Time and again those engaged in mercantile pursuits were encouraged to take up natural history as a relief from the hurly-burly of the counting house. Natural history would extend them intellectually, promote social intercourse, instil moral direction, and refresh the wearied body. Field clubs, in particular, stressed the benefits of social interaction and that their excursions promoted health.

With their vast collections and concentration on objects rather than processes, museums epitomize rational amusement and give form to the idea of useful entertainment which both educates and amuses.

Materialism

The heresy that both natural theology and rational amusement sought to combat was materialism—the scourge of the Victorian era. Ultimately, the clash was between two explanations for the order observers found in the natural world. While materialists reasoned that the mechanical aspects of the universe indicated it to be a machine, or at least machine-like, natural theologians offered a teleological explanation for the universe. The concept advanced by the materialists of a universe constructed as a gigantic clockwork machine, devoid of a benevolent and interventionist God, was bound to incur the wrath of theologians because such a notion attacked the very heart of their dogma. Materialists asserted that the universe was explicable solely in terms of matter. Immaterial objects such as the soul, if not reducible to physical objects or processes, did not exist. Materialists extended their ideas to natural history by treating animals and humans as complex machines, and attempting to link physiological processes with human cognition. They believed that natural history or biology could be explained in terms of chemical compounds and reactions which were in turn explicable by physical laws. A radical element of materialism was that it advocated tearing down the barriers which had previously separated the animate and inanimate, animal and vegetable, and most controversial of all, humans from the rest of the animal kingdom. The animate–inanimate boundary, although not breached during the century, was attacked conceptually. The animal–vegetable distinction became ambiguous with the observation of microscopic motile organisms possessing chloroplasts, and debate after the publication of Darwin's *On The Origin of Species* called into question the separation of humans from the rest of the animal kingdom. The challenge that materialism presented to orthodoxy in the nineteenth century was greater than the threat posed by evolution. This is indicated by Thomas Huxley's vehement denial of any sympathy for materialism in publications which preached the evolutionary cause.

The stark portrayal of science and religion at odds with each other, which found so prominent a place in Thomas Huxley's scientific propaganda, was, however, considerably overstated. Few practising scientists of the mid-nineteenth century saw a direct conflict between science and religion, and many remained committed Christians. Although much of the science carried out during the century was explicable in purely materialistic terms, there were few scientists who openly espoused materialism. Science could be described in materialistic terms but the world view of scientists was nevertheless theologically based. Charles Lyell, for instance, accepted progressive development but wrote of a higher agency directing it.[20] Any perceived tension between science and religion was reduced by limiting science to investigating secondary causes, while assigning the first cause to theology. This was considerably easier in the physical sciences than in natural history because the place of man in the natural world was necessarily involved with theological concepts.

Positivism

Clearly not synonymous with materialism, although often lumped together with it by critics, were the ideas of positivism. Much of science in the latter half of the nineteenth century was, if not grounded in positivism, a product of the intellectual climate that allowed positivism to flourish. A legacy of the eighteenth century empiricism of Hume and Berkeley, the basic precepts of positivism were outlined in the work of Auguste Comte during the 1830s and 1840s.

At the heart of Comte's philosophy was the idea that human thought passed through three characteristic stages. During the first or 'theological' stage, humans attributed events to supernatural causes: 'God breathed life into animals'. As man progressed intellectually he began to explain phenomena in metaphysical rather than theological terms; previously supernatural causes become abstract qualities: 'Animals contain a vital animating force'. In Comte's hierarchical plan, the culmination of man's intellectual development was reached in the final positive or scientific stage. Here all knowledge was based on 'positive' experimental data. Questions framed in theological or metaphysical terms were rendered meaningless for they were outside the realm of science. Those engaged in positivist science found it sufficient to observe whatever regularities could be found in the chaos of nature and reduce them to predictive rules. Theories, rather than being unalterable laws, became no more than useful instruments of prediction. Facts, unencumbered with ornate rhetoric, became the gods of the positivists, in intent if not always in practice.

This was a philosophy that underpinned the approach to research which became prevalent among professional biologists towards the end of the century. Whereas the amateur naturalist sought to humanize nature, to interpret the natural world in a human framework, the professional attempted to free nature from man and to view it dispassionately. As a theoretical concept this was enviable, but posed the question of how the individual scientist was to implement it. The answer lay in scientists trying, conceptually at least, to free themselves from the notion that 'man was the measure of all things'. By adopting a remote (or disinterested) vantage point, focusing on discrete and usually narrowly defined problems, but most of all by questioning how nature functioned rather than merely observing it, the scientist attempted to liberate science from theological and philosophical frameworks.

Baconian tradition

The nineteenth century, particularly the period from 1830 to 1870, saw a shift in the theoretical foundations of the natural sciences. The most obvious challenge to the theoretical foundations was the evolutionary thesis of Charles Darwin and his supporters. The transition from the design argument of natural theology to evolutionary theory was, however, only one facet of more significant changes that included interrelated transformations in technique and methodology, and the relationship of theory to practice. This was the displacement of the 'Baconian' methodology that had previously been accepted as the correct procedure for scientific investigation.[21] Whether this Baconian tradition accurately reflected the ideas of Francis Bacon (1561–1626) is not particularly crucial here. Well into the nineteenth century a tradition of 'doing' science existed and it was described by that name.

The Baconian method, as construed by most early nineteenth century scientists, preached the gospel of induction—although exactly what was meant by induction generally varied with each individual author.[22] Most, however, agreed that induction involved gathering a vast corpus of facts which, when analyzed, would produce a hierarchical series of ever more encompassing generalizations, the highest of which would be laws of nature. In this sequence, the accumulation of facts was called natural history or science, and the second stage, the generalization of facts into theory, was labelled metaphysics or philosophy. In the rush to make science fact-based the second metaphysical stage was to be, if not discarded, actively discouraged as premature.

Early Australian philosophical societies and journals included frequent references to this Baconian tradition. The Reverend Charles Wilton, in an article claiming pride of place in the first issue of his *Australian Quarterly Journal*, declared that in the present age, 'fact is for the most part substituted for hypothesis, and the results of a careful investigation for visions of fancy . . .'.[23] In 1830 the Van Diemen's Land Society heard Matthew Friend, fellow of the Royal Society, admonish them to 'Avoid theories unless you have ample materials and shun hypotheses at all times'.[24] Fact was to be given primacy over theory. Twelve years later explicit reference was again made to Baconianism in the manifesto of the Tasmanian Society. John Lillie's 'Introductory Paper' stated that 'it will be our aim to adhere, as much as possible, to a simple exposition of facts, as they present themselves in Nature; and especially to shun all unnecessary dubious and undetermined questions of theory . . .'.[25]

By the latter part of the century Baconian methodology was not so much overturned as relegated to a menial role. The *Encyclopedia Britannica* (1875) declared, 'The inductive formation of axioms by a gradually ascending scale is a route no science has ever followed, and by which no science could ever make progress'.[26] In a complete reversal, science demoted fact collecting, making it subordinate to theory. The Baconian tradition was not discarded in this process, but the task of collecting scientific information was increasingly carried out by a lower echelon of scientists who were divorced from the theoretical analysis of their data.

Specific Issues in Natural History

Classification

The central core of natural history was always classification. During the early years of the nineteenth century, the dominant classification scheme, developed by Linnaeus from the 1730s, was gradually replaced. The Linnaean system of binomial nomenclature, under which every organism is denoted by a generic and specific name, survived to form the basis of modern scientific nomenclature, but the classification scheme Linnaeus proposed for botany—he was primarily a botanist—gave way to natural classification systems. The Linnaean classification, acknowledged by Linnaeus himself as a preliminary scheme, relied on an artificial system.

The difference between natural and artificial classifications is often a matter of emphasis rather than kind. Natural classifications attempt to evaluate simultaneously a broad range of characteristics from the objects in question. Artificial classifications, on the other hand, restrict themselves to the use of only one or, at most, a few distinctive characteristics to determine an object's taxonomic position. However, just as an artificial classification may use more than one characteristic to classify an object, natural classifications of any practical use restrict the number of characteristics analyzed, and place greater emphasis on some criteria than on others. The advantage of pure natural classification systems is that no one criterion is all-important, and organisms possessing a near commonality of characteristics are classified together. Artificial classifications, with their either/or structure, frequently separate taxa which under natural classifications would be closely grouped. The Linnaean botanical system, published in *Systema Naturae* (1735), centred on the sexual characteristics of plants. Flowering plants were broken up into classes on the basis of the number, position and morphology of the stamens, the male sexual organs. Subdivision of classes into orders was dependent on the female sexual organs of the plant. Although further classification to genus and species required the determination of other characteristics, it was the use of one characteristic in isolation, the stamens or stigmata, that made the Linnaean classification an artificial system. Despite being easy to use, the system had the disadvantage of sometimes separating plants which by other systems of classification (and by common sense) seemed very similar.

By the beginning of the nineteenth century classification systems based on natural affinities began to gain ascendancy over artificial classifications. Subsequent to the publication of Darwin's *On The Origin of Species* in 1859, the term 'natural affinities' has implied common descent, but before *Origin* a species was considered to show affinity with another if they exhibited similar characteristics. The botanical dynasty of the de Jussieus and Augustin-Pyramus de Candolle championed the cause of natural classifications in France, and Robert Brown became a major publicist of natural classification in England when he published *Prodromus Florae Novae Hollandiae* (1810).

The displacement of Linnaean classification and the transitional period, before natural affinity systems were firmly entrenched, allowed other classificatory schemes to be mooted. One of these, of relevance to Australia both because it was formulated by William Sharp Macleay, one of Australia's better-known naturalists, and because the system was used to classify some taxa of Australian birds, was the quinary system. The quinary system forms a curious intermediary between artificial and natural classifications.

In 1819 William Sharp Macleay published *Horae Entomologicae*, an essay reworking the taxonomy of a small group of insects and advancing the rudiments of the quinary system. The term 'quinary' arose from the invariable division of the system into units of five. Although claiming status as a natural system, the quinary system appears distinctly artificial within its rigid emphasis on dividing taxa into units of five.

In 1821 Macleay published the second essay of *Horae Entomologicae*, which broadened the quinary system from its original narrow focus on insects to include both the animal and plant kingdoms. In succeeding years, Macleay expanded and defended the quinary system in articles printed in various English publications, particularly the *Transactions of the Linnean Society of London*.[27] Others, particularly entomologists and ornithologists, rallied to his support. A zealous ornithological ally appeared in Nicholas Vigors, who proceeded to convert the entire class Aves to the quinary system.[28] Vigors and Horsfield presented a paper classifying the Australian birds in the collection of the Linnean Society according to the quinary system, and such was the support for the classification that, when the paper was published in 1827, the authors presumed that there was little need to justify its use.[29] The meetings of the zoological club of the Linnean Society and its publication, the *Zoological Journal*, provided a forum for the advocacy of the system during most of the 1820s. By 1829 the quinary system was in retreat.[30] Even during its prime in the mid-1820s, the French naturalist Nicolas Desmarest had defended traditional Linnaean taxonomy against the quinary system, and particularly its use in ornithology.[31] The reaction of the advocates of the quinary system to such criticism was often so venomous that William Swainson, who accepted and used the quinary system himself, found it necessary to defend some of its critics from their intemperate attacks.[32] The quinary system continued to be used by isolated individuals until the 1840s, but by then it had been thoroughly discredited.

Fixity of species

The growing acceptance of natural affinity classification systems at the commencement of the nineteenth century renewed attention on the question of the fixity of species. It had been a matter of faith for most naturalists before the nineteenth century that species were constant and unchanging (although Linnaeus developed a theory founded on the divine creation of a limited number of original species which later hybridized with each other to form new species). However, the search for multiple affinities (in the pre-1859 sense) focused attention on just what constituted a species.

Jean-Baptiste Lamarck was one of the naturalists who had investigated natural systems of classification in the closing decades of the eighteenth century. Before 1800 Lamarck believed in the fixity of species, but during the first decade of the nineteenth century he proposed a theory of progressive development which brought the issue to the fore.[33]

Lamarck proposed that species were gradually transmuted over time in response to their environment, and exhibited a 'natural' tendency towards increased complexity. This proposition challenged the current view that new species represented successive acts of creation. As an example of his thesis, Lamarck described a mechanism for the development of the extraordinary body of the giraffe. Giraffes, in continually striving to reach leaves high in trees, constantly stretched their forelegs and neck. This stretching caused the limbs and neck to lengthen; characteristics which were passed on to their offspring. Incremental gains in the length of the body over successive generations produced the present giraffe. Lamarck's transformation thesis was predicated on several assumptions: that an internally driven tendency to greater complexity existed in organisms; that a need created a new organ (with development of that organ proportional to its use); and that changes in an individual of a species could be passed on to the next generation. Although Lamarck's theory was given short shrift by prominent naturalists of the day, the idea of the mutability of species persisted during the first half of the century.

Status of fossils

Much of the argument for the mutability of species came to depend on fossil evidence, for as those who maintained their faith in the constancy of species were quick to point out, no one had ever observed the transformation of one species into another. Gone were the days when fossils could be dismissed as mere curiosities, the issue of creative forces within the earth, or spontaneous productions of nature. There were many who still insisted that fossils were no more than the impressions of organisms buried in the Biblical deluge, but by the early nineteenth century a tentative integration of fossils with geological theory was underway. William Smith was using fossils to connect spatially separate strata, and Cuvier and Brongniart would soon employ fossils to define geological strata.

Much of the impetus given to palaeontology throughout the century was a result of the work of comparative anatomists. By the early 1800s, Georges Cuvier had formulated his principle of correlation which gave theoretical legitimacy to the reconstruction of entire animals from a single bone fragment or tooth. Loosely stated, the principle of correlation suggested that each morphological structure in an organism was integrated with all other structures and organs, and that there could be no modification of one organ without an effect on the rest of the organism. With this theoretical basis the configuration of the body and the digestive organs could be inferred from the shape of a single tooth. The first requirement in the reconstruction of an animal—Cuvier worked principally on quadrupeds—was to determine the shape of the molar teeth. Comparison of fossil molars with those of extant animals indicated whether the animal was carnivorous or herbivorous, and suggested the general shape of the body. Further morphological analogies allowed the unknown fossil animal to be fleshed out gradually. Only extremely competent comparative anatomists could make the required analogies, but some of Cuvier's reconstructions were quickly vindicated by more complete fossil discoveries. Later in the century, Richard Owen was to use Cuvier's methodology to similar good effect in England.

The antiquity of man, a palaeontological problem that was the subject of prolonged and heated debate during the latter half of the century, attracted limited scientific interest before the 1840s. The discovery of human skeletons in association with fossil animals was typically explained away by asserting that they were recent skeletons superimposed on fossils from an earlier creation. Studies which indicated human skeletons to be contemporaneous with extinct animals were generally ignored. It was not until after 1840 with the reworking of the Abbeville deposits of northern France, where palaeolithic fossils were unearthed, that human contemporaneity with extinct animals began to be recognized.

CHAPTER TWO

the beginning of an infrastructure

NEW SOUTH WALES, 1820–26

The second decade of the nineteenth century saw a qualitative change in natural history as practised in the fledgling colonies of New South Wales and Van Diemen's Land. Before the early 1820s natural history was carried out by individuals; men such as David Burton, George Caley or Allan Cunningham, working in isolation.[1] All too infrequently the tedium and problems of working alone were broken by the arrival of that hallmark of early nineteenth century science—the globe-girdling scientific-exploratory expedition. When Matthew Flinders' *Investigator*, with botanist Robert Brown aboard, touched at Sydney for a second time in 1803, George Caley wrote to his patron, Joseph Banks:

> I know I shall be much benefitted by Mr Brown, for in general, until the present, I have had nobody to discourse upon the same pursuit, for want of which, the pleasures of the study were obstructed.[2]

Yet the arrival of colleagues brought its own share of problems, including the introduction of rivals into areas which the resident naturalists considered to be their exclusive domain. Governor Philip Gidley King noted that the irascible Caley, despite his desire for discourse on botany, objected to interloper Robert Brown's presumption in collecting in what Caley considered to be his own territory: 'I believe he is very angry at having Mr Brown here, who he cannot help considering as a laborer in the field that ought to be wrought by himself'.[3]

During the early years of Australian settlement the number of naturalists resident in either New South Wales or Van Diemen's Land was insufficient to spark the development of the formal infrastructure normally associated with science. There were no scientific societies, museums or scientific journals. This initial period was the Banksian era of Australian natural history, a time devoted to the collection of specimens for despatch to England, usually to Joseph Banks, who then dispersed them to European naturalists. Only a limited number of individuals domiciled in New South Wales in January 1820 could claim more than a peripheral interest in natural history, among them: Allan Cunningham, Charles Fraser, Phillip Parker King, John Oxley, John Jamison and George Harper. A majority of this group, Cunningham, Fraser, King and Oxley, were often away from Sydney on extended exploratory or collecting expeditions. In the coming decade, however, the number of those interested in natural history and who were resident in New South Wales expanded considerably. This increase led to the beginning of an infrastructure for natural history with the formation of a museum and a scientific society, and the commencement of the scientific organization of the Botanic Gardens. The decade witnessed a further change. The frontier of natural history, the continual discovery of new plant and animal species, was pushed beyond the doorstep of Sydney and out into the hinterlands. Natural history could now be organized, plucked from the realm of the heroic and seated in the prosaic. The camaraderie of a shared interest partially replaced the excitement of discovery. A social history of natural history could begin.

The influx of scientific talent into New South Wales around 1820 was tied to political and social changes in both Europe and the colony. Important among European events was the defeat of Napoleon at Waterloo in 1815. The military was a traditional source of individuals interested in natural history. After Napoleon's defeat many British officers were placed on peacetime half-pay and to supplement their finances, numbers of these officers sought civil service in the colonies.[4] A second event of consequence was the death in June 1820 of Joseph Banks, marking the close of the Banksian era. Natural history in Australia was never again to find shelter under such a powerful and autocratic patron. Neither the vice-regal patronage of local governors nor the botanical empire which arose around William and Joseph Hooker subsequent to the 1830s, exercised the overweening influence of Banks.

Locally, although the infamy of the phrase 'Botany Bay' was to linger on for many years in the minds of the English public, the colony was no longer exclusively a penal settlement. Free settlers made up an increasingly large percentage of the population. After the hesitant arrival of the first thirteen free settlers in 1792 their numbers quickly expanded to over 6,000 by 1814, and some 16,000 in 1819. By 1820 English newspapers touted New South Wales as a potential home for men of capital. This influx of free settlers brought two vastly different classes of immigrants: financially secure capitalists who acquired large land grants, and the less wealthy free settlers such as mechanics and operatives. The interests of the labourers increasingly diverged from those of the large landowners. Lachlan Macquarie's tenure as governor (1810–21) witnessed the rise of a third group, the emancipists, prisoners who had served out their sentences. Whatever their subsequent success, as their opponents loudly and frequently proclaimed, emancipists still bore the stain of their legal conviction. By the 1820s dissension between the two major political factions—the exclusives who advocated a landed gentry controlling power in the colony, and the emancipists who wanted full rights and power sharing—dominated the colony. The bitterness of the struggle between these factions dogged the latter years of Macquarie's governorship and resulted in the appointment by the British government of John Thomas Bigge to a commission of enquiry into the state of the colony. Bigge toured New South Wales from 1819 to 1821 before returning to England to draw up his report. His recommendations, based on evidence largely supplied by the exclusive faction with which he clearly sympathized, curtailed the growing power of the emancipists, but not their pugnacity. Bigge's two crucial recommendations called for convicts to be removed to rural districts through assignment to large landowners, and for free settlers who had sufficient capital, to be tempted by land grants to emigrate to the notorious Botany Bay. New South Wales, founded as a depository for Britain's undesirables, had begun its slow transition to respectability. Its Tory gentility had begun an ascendancy in the colony, much to the discomfort of the Botany Bay Whigs who, despite increasing wealth, were denied commensurate political power. A major effect of the Bigge report was a hardening of attitudes of the emancipist and exclusive alike.

Philosophical Society of Australasia

The factionalism of the 1820s affected the course of natural history in New South Wales. It influenced formal organizations such as the Philosophical Society of Australasia as well as individual naturalists. Most of those in the colony with an interest in natural history were closely associated with the exclusive faction, but there were sufficient exceptions to render natural history a pawn in the struggle for power.

The first hesitant steps in the process of formalizing science in New South Wales took place on two consecutive Wednesdays in mid-1821, 27 June and 4 July. During that fortnight, in a land so newly settled and seemingly remote from the pleasures of philosophic discourse, the first scientific society in the colonies was established: the Philosophical Society of Australasia.[5] In contrast to the new narrowly based, specialist societies of metropolitan London (the Linnean Society of London, 1778; the Geological Society of London, 1807; and the Astronomical Society of London, 1820), and in keeping with its remote location, the Philosophical Society took the broad-based provincial philosophical societies such as the Manchester Literary and Philosophical Society (1781) as its models.

Initiated by the military and administrative officers of the colony, in effect the social élite of New South Wales, the meetings of the Philosophical Society on 27 June and 4 July brought together James Bowman, Henry Douglass, Barron Field, Frederick Goulburn, Francis Irvine, John Oxley and Edward Wollstonecraft, with Douglass serving as secretary.[6] Only two of the seven, surgeons James Bowman and Henry Douglass, had any formal training to augment their work as naturalists. Another, surveyor and expedition leader John Oxley, had practical experience but the other four original members were confederates of natural history rather than practitioners. Yet they set out to

> form a Society, for the purpose of collecting information with respect to the natural state, capabilities, productions, and resources of Australasia and the adjacent regions, and for the purpose of publishing, from time to time, such information as may be likely to benefit the world at large.[7]

Acknowledging that science in the colonies had hitherto lacked a focal point which could bring attention to newly acquired knowledge of the region, the Society sought to become that focus.

The formation of this scientific society was an indication of Sydney's growing sophistication and was one wave of a rising intellectual tide. At much the same time as the inception of the Philosophical Society, a private lending library was established in Sydney, and publication began of the *Australian Magazine*. The library listed among its founding members half the originators of the Philosophical Society. The *Australian Magazine* was styled a 'Compendium of Religious, Literary and Miscellaneous Intelligence', and its miscellaneous category included scientific articles ranging from a 'History of water snakes, sea snakes, and sea serpents', to 'Remarks on the comets of 1807 and 1811'.[8] These articles were extracted from European journals or books, and even 'The Duckbilled Platypus' came from Shaw's *Naturalist's Miscellany*. The major local contribution to the magazine in matters scientific was the monthly meteorological diary prepared by a 'respectable gentleman', obviously Frederick Goulburn for the data was later printed under his name in Field's *Geographical Memoirs of New South*

Wales. The *Australian Magazine* drew an unfavourable response in London where the Wesleyan Committee prohibited its editor, the Reverend Ralph Mansfield, from further publication.[9]

The impetus for many of these attempts to beat back the wilderness, particularly in the case of the Philosophical Society, was the arrival in Sydney of a number of relatively well-educated men in 1819 and 1820. Five of the seven founding members of the Society reached Sydney in the period between September 1819 and May 1821.[10] But the Philosophical Society was not just a symbol of the tempering of rude conditions of Sydney. It also functioned as an alternative social club open to those opposed to Governor Macquarie.[11] With the exception of the recently disembarked Goulburn and Douglass, the original membership was wholly antipathetic to Macquarie's policies. Bowman, Field, and Oxley, in particular, were openly hostile to Macquarie, and early additions to the membership further strengthened the anti-Macquarie faction.

The seven founding members of the Philosophical Society quickly adopted organizational by-laws, the most important of these specified that each member was to read a paper, exclusive of religion or politics, before the Society in a monthly rotation. Other by-laws were that the Society was to meet weekly on Wednesday evenings; the proposal and seconding of new members was to take place only on the first Wednesday of each month; and prospective members were to be elected by ballot (one blackball to exclude).[12] This last regulation emphasized the élitist and potentially exclusive tendencies of the Society, for there was to be no democratic majority vote on membership. The restriction on discussion of politics and religion had been common to scientific societies since the establishment of the Royal Society in the seventeenth century, and had been reinforced by the British Parliament's proscription of seditious meetings in 1795 and again in 1817 and 1819.[13]

Over the next two weekly meetings (11 and 18 July) additional by-laws were enacted: papers read before the Society were to be disseminated for discussion, experiments cited in papers read before the Society were to be repeated at the meeting (or documentation on the experiment provided); and a £5 levy was applied to members to fund the formation of a museum and library. Frederick Goulburn, the colonial secretary, put forward and had accepted an offer of a room in his office for use as the proposed museum and library.[14] A further suggestion was that a memorial be erected on the shores of Botany Bay to the scientific pioneers of Australia, James Cook and Joseph Banks. In the middle of all this activity, however, there was an omen of future problems. At the meeting held on 18 July a resolution was passed specifying that an invitation to dine at Government House was not sufficient excuse to miss a gathering of the Society (failure to attend a meeting attracted a fine). Edward Wollstonecraft, who dined with Governor Macquarie that very night, was the culprit.[15] Although a small point, the resolution was indicative of the antipathy of many of the original members of the Philosophical Society of Australasia towards Governor Macquarie. The ill-feeling was mutual. In a private memorandum, Macquarie classified the following members and potential members of the Philosophical Society as 'Fractious and dissatisfied': the Reverend Samuel Marsden, Dr Robert Townson, William Howe, John Oxley, Dr James Bowman and Judge Barron Field.[16]

The Society was unwilling to forgive dining with the governor, but ready to ignore inconvenient by-laws. Patrick Hill, surgeon, was proposed for membership at that same meeting by Bowman and, a week later, the name of the Reverend Samuel

Marsden was submitted by Field. Both nominations disregarded the existing by-law which specified that new members could only be proposed on the first Wednesday of the month. Hill was quickly admitted to the Society while Marsden's application was first postponed and then withdrawn at his own request. At future meetings, Alexander Berry and Phillip Parker King were nominated and accepted into the Society, King's accession to membership occurring during his absence on the fourth of his circumnavigations of Australia. Another addition to the membership came when Douglass proposed and Goulburn seconded the nomination of William Howe, a gentleman farmer who appears to have had little interest in the Society. Howe was to attend only three of the next thirty-eight meetings. This apparently innocuous addition to the membership was an attempt to boost the strength of one of the cliques that were now forming in the Society. Those few meetings that Howe did attend were held at the home of either Goulburn or Douglass.

The membership of the Society expanded and the Society proceeded with business. A letter drawn up to announce the formation of the Philosophical Society of Australasia was despatched to various literary and philosophical societies, ranging from the Royal and Linnean societies to smaller organizations in Java and Ceylon (Sri Lanka). The museum room was refurbished, and eventually its acquisitions included mineralogical specimens brought from Port Macquarie by Oxley, two antique Peruvian bottles contributed by Field, and mineral collections from Port Dalrymple, Port Hunter and Port Macquarie.[17] Collecting instructions were compiled for dissemination to ships' captains and surgeons, and an English inscription for the proposed Cook–Banks memorial was substituted in place of the original Latin. During the course of its existence, the Society heard seven papers, several of which were later published in Barron Field's *Geographical Memoirs of New South Wales.*[18]

But the factionalism that so tormented New South Wales in the early nineteenth century began to intrude into the affairs of the Society. This sectarianism, which eventually resulted in the organization's demise in little over a year, mirrored that in the colony at large. An early example of the surfacing tensions came with the resignation of James Bowman from the Society in November 1821, only four months after the organization's formation. Ardent exclusivist, and friend and protégé of Commissioner Bigge, Bowman's political views set him at odds with Henry Douglass who was mildly sympathetic to the emancipist cause.[19] On 16 October 1821 Bowman, in his capacity as principal surgeon of New South Wales, wrote to Douglass, then superintendent of the Female Factory at Parramatta, accusing him of neglect of his official duty and causing patients to suffer unduly by his frequent absences. Bowman continued,

> You must be sensible that it is very annoying to hear these complaints and to be constantly urging you to your duty. I was in hopes from the recommendations you brought and your apparent Piety when you came here, you would prove a valuable acquisition to the Medical Staff of the colony but these hopes I am very sorry to say have not been realized.[20]

Bowman never substantiated his charges and Douglass continued his work at the Female Factory for some years. But Bowman's accusation of dereliction of duty by Douglass caused the two men to sever their social connections and Bowman resigned his membership in the Philosophical Society soon after writing the letter castigating Douglass.

Despite increasing strain between members, the animosity had not yet built up to the degree it was later to assume. Frederick Goulburn was able to pen a light-hearted note to merchant Edward Wollstonecraft, noting

> It was not from any momentary flash of extravagance that I took the liberty of going into your yard the other day, when I had the pleasure of meeting Mr Berry, but because our friend Douglass was in want of a gig to drive philosophically from Parramatta to Sydney more regularly on Wednesday than heretofore.[21]

Most of the original membership of the Philosophical Society had actively disliked Governor Macquarie, but with the arrival on 7 November 1821 of his successor, Thomas Brisbane, the organization's relationship with the office of the governor dramatically turned about. At the 26 September 1821 meeting the Society agreed to invite Brisbane to become president (in a backhanded slight to Macquarie, the presidency had until then been left vacant). A month later the Society received Brisbane's courteous reply accepting the office, although Brisbane included the caveat that the pressure of public duty might limit the time he could devote to the Society.[22] Brisbane attended less than one third of the subsequent meetings. His presidency of the Philosophical Society, however, cemented the group's relationship with the power structure of the colony. The three most influential figures in the colony, Governor Brisbane, Colonial Secretary Goulburn, and Supreme Court Justice Field, were all members.[23]

The pressure of weekly meetings was having its effect on attendance by the beginning of 1822. With some members resident in Sydney and others, including Brisbane and Douglass, in Parramatta, attending weekly meetings involved a good deal of travel. On many Wednesday evenings the attendance numbered fewer than four, and occasionally was limited to two.[24] The majority of members of the Society gathered infrequently. The *Sydney Gazette* of 22 March 1822 recorded one such occasion when the members of the Philosophical Society first went to the southern head of Botany Bay to install the commemorative tablet for Cook and Banks, and then retired to a natural arbour to drink a toast to their scientific predecessors.[25]

By mid-1822 the Philosophical Society was moribund. On 5 June a resolution was passed repealing the by-law requiring members to regularly read papers before the Society. The preparation of further papers was to be left to the interest and zeal of the members. The 3 July 1822 Anniversary Dinner held at Government House attracted a large attendance, but Brisbane, who often travelled from Parramatta to Sydney on Wednesday mornings, generally returned west in the afternoon and so missed the weekly meetings. Furthermore, the Philosophical Society of Australasia now had a competitor. On 5 July 1822 the Agricultural Society of New South Wales was inaugurated with Brisbane as its patron, Goulburn as its vice-patron, John Jamison as president, and more than seventy 'gentlemen of the 1st rank and opulence in the territory' taking up membership.[26] From then on Brisbane transferred his allegiance to the Agricultural Society. At its first meeting he promised a land grant for an experimental farm, stationery for the Society, and a list of agricultural experiments undertaken by the Botanic Gardens.

Forty-five years after the event, the Reverend W. B. Clarke attributed the Philosophical Society's break-up to currency reform instituted by Brisbane, and the tensions this aroused among members of the Society.[27] Barron Field, in the preface to his *Geographical Memoirs*, regretted that the 'infant society soon expired in the baneful atmosphere of distracted politics'.[28] Field's description of the vituperative atmosphere that characterized the colony was more indicative of the events surrounding the Society's demise.

The incident that finally closed the Philosophical Society of Australasia originated from an accusation by Dr James Hall that Henry Douglass had made many attempts to seduce the convict Ann Rumsby by taking indecent liberties with her person.[29] Hall's allegations, in letters to the Reverend Samuel Marsden, Governor Brisbane and Judge-Advocate Wylde, produced a variety of responses. Marsden and his fellow Parramatta magistrates, including Hannibal Macarthur, nephew to that nemesis of colonial governors, John Macarthur, seized the Rumsby affair as a *cause célèbre*. The charges were of the type to excite the impetuous Marsden in his search for the taint in men's souls. Others less concerned with God turned the incident to political advantage. Douglass had shown a marked sympathy to the emancipist faction, in opposition to the exclusives led by John Macarthur. Here was a chance for the exclusives to drag Douglass down into the mire.

Douglass chose not to appear before his fellow magistrates on 19 August when they assembled to hear the complaint against him. At the hearing the convict girl denied that any of the events outlined by Hall had taken place, whereupon the magistrates promptly commended Hall for the propriety of his conduct, his 'disinterested, laudable and honorable' motives, and condemned Rumsby for wilful perjury and prevarication. Additionally, Marsden, Macarthur and company resolved not to sit on the bench with Douglass in future and so informed Governor Brisbane. Vexed by the whole issue, Brisbane suggested that the recalcitrant magistrates resign, but after gaining the support of other judicial officers, including Field, Wollstonecraft and Oxley, the Parramatta magistrates continued to decline either to sit with Douglass or to resign. Brisbane then dismissed all the Parramatta magistrates and informed his Colonial Office superiors that

> ... the little command of temper, that is exercised in this Colony, would never have permitted the whole six to have remained in the same Commission, and acted in the same neighborhood, without their becoming violators instead of Conservators of the Peace.[30]

Brisbane clearly sided with Douglass in the affair and his despatch to Bathurst in London obliquely implied that it was Hall who had taken advantage of Rumsby, rather than Douglass.

The affair had barely subsided before Hall again stirred up trouble. This time it was Colonial Secretary Frederick Goulburn, friend and defender of Douglass, whom Hall had in his sights. Hall spread rumours that Goulburn, with the complicity of Governor Brisbane, had ordered convict women to be sent to the Emu Plains convict establishment to satisfy the men's carnal appetites; all to prevent the great terror of what the writers euphemistically called 'unnatural crimes' between men.

The Philosophical Society of Australasia, doomed by Hall's charges, split into three factions: the aggrieved Douglass and Goulburn; the exclusives (Field, Oxley, Wollstonecraft, Berry and Phillip Parker King), and a middle group of Brisbane and his supporters, who could satisfy neither faction. The last weekly meeting of the Society to be recorded in its minutebook took place on 14 August 1822, two days before Hall's initial accusations were made public. If the Society continued to meet subsequent to this date, the meetings went undocumented.[31] Douglass, secretary of the Society, was unlikely to have attended further meetings.

The break-up of the Philosophical Society reflected the chaos which afflicted society in New South Wales during the governorship of Thomas Brisbane. The exclusive faction had lost its internal cohesion and its members only occasionally stopped savaging each other to snipe at the emancipists. Field split the exclusive faction early in 1822 by reminding Brisbane of John Macarthur's complicity in the Bligh insurrection and therefore of Macarthur's unsuitability for a magistrate position. Magisterial appointments were an important source of power in the colony and at various times Philosophical Society members Berry, Bowman, Douglass, Field, Macleod, Oxley and Wollstonecraft all held such positions. Bowman, son-in-law to Macarthur, further divided the exclusives when he quarrelled with John Jamison in 1822.

Brisbane was increasingly caught in the middle of the sectarian strife. He had quickly become dissatisfied with the constant intriguing of Field, and in 1824 complained to the secretary of state for the colonies that Field never missed an opportunity to falsely and foully slander him. Brisbane also cast doubt on Field's ability to rise above party factionalism in delivering his judicial decisions and sought to remove Field's fellow exclusives, Oxley and Bowman, from their positions as magistrates. John Jamison, another of the exclusivist clique also came in for criticism from the governor and was described as 'a Blackguard fellow . . . [who] has been sending home foul statements respecting my conduct'.[32] The exclusives' opponents caused Brisbane just as much trouble and by early 1824 Brisbane wanted Frederick Goulburn replaced as colonial secretary.[33] Such was Brisbane's dissatisfaction with his colony that in February 1823 he wrote home to England that the fabric of the social order of New South Wales had been destroyed, and what little culture had formerly existed in the colony had now fallen prey to scandal, factionalism and pure malevolence.[34]

The Rumsby affair was not to be the last confrontation between Douglass and the exclusives. In 1823 Douglass again clashed with Marsden when the latter accused Douglass of an over-readiness to resort to the lash to extract confessions from convicts. Again the affair degenerated into personal insult and factional rivalry.

The final episode in the short history of the Philosophical Society of Australasia came three years after the Society collapsed. In 1825 Barron Field published a collection of papers presented before the Society, their scant number fleshed out with extracts from the journals of explorers, under the title *Geographical Memoirs of New South Wales*. Seeking to obtain permission to include Berry's paper on the geology of New South Wales in his compilation, Field alluded to the Philosophical Society and commented parenthetically, 'Now alas! no more'.[35] After 1822 the members of the Philosophical Society scattered. Phillip Parker King was recalled to England in 1822, and Field embarked for England two years later. Berry was often resident at his land grant and Douglass, nominated for a position on the Court of Requests, was sent to England for instruction and to try to offset the continuing mischief caused by letters to the Colonial Office from disgruntled exclusives. This dispersal failed to stop the political intrigues of former members of the Society.

In 1824 Field, his pen dipped in gall, wrote his friend Samuel Marsden a series of letters about events in London. At the end of June 1824, Field indicated that Bathurst had given him permission to publish his *Geographical Memoirs*. In his interview with Bathurst, Field pressed the issue of the Douglass affair, but despite his eloquence, the secretary of state for the colonies continued to believe that although the Parramatta magistrates had been deceived by Ann Rumsby, they had dealt with her too harshly. Field voiced his complaints about Brisbane, but Bathurst sided with his governor and again slipped away without committing himself. Thwarted in his political machinations, Field could only vow to expose Brisbane publicly some day. Field also asked Marsden to convey to his good friend Allan Cunningham the news that Cunningham's route from Bathurst to Liverpool Plains had been publicized in England.[36] A few months later Field again conveyed news of his plotting to Marsden. His co-conspirator in the concentrated campaign of character assassination in London, Phillip Parker King, had supported his accusations. By now Field had found time to reflect on the Rumsby case. He saw that the exclusives' cause had been lost for not being opportunely fought. Douglass had bettered them by insinuating himself into the Colonial Office.[37]

Lieutenant Phillip Parker King, recalled to England in 1822, arrived in London in May 1823, and associated with Field and Thomas Scott, former secretary to Bigge and later to become archdeacon of New South Wales. All three were involved in attempts to undermine Brisbane's administration for the benefit of the exclusive faction. Phillip Parker King had reason to be dissatisfied with Brisbane when they quarrelled over the usual source of contention in the colony, a land grant. In addition to his political intriguing, King found time to become active in natural history circles in England. He donated botanical specimens to Aylmer Lambert, attended meetings of the zoological club of the Linnean Society, and provided geological information to Charles Lyell.[38] King was elected a fellow of the Royal Society of London in 1824.

Alexander Berry

There were no typical members of the Philosophical Society of Australasia, for the membership was never large enough to allow the definition of an average member. However, Alexander Berry might be considered representative of the more scientifically inclined of the Society's membership. In common with many involved in colonial science, Berry had studied medicine, in his case, at the Scottish universities of St Andrews and Edinburgh. After a brief stint as a surgeon's mate with the British East India Company, Berry chose to devote his attention to commercial ventures of a more lucrative nature. He visited Van Diemen's Land and New South Wales in 1808 as supercargo aboard a merchant vessel. In 1819, after Berry entered into a partnership with Edward Wollstonecraft, the pair decided to chance their future in New South Wales, and reached the colony in the middle of that year.

Despite the need to establish the joint venture, Berry found time enough to pursue natural history, particularly geology. In February 1820 he gave evidence before the Bigge Commission on the geological structure of New South Wales, elaborating on observations of the basic sandstone structure of the region west of the Blue Mountains, and the results of chemical tests on the purity of limestone outcroppings.[39]

Shortly after, leaving his partner to run the business in New South Wales, Berry embarked for England (he was thus not a founding member of the Philosophical Society). He was back in the colony by 1822, and engaged in a series of excursions that were to give him an overview of the geology of New South Wales. The diaries he kept on these trips form the basis for articles on geology which he published in later years. In mid-1822 Berry and Wollstonecraft took up land grants at Crookhaven on the south coast, and from that date Berry spent much of his time developing the grants while Wollstonecraft carried on their joint business in Sydney. Berry came to Sydney sufficiently often to hold office as joint secretary of the Agricultural Society of New South Wales.

During its brief existence, Berry read two geological essays before the Philosophical Society. The second, 'Geology of the coastland between Newcastle and Bateman's Bay', indicated Berry's approach to natural history. He saw an advantage in the delayed colonization of Australia, for the process could now be based on the just and rational principles of the progressive nineteenth century, rather than mere experiment, or even worse, from 'the offspring of false theory'.

Berry retained his interest in geology long after the demise of the Philosophical Society. His association with Hamilton Hume, employed by Berry as an overseer for a number of years, resulted in Berry's examining the geological specimens Hume brought back from his 1824–25 expedition in conjunction with Hovell. Additionally, Berry championed the Huttonian (or vulcanist) argument in the colony, despatched geological collections to the University of Edinburgh museum, and contributed an essay on geology to the *Sydney Gazette* in 1827.[40] The inaugural issue of the *South-Asian Register* (1827) reviewed Berry's 'Geology of the coastland between Newcastle and Bateman's Bay' (published in Field's *Geographical Memoirs*), and quoted extensively from the article, but criticized Berry for not carrying out his investigation in sufficiently comprehensive detail.[41] That same year Berry wrote a description of Broken Bay, presumably for the Agricultural and Horticultural Society.[42] After the 1820s, as was typical of much of science in New South Wales, Berry's geological interests became essentially a private pursuit. When W. B. Clarke arrived in 1839, the two geologists became friends, and Berry not only contributed geological specimens to Clarke's collection but, as a member of the legislative council, proposed that the council fund the publication costs of Clarke's scientific work. Berry, a member of the Philosophical Society in 1822, was elected to the council of the next broad-based scientific society in New South Wales, the Australian Philosophical Society, when it was established in 1850.

A second scientific interest of Berry's was the study of phrenology, popularly perceived as an attempt to correlate personal characteristics of humans with the morphology of the skull.[43] During 1819 and 1820 Berry originated a correspondence with the Reverend Robert Knopwood of Hobart, one object of which was to procure the skull of a Van Diemen's Land Aborigine.[44] When Knopwood apologized for being unable to fulfil the request, Berry revealed to him that Thomas Scott, secretary to Commissioner Bigge, was a fellow craniologist and entreated Knopwood's help in providing Scott with an Aboriginal skull. Berry facetiously advised Knopwood to warn friends doubtful of their own heads to prohibit Scott from examining their bumps lest he should decipher what was inside of them.[45] Berry's interest in craniology continued well into the late 1820s. In 1827 he explained to a correspondent that he had obtained the skull of an Aborigine and hoped that it would reveal sufficient scientific data to atone for the bloody crimes the man had committed. Berry suggested that the configuration of the skull might be correlated with the Aborigine's high rank and his blood-thirsty character.[46] The skull had been obtained by exhuming the body from its burial place.

Berry's political propensities were conservative. Soon after his arrival in New South Wales, he commented favourably on Bigge and Scott who were even then formulating the report which would provide a blueprint for the colony's development along exclusivist lines.[47] Dissatisfied with Macquarie's administration, Berry felt the early changes initiated by Macquarie's successor, Brisbane, were judicious and was similarly impressed with the talents of the newly arrived Frederick Goulburn. Within a year, however, Berry was critical of both; Brisbane was 'too accustomed to look at the moon through a telescope to have much pleasure in looking at the earth through any other medium' and had abdicated his responsibilities to Goulburn. Goulburn in turn was uneducated in economics but tried to remedy his shortcomings by reading Adam Smith and other writers on political economy, which merely filled his head with crude and undigested theories.[48] Referring to the break that eventuated between the two administrators of the colony, Governor Brisbane and Colonial Secretary Frederick Goulburn, Berry noted that both men despised each other, and Brisbane's dereliction of duty allowed Goulburn's policies to threaten to ruin the stranglehold that the exclusive faction had on the colony.

Agricultural Society

The demise of the Philosophical Society was not the end of societies in New South Wales during the 1820s. A 'Literary' or 'Literary and Philosophical Society' was mooted in 1829, but failed to eventuate.[49] Other attempts to found societies took on a markedly different character.[50] No longer were there to be philosophical societies which encompassed all science. The successors to the Philosophical Society were narrowly based and focused on agriculture, such as the Agricultural Society of New South Wales. Successive permutations and variants of this agriculturally based society existed well into the latter half of the century, but it was not until 1850 that another broad-based group, the Australian Philosophical Society, was again formed.[51]

The Agricultural Society of New South Wales was not the first attempt to form an agrarian society in the colony. Evidence given by Archibald Bell before the Bigge Commission revealed that a previous proposal to form an agricultural society had been vetoed by Governor Macquarie. Individuals involved in the unconsummated proposal included the Blaxlands, Townson, Jamison and Wylde. Hearsay evidence from Bell indicated that Macquarie objected to the proposal on the basis that admission was by ballot, a feature designed to preclude emancipist involvement. Although there was no specific by-law to exclude emancipists, Bell agreed that the principals behind the proposal concurred on the exclusion of emancipists. Bell continued that emancipists 'having once been tainted, [were] unfit for associating with afterward'.[52] When questioned by Bigge on the charge of obstructing the formation of the Society, Macquarie stressed that he had never refused to sanction the Society, and would have been only too pleased to encourage any society founded on liberal principles.[53] It was Macquarie's replacement by Brisbane in 1821 that allowed the successful revival of the idea for an Agricultural Society. It too commenced with exclusivist tendencies, but eventually included emancipists such as Samuel Terry on its executive committee.

The Philosophical and Agricultural societies of New South Wales had many common members, yet the Agricultural Society survived the factionalism that tore the Philosophical Society apart. The Agricultural Society could tolerate radically opposed individuals both through its buffer of numerous members and because the circumscribed agenda of the organization which focused on improvements in agriculture, a feature which appealed to supporters of emancipist and exclusive alike. The Society's durability was also partly due to the vice-regal patronage of Brisbane, who gave generous support in the form of a £100 donation to its treasury in October 1823, and in 1825 inaugurated an annual Brisbane Medal to be awarded through the Society for the best colonial produce.[54] These factors combined to emphasize the Agricultural Society's role as a society rather than a scientific–social club, such as that which took the name of the Philosophical Society of Australasia.

Yet even in the Agricultural Society there was political fallout from Hall's accusations against Douglass. John Jamison, the president, resigned abruptly in the week of 23–30 August 1822.[55] The timing of his resignation was hardly coincidental, Jamison, along with Hall, was one of the individuals who heard Rumsby's initial complaints. Jamison was replaced as president by Barron Field, with Hannibal Macarthur taking Field's former position of vice-president. Despite his support for the Society, Brisbane had one enemy of his administration replace another as its president.

There were other examples of politics intruding into the Agricultural Society. Before Field's return to England in 1824 an address to the Agricultural Society referred to his judicial impartiality. Governor Brisbane took issue with this dubious and unacceptable reference and censored it from the subsequent printed address on the grounds that the Society had a specific by-law prohibiting political commentary.[56] While the original address certainly contravened the spirit of the Agricultural Society's charter and was blatantly political, Brisbane over-reacted and left himself open to criticism. Despite these skirmishes the Agricultural Society and its successors survived.

Fraser and Cunningham

Comparison of the membership of the Philosophical Society of Australasia with those who can be considered professional naturalists produces a curious result. There is no evidence that individuals such as Allan Cunningham and Charles Fraser, who derived much of their income from their natural history activities, were ever considered for membership in the Philosophical Society. The apparent exclusion of Fraser and Cunningham again emphasizes the Philosophical Society's role as an élite social club rather than a scientific society. Neither Cunningham nor Fraser had the social stature necessary to become a member. The exception of a professional scientist joining the Philosophical Society was Charles Rumker who had, initially at least, the approval of Governor Brisbane. Cunningham and Fraser, like their predecessors Burton and Caley, were representative of a very different social stratum to the members of the Society. Those who acquired membership of the Society had raised themselves from the petty bourgeoisie by military service, medical training or mercantile activity.

Both Fraser and Cunningham had at least some claim to status. Fraser had accompanied Oxley on his 1817 expedition west of the Blue Mountains, and had taken part in Oxley's second expedition slightly over a year later. Subsequent to these exploratory ventures he took charge of the Botanic Gardens in Sydney and on 1 January 1820, Macquarie appointed Fraser to the position of colonial botanist.

After an apprenticeship at Kew, Cunningham had been chosen by Joseph Banks as a botanical collector for the Royal Gardens, first in Brazil, then in Australia. Once in New South Wales, he found himself in a far different position from that to which he had been accustomed in England. He was styled the king's botanist and, with the backing of Joseph Banks, could not be regarded as a mere gardener. On occasion he was invited to dine with Governor Macquarie, although many in the colony felt this a dubious distinction, for emancipists were also invited to the gubernatorial table.

Cunningham had one further recommendation that may have been favourably viewed by the anti-Macquarie membership of the Philosophical Society. Within months of setting foot in the colony, Cunningham managed to alienate Macquarie by complaints to Joseph Banks of his treatment at the hands of the colonial government.

News of the accusations surreptitiously reached Macquarie, and Cunningham and Macquarie had correct but hardly fraternal relations for the duration of Macquarie's tenure.[57] The quarrel resulted in Macquarie's increasing patronage of his own botanist, Charles Fraser, and in a sense Cunningham's complaints sparked the growth of the Botanic Gardens in Sydney.

Both Fraser and Cunningham had early come under the influence of the exclusive faction in the convoluted politics of New South Wales. Each had spent a portion of his initial years in the colony in close association with an exclusivist; Fraser under the command of John Oxley on his two expeditions into the interior, and a later excursion to Port Macquarie; Cunningham, with Oxley on his first inland exploration and then with Phillip Parker King on his circumnavigations of Australia. Both Cunningham and Fraser became involved with the Bigge enquiry of 1820. Cunningham submitted a proposal for Botanic Gardens to Bigge, while Fraser accompanied Bigge to Bathurst and gave evidence before the enquiry on a variety of subjects, including the abuse of government property.[58] Bigge commended Fraser's zealous efforts at the Botanic Gardens, made donations to him of some £50 (approximately equal to half Fraser's annual salary), and submitted a recommendation to Macquarie that Fraser be given a land grant of 500 acres.

Fraser seems to have been able to get along with most of the diverse elements of the colony.[59] Governor Brisbane, under instructions to reduce expenses, continued to support the expansion of the Botanic Gardens, and recommended Fraser for his zeal, talent, and enthusiasm.[60] Fraser was also keenly appreciated by the exclusives, and not only for his supply of gum leaves for their pet koalas.[61] William Macarthur commented to his brother John Macarthur jnr,

> To the Botanic Gardens of Sydney I shall always send a portion of every paper of seeds we receive. I know they will be carefully tended and whenever they are sufficiently increased they will be spread gratuitously through the Colony. Mr Frazer deserves much praise for his industry and liberality, unlike most persons of his profession he makes a point of giving to every one who will promise to take care of them whatever plants can be spared without injury to the Gardens.[62]

Fraser's liberality was maintained throughout his career at the Botanic Gardens. Robert Dawson, chief agent of the Australian Agricultural Company, was also to commend him in 1830.[63] But in 1823 Fraser fell prey to the divisiveness that dominated the colony. Before his recall to England, Macquarie approved Bigge's recommendation for a land grant of 500 acres for Fraser in recognition of his work during the Oxley expeditions, and in 1823 Fraser applied to take up his grant. But as William Macarthur related,

> About twelve months since, being desirous to establish a Garden near Sydney on his own accord, he applied to Goulburn for an order to have his land measured on some unlocated land in the neighborhood. The answer received was to this effect 'Mr Frazer I have myself lately returned from Bathurst, whither I attended His Excellency the Govr on an excursion in my official capacity. When I receive a Grant of land to compensate me for my services, you shall have one also'. To a decent respectable man to whose general good character and to whose utility to the colony every person in it will I am sure give testimony, could any answer be more insulting after the privations he had endured? And with General Macquarie's written promise in his pocket too be it remembered.[64]

Fraser's custom of freely dispensing plants to members of the exclusivists, with whom Goulburn was locked in bitter battle, was perhaps the cause of the latter's peevishness.

Unlike Fraser, who was tied to the Botanic Gardens and normally away from Sydney for only short periods, Cunningham had the independence to prefer unsurveyed Australia to that under the control of the colonial administration. His problems with Macquarie in 1817, but also the far greater opportunities for specimen collection on the expeditions of the congenial Phillip Parker King, influenced Cunningham to spend considerable time in the field. The lure of the country and the possibility of geographic discoveries also took him away from Sydney, for like many of the naturalists who traversed the colonies, he had a strong inclination towards geographic exploration. Initially on the heels of exploratory expeditions, and later at their head, Cunningham spent much of his time in the hinterlands. Thomas Brisbane was always appreciative of his exploration interests, and at a time when Brisbane was under continual pressure from the Colonial Office to reduce expenditure, he was unstinting in his support for Cunningham, giving him access to horses, convict servants and equipment, as well as general encouragement.[65]

In December 1820 Cunningham had returned from the third of Phillip Parker King's series of exploratory voyages to find that the Banksian botanical empire had fallen. Joseph Banks was dead. Perforce Cunningham had to become his own man. No longer was he to have the shadow of a distant Joseph Banks looming over his meetings with the governors of the colony. Banks' successor at Kew, William T. Aiton, lacked the political connections and the social background that were the real source of Banks' power.

Cunningham was now his own master in the colony and sought to establish his independence. He wrote to Aiton noting that the colonial administration had suggested that since he was paid by the English Treasury he should send duplicates of his collections to the Sydney Botanic Gardens and also report any potentially commercial plant species.[66] These requests seem reasonable but Cunningham wanted no part of them, and played on Aiton's fears to ensure Aiton gave no sympathy to the idea.

Although ostensibly a friend and colleague of Fraser's, Cunningham was not above intimating that Fraser sold packets of seeds to ships' captains and pocketed the profit. If, therefore, Cunningham supplied plants to the Botanic Gardens, commercial nurseries in England might obtain new species via this route before Kew received them. Aiton informed Cunningham that it was entirely up to his own discretion as to whether he gave duplicates to the Botanic Gardens.[67]

While Aiton was his official employer, it was Robert Brown to whom Cunningham turned initially for direction. Cunningham followed Brown's lead in taxonomy and expanded on Brown's biogeographical work. When he published a botanical appendix to Phillip Parker King's *Narrative of a survey of the intertropical and Western coasts of Australia* (1826), Cunningham paid homage to his mentor carefully explaining that much of the work followed in the steps (both literally and metaphorically) of Brown. Although he still knuckled his brow to the science of Europe, Cunningham increasingly chafed at the constraints he worked under. He wrote to his brother,

> I wish I could *fairly* (situated as I am in relation to Kew) send periodically to Dr Hooker specimens of my plants after supplying Mr Aiton and Mr Brown's Herbaria. I wish to act uprightly to all concerned but when I consider that those persons to whom I am *bound* to send my plants do not publish them but rather sedulously study to keep them from the public thereby giving full opporty for others to claim the merit of Discovery I regret it much and I feel disposed to give them to others who would do justice to any thing

interesting I might send. I have no hesitation in saying that so soon as I am released from my present tie I shall not scruple to act as I have said.[68]

The departure of Barron Field for London in February 1824 initiated an exchange of correspondence which highlights the quarrels and jealousies of the period. Richard Cunningham, brother to Allan and later to succeed Charles Fraser as colonial botanist, was throughout the 1820s an employee of Kew Gardens. It had long been Allan Cunningham's practice to forward Australian specimens, many obtained while he was on Phillip Parker King's circumnavigations of the continent, to his brother, in addition to official shipments to Kew. With both Field and King in London preparing books on Australia, *Geographical Memoirs of New South Wales* and *Narrative of a survey of the intertropical and Western coasts of Australia* respectively, and William Hooker, Robert Brown and William Aiton all keen to obtain and describe Australian plants, priority and access to these specimens became important. Aiton considered that all the specimens belonged to Kew and by extension to himself, while Robert Brown rightly saw himself as the acknowledged expert on Australian botany. Richard Cunningham became a go-between for several of the concerned parties, and his correspondence, although aimed at securing his brother's reputation, proved both duplicitous and manipulative.[69] He sent botanical specimens to Hooker, to whom he showed considerably more loyalty than to his employer Aiton, and helped Phillip Parker King prepare botanical descriptions (derived from Allan Cunningham's journals) for his book.[70] The botanical appendices that grace King's *Narrative* were an afterthought devised by Richard to allow his brother's work to appear in print. Richard was worried that Brown would credit William Baxter as the collector of new specimens rather than Cunningham.[71] Richard Cunningham also negotiated with Barron Field for the inclusion of descriptions of Australian specimens in *Geographical Memoirs*.[72] When Field's book with its botanical appendix authored by Allan Cunningham appeared, Robert Brown attributed the article to the pen of William Hooker and regarded it as an invasion of his own territory.[73] The mentor refused to acknowledge the work of his student.

After his arrival in New South Wales, Allan Cunningham had quickly become attracted to the exclusivist faction of the colony. Conditioned to the patronage system of Banks, able both by the nature of his position and his quarrel with Macquarie to set himself apart from the colonial administration, and thrown into proximity with stalwarts of the exclusive faction for most of his first six years in the colony, Cunningham became a close associate of Oxley and Phillip Parker King. Other friends of Cunningham included George Suttor (another Banks-assisted émigré) and Samuel Marsden, both fervent exclusivists.

Events of 1825 illustrate Cunningham's connection with the exclusive faction. The cause was again the Douglass case, a continuation of the Marsden allegations that Henry Douglass had cruelly flogged convicts to obtain information. Cunningham was a member of a Parramatta quarter sessions grand jury which dredged up purported incidents showing Douglass to be ruthless with the lash in extracting confessions. The grand jury, led by Hannibal Macarthur, concluded that Douglass had acted with 'magisterial authority beyond the law, opposed to the principles of reformation and the interests and welfare of society'.[74] The allegations were leaked to the press and published in the *Sydney Gazette*. The political nature of the attack was obvious, for just prior to the sitting of the grand jury a committee established at the behest of Lord Bathurst to enquire into these same allegations had failed to find any evidence to

support them. After the accusations found their way into the *Gazette*, Douglass'
lawyer, the firebrand W. C. Wentworth, claimed in letters to the attorney-general
that Cunningham had been one of the individuals behind the libellous publication of
the allegations. On behalf of Douglass, Macleod and Lawson (Macleod and Lawson
supported Douglass), Wentworth sought to file a libel suit against the members of the
grand jury.[75] Specifically, Wentworth claimed that Cunningham and John Blaxland
had called at the office of Robert Howe, editor of the *Gazette*, to urge that the allegations, previously given to Howe by Hannibal Macarthur, be published.[76] Although
Wentworth indicated that he would produce written evidence that the grand jury had
sanctioned the publication of the allegations, the libel suit never eventuated.[77]

Brisbane's departure

The constant political intriguing finally took its toll on the administration of
Governor Thomas Brisbane. The arrival of despatches in December 1824 brought a
shock for Brisbane: the announcement of his recall. News of the continual sniping
between Brisbane and Goulburn had found its way back to the Colonial Office. Brisbane, who had angled for Goulburn's replacement, was mortified when he, too, was
replaced. In response to the news of his recall, however, Brisbane wrote to Bathurst, 'I
hope I shall not be deemed insincere if I assure your Lordship that I receive His
Majesty's Commands without regret. The government of this colony is onerous and
peculiar . . .'.[78] Brisbane's experience in New South Wales had fulfilled the prophecy
of George Caley, former colonial botanist, on hearing in 1821 of Brisbane's appointment as governor. 'I must confess that I think a man of Science is an unfit man for your
Governor. If I was a prime minister I would place such men in sinecure situations as
then they would be of benefit to the public—But the Governorship of N.S.W. is not a
sinecure . . .'.[79] Tossed into the maelstrom of the inadvertent social experiment conducted by the Colonial Office, the transition of a colony founded on penal servitude
into a free society, Brisbane had coped as best he could.

   When Brisbane sailed from New South Wales in 1825 he left behind political
turmoil but also a scientific legacy; his patronage had temporarily legitimized science
in the colony. Brisbane was ultimately more successful with the heavens of New
South Wales than with the earth. Midway through his governorship, Brisbane had
boasted that 'Science has not been allowed to flag here as the Scientific Journals of
Gt Britain & the continent of Europe will testify'.[80] But these very claims formed the
basis of an attack on Brisbane's administration. In August 1824 the English *Morning
Chronicle* published a letter containing a wide-ranging indictment of Brisbane's conduct of colonial affairs. One of the charges aired was that Brisbane spent most of his
time either shooting parrots or at his observatory. Attempting to reply to the charges
published in the *Chronicle*, Brisbane indicated to his Colonial Office master, Bathurst,
that his time had been so occupied with civil duties that his health had been impaired,
and he never passed so much as a quarter of an hour a day in his observatory (although
he included the caveat 'from sunrise to sunset').[81] It may be no coincidence that
Brisbane's arch critic, Barron Field, had arrived in London by June 1824 just a few
months before the *Morning Chronicle* allegations. In fact many others arrived at this
conclusion and the *Sydney Gazette* later declared 'We are authorised to state, upon
good authority, that Mr Justice Field was not the author of the memorable letter
which appeared in the *Morning Chronicle*'.[82] Despite the *Gazette*'s denial, Field remains
the chief suspect for authorship of the letter.

Darling and Macleay

The arrival of Brisbane's successor, Ralph Darling, and Goulburn's replacement as colonial secretary, Alexander Macleay, began a new episode in natural history in the colony. Darling had none of Brisbane's interest in science but Macleay brought impeccable scientific credentials to New South Wales. Elected to the Linnean Society of London in 1794, Macleay had succeeded Marsham as its secretary in 1798, and remained in that office until 1825 when he accepted the position of colonial secretary of New South Wales. He also became a fellow of the Royal Society in 1809 and a member of its council in 1824. As well as his organizational skills and his acquaintance with most of the naturalists of Britain, Macleay brought to the colony two physical instruments of natural history, his large entomological collection and an impressive library. When it came under the auction hammer in 1846, the library included 189 zoological, seventy-three botanical, and nineteen geological titles. Most of the zoological books concerned entomology, and the remainder were classic texts of the time including Buffon, Cuvier, Latham and Pennant, as well as collections of scientific journals.

Barron Field suggested in his *Geographical Memoirs* that Macleay's appointment as colonial secretary would materially advance natural history in New South Wales, a view shared by the naturalists of Britain. Nicolas Vigors and Thomas Horsfield published an important paper on the ornithology of Australia in 1827, and recorded their expectation that the lack of knowledge and specimens from New South Wales would be speedily remedied by Macleay.[83] Macleay did forward specimens to England, especially to the Linnean Society, but he was never to supply the quantity of specimens many had hoped for.

Alexander Macleay's close association with organized natural history in Britain had only a limited effect in the colony. Scientific societies did not re-emerge in New South Wales until the 1850s. Further additions to the infrastructure of science in the colony including the establishment of the Australian Museum and the continued scientific organization of the Botanic Gardens occurred in the late 1820s and 1830s, but progress was slow and fitful. Macleay considered natural history to be a private pursuit of gentlemen rather than the concern of government.

Soon after the replacement of Brisbane by Darling, Allan Cunningham regretted the 'lamentable degree of apathy . . . manifested by the Govt in matters connected with science'.[84] Although Cunningham was primarily concerned with the lack of support for his own work, his statement was prophetic of the relative poverty into which natural history would fall in New South Wales subsequent to the departure of Brisbane. Natural history was pursued predominantly as a private interest of gentlemen. The result was that the centre of activity of natural history moved from New South Wales to the colony of Van Diemen's Land. Science followed vice-regal patronage. New South Wales was not to afford this kind of government patronage again until William Denison became governor in the 1850s.[85]

CHAPTER THREE

a rash of cultural institutions

VAN DIEMEN'S LAND, 1826–50

In December 1825, about six months after the decision had been announced in London, news arrived in Hobart Town that Van Diemen's Land was to be separated from the jurisdiction of New South Wales and to acquire its own legislative council. Recognition of its separate identity started two processes which decisively affected the hitherto torpid state of natural history in the colony. First, there was the establishment of a rash of cultural institutions in the colony, and this despite the intention of recently appointed Lieutenant-Governor George Arthur to maintain the island as a gaol for the British empire. Second was the consolidation of malignant political factions in the colony. In Van Diemen's Land throughout the 1820s, the catch-phrase of the era, exclusivism, referred not to the free settler–convict division but to the tension between the 'aristocracy' of the colony, consisting of the military and colonial officers, and tradespeople. It was not until a decade later that institutions in the colony had to contend with the problem of emancipists who wanted to join. Like the New South Wales experience, exclusivism, in both its early and later manifestations, tore apart a number of Vandemonian institutions, including some with an interest in science. In the confined colony, political issues coloured all events. From the moment of their conception, science-oriented institutions in the colony were a battlefield for political warfare. These organizations were not the main arena for factionalism (generally staged in the island's press), and in most cases their battles were incidental to tensions in the colony, but few organizations, if any, were spared from political machinations. This factionalism, in conjunction with other factors, eventually eroded the pre-eminent position Van Diemen's Land had achieved in Australian science in the late 1830s and early 1840s.

Mechanics' Institute I

One of the early cultural initiatives in Van Diemen's Land was the establishment of the Van Diemen's Land Mechanics' Institute. Originally mooted at a meeting of tradesmen in early January 1827, the formal organization and first meeting of the Mechanics' Institute did not occur until three months later. On 20 March 1827 newspaper editor James Ross chaired the inaugural meeting of the Institute which attracted some 130 individuals and declared its objective to be the promotion of arts and sciences among the mechanics of the colony. This initial meeting of the Mechanics' Institute received favourable publicity from the colony's press, including an offer from the editor of the *Colonial Times* to print a *Tasmanian Mechanics' Magazine*.[1]

The subsequent issue of the *Colonial Times* commended the Institute for its liberal character. The intent of the Institute was to transcend the all-too-prevalent factional tendency in Hobart and so avoid any exclusionary or party feeling. The *Colonial Times* entertained a continuing interest in preventing exclusive principles from gaining ascendancy in the colony. This was hardly surprising as the proprietor of the publication, Andrew Bent, was an emancipist. Just a week previously the paper had printed a letter from a pseudonymous 'Emancipist' regretting the sharp line drawn between the emancipist and the free settler in the colony, and citing the Agricultural Society as an exclusivist example.[2] Antagonism between emancipists and free settlers in the Mechanics' Institute never reached the intensity it assumed in other Van Diemen's Land organizations, but soon after the establishment of the Institute another division in the colony was revealed.

The original meeting of master tradesmen that had called for the formation of a Mechanics' Institute had had less ambitious objectives than those of the mechanics' institute movement in Britain. A newspaper report cited the purposes of this preliminary meeting as the protection of trade and the promotion of useful knowledge in the various branches of science. An editorial comment accompanying the report expressed the pious hope that the intent of the organization was not to control, and therefore increase, the price of labour.[3] In fact, this was probably one of the major reasons behind the original meeting. Free tradesmen in the colony were constantly complaining that assigned convicts were undercutting their prices.

When it was first established membership of the Mechanics' Institute may have been open to all (barring convicts and emancipists), but the Institute was quickly dominated by men with cultural aspirations. In line with colonial protocol Lieutenant-Governor Arthur was invited to be the patron of the institution, chief justice John Pedder assumed the presidency, and James Wood was appointed secretary. Colonial Secretary John Burnett and prominent citizens W. Bethune, W. Gellibrand, J. T. Gellibrand, J. Lakeland, J. Ross, J. Scott, and A. Stephen were all elected vice-presidents.[4] These officers had little to do with the running of the Institute in future years, but even among the committee of management there was a noticeable lack of mechanics. This absence was soon noted by the pseudonymous and self-styled 'Numbskull' in correspondence addressed to newspapers. His initial letter, of 20 July 1827, deplored the circumstances to which the Mechanics' Institute had been reduced.[5] It was an institution not of and for mechanics, but of and for gentlemen—public officers, merchants and others of considerable wealth. This attack drew a rebuttal from 'Opifex' who slated 'Numbskull' for claiming the existence of adversarial factions in the Mechanics' Institute.[6] Although it was true that mechanics had founded the institution, 'Opifex' admitted they had subsequently thrown the Institute open to the public. 'Numbskull' resumed his attack in August, accusing those gentlemen who had elected themselves officers of wresting control of the institution from the hands of the mechanics who founded it. The mechanics of Hobart were afraid to protest against this takeover, 'Numbskull' continued, for these same gentlemen occupied positions of power in the colonial administration and could deny them work. 'Numbskull' insisted that the Mechanics' Institute should be left in the hands of mechanics. Bent, the editor of the *Colonial Times*, supported this view and recommended that lectures at the Van Diemen's Land Mechanics' Institute should be 'practical lectures by practical men', not arcane and obscure pedantry.

The events to which 'Numbskull' alluded probably began with the 19 June meeting of the Institute, chaired by George Augustus Robinson, which had sought to elect officers for the following six months. Newspaper reports of the first formal meeting of the Van Diemen's Land Mechanics' Institute had cited Robinson as the prime mover in the Institute's foundation. Letters to and from Robinson (who was later to achieve a measure of fame as conciliator to the Aborigines) record his tenure as chairman of the Mechanics' Institute from early to mid-1827.[7] However, the 19 June meeting broke up early after 'some unpleasantness in opinion having arisen respecting the foundership'.[8] The following day the meeting reconvened under the chairmanship of W. Gellibrand and proceeded with the election of officers and amendments to the proposed rules. Instead of two vice-presidents there were now to be eight and, crucially, the committee of management, increased from twelve to twenty, would draw only half its members from the ranks of mechanics rather than the originally specified two-thirds. Power in the Mechanics' Institute was effectively transferred at this meeting to 'gentlemen' and Robinson, a builder by trade, was deposed. Although he was appointed to the committee of management he soon severed his connection with the Institute.

Discontent with the social hierarchy in the Van Diemen's Land Mechanics' Institute was a continual problem. In the early 1840s the *Hobart Town Courier* noted that the term 'Mechanics' Institute' was a misnomer: the Institute, as then constituted, was closer to a literary and scientific society than a true mechanics' institute.[9] Ten years later the *Hobart Guardian* reported on a meeting of one hundred individuals to discuss the formation of an organization sympathetic to the needs of mechanics. Joseph Hone, vice-president of the Mechanics' Institute, pointed out that such an organization already existed but W. Smith dismissed the Institute as no more than an exclusive library or scientific institution which catered to neither the interests nor the needs of mechanics. The meeting resolved to establish a Van Diemen's Land Mechanics' School of Arts.[10]

It was not uncommon for mechanics' institutes to be alienated from the working classes during the mid-nineteenth century. In 1851 J. Hudson's *The History of Adult Education*, an early chronicle of English mechanics' institutes, described the complaint that the institutes were attended by those of a higher rank than had been intended as universal.[11] Similarly Friedrich Engels, after noting that his heroic proletariat had established schools where children could obtain a truly proletarian education, continued

> These arrangements are very dangerous for the bourgeoisie which has succeeded in withdrawing several such institutions, 'Mechanics' Institutes', from proletarian influence, and making them organs for the dissemination of sciences useful to the bourgeoisie.[12]

Engels perceived that science had the capacity to distract the working class from its proper goal of opposing the bourgeoisie. (Recently a well-documented case has been made for the use of mechanics' institutes as agents of social control in the first half of the nineteenth century in Britain.[13])

Despite its bourgeois focus, the Van Diemen's Land Mechanics' Institute espoused the rhetoric typical of the movement. Its objective of promoting useful scientific knowledge was to be achieved by following the universal formula of mechanics' institutes: the voluntary association of mechanics, the organization of a library, a reading room and a museum, lectures on natural and experimental science, and the introduction of elementary schools to teach arithmetic, geometry and trigonometry.[14] During 1827, in an attempt to achieve some of these aims, a course on elementary arithmetic and geometry taught by James Thompson, schoolmaster of the Hobart Town Academy, was announced and lectures were given on mechanics (James Ross), astronomy (W. Gellibrand), steam engines (J. Hackett), astronomy again (R. Griblin), and chemistry (A. Turnbull).

The initial enthusiasm associated with the formation of the Van Diemen's Land Mechanics' Institute soon waned and the organization was dormant until 1829. That year science in the colony received a much-needed boost from a combination of events, including the revival of the Mechanics' Institute following the return of its secretary, James Wood, who had embarked for England soon after his appointment. After a year's suspension the lecture series recommenced in September 1829. The initial lectures for that year, given by Adam Turnbull, proved popular. Indicative of the genteel nature of the Mechanics' Institute, these talks attracted few mechanics but a number of ladies.[15] By the annual meeting of the organization in March 1830 it could claim a membership of 200, the attendance of the lieutenant-governor at lectures, the foundation of a library, and the purchase of demonstration scientific apparatus from England.

Henderson and the Van Diemen's Land Society

In the 1820s, Van Diemen's Land society consisted of an upper stratum of military and colonial officers, a middle stratum of free settlers, and a bottom layer of emancipists and convicts. The Van Diemen's Land Mechanics' Institute, captured initially by an élite coterie, soon developed into a middle-class institution but continued to see its *raison d'être* as the improvement of the working man. With its ostensibly intimate connection with mechanics, its emphasis on education rather than experiment, and its relatively open membership policy, there was room for a more exclusive scientific club. In a land still peopled for the most part by thieves, whores and murderers, the lack of organizations which differentiated the élite from the masses was strongly felt.

At the end of August 1829 an individual stepped ashore at Hobart who was to stimulate scientific activity in Van Diemen's Land. Dr John Henderson, late military surgeon to the Bengal Army, disembarked to convalesce. Henderson descended on the colony like a whirlwind. Keenly interested in natural history, Henderson recognized the need for a society which would collect and publish information peculiar to Van Diemen's Land.[16] Within four months of Henderson's arrival, the *Hobart Town Courier* announced the formation of such a fellowship. under the title 'The Van Diemen's Land Society'.[17] Similar to its short-lived predecessor, the Philosophical Society of Australasia, the Van Diemen's Land Society's published objectives included the collection of information on the colony, the establishment of a natural history museum and an experimental garden, and the inauguration of correspondence with similarly inclined overseas societies. Henderson pushed events along quickly. A deputation called upon Lieutenant-Governor Arthur, who agreed to their request to become patron, and a committee of management was formed.[18]

James Ross was always to be a strong supporter of the Van Diemen's Land Society and throughout its existence the Society continued to receive sympathetic treatment in his *Hobart Town Courier*. The more radical *Colonial Times*, although initially wishing the Society well, was less optimistic about its prospects. The public of the colony was too indifferent and apathetic to encourage such an organization. And who would pay the piper? Would the expenses incurred in running the Society be met by subscription or, less palatably, was there any truth to the rumour that the lieutenant-governor had recommended that the Society be given a grant from the Treasury?[19]

Henderson's Society attracted the élite of the colony to its inaugural annual meeting held during the afternoon of Saturday, 16 January 1830. Lieutenant-Governor Arthur and his wife were included in the attendance of almost one hundred. Henderson's 'Presidential Address' delivered before this audience was a rigorous scientific lecture. His wide-ranging oration discussed the state of local natural history, gave a geological sketch of the colony and outlined an ambitious reformation of botanical nomenclature.[20] Few of the listeners, however, could claim any scientific expertise and Henderson was later to realize that he had 'collected amongst the members a number of spectators'. The reception to Henderson's revision of botanical systematics was mixed.[21] Adam Turnbull considered the scheme to be sufficiently worthwhile to be given a trial on the botany of Van Diemen's Land. James Ross, something of a botanist himself although apparently a conservative one, opposed the introduction of the scheme and argued for the retention of the antiquated Linnaean system. Henderson's scheme was never given a trial in Van Diemen's Land and he later submitted it to the Institute of France.[22]

After the intellectual labour of the afternoon the Van Diemen's Land Society reconvened that evening to entertain the governor at dinner. Replying to the interminable rounds of toasts, the governor admitted that he had sanctioned the formation of the Society on the conviction 'that it might very probably do a great deal of good, but could in no way do any harm'. In fact, as newspapers other than the *Hobart Town Courier* were already reporting, the Van Diemen's Land Society was causing a great deal of trouble and adding to the divisiveness in the colony.

At a meeting the previous day (15 January) a small group of twelve members of the Society had voted on nominations for new members.[23] Several names, including J. Dunn and C. Bilton, were found to have received three or four blackballs, thus barring them from admission. Considerable embarrassment ensued, for both Dunn and Bilton had been solicited as members by the Society's secretary, Adam Turnbull, and had been invited to attend the dinner with the governor following the annual general meeting.[24] The *Colonial Times* suggested that the reason Dunn and Bilton had been blackballed was their connection with the 'retail trade', an association which may indeed have been sufficient to bar the two men at a time when the old guard, the exclusivists of the colony, were reacting to the newly monied bourgeoisie. Following the rejection of Dunn and Bilton, J. T. Gellibrand, member of the committee of management, withdrew from the Society and John Burnett, vice-patron, requested that the Society's secretary call a special meeting to reconsider the events of the 15 January meeting.[25] On 12 February Burnett despatched a circular letter to the members calling on them to attend the special meeting if they objected to the general practice of blackballing and to the recent blackballing in particular.[26] While this manoeuvring was taking place, the *Hobart Town Courier* raised the suspicion that the blackballs had been cast by newcomers to the colony, a thinly veiled reference to Henderson, Captain Swanston and Ensign Betts, all military officers recently arrived from India. The more radical *Tasmanian* could scarcely contain its glee. The exclusive Van Diemen's Land Society had amply fulfilled all expectations, it had mortally wounded itself by its factious behaviour.[27]

The special meeting of the Society requested by Burnett took place on 10 February. Obeying the summons of Burnett's circular, forty members attended and devoted their time to considering both the admission policy of the Society and a motion put by Burnett that the proceedings of the fateful 15 January meeting be rescinded.[28] Amendments and opposition to Burnett's motion occupied the evening until Alfred Stephen, solicitor-general of the colony, finally moved for adjournment. It was the only decision reached that day. In the course of the meeting, Henderson insulted Colonial Secretary Burnett, and the latter declined any further acquaintance with him. Henderson had now alienated enough of the powerful members of the colony to ensure the doom of his Society.

The adjourned meeting reconvened five days later but attracted only twenty members. Swanston addressed the meeting and indignantly stated that despite the snide insinuations and ill-treatment that he and his associates from India had suffered at the hands of the local press, neither he nor any of his friends had blackballed anyone. He then quit the meeting.[29] With Swanston's declaration it became evident that at least some of the long-resident colonial members of the Society had wielded the contentious blackballs. Burnett reintroduced his motion to eliminate blackballing altogether, but Alfred Stephen countermoved that blackballing be retained (with the requirement that it needed a majority of a quorum of twenty members to block admission).[30] When the question was put to a vote, the anti-blackball faction had a majority of one. Stephen's son immediately rose to successfully challenge the membership of one of the anti-blackball faction and demanded a new vote. The vote was tied and when the chairman indicated he would vote with the pro-blackballers, Burnett and several others resigned from the Society.[31]

Within two months of its formation the Van Diemen's Land Society had been crippled. The Society, albeit with considerably reduced numbers, continued to hear occasional papers, acquire a few specimens for its museum, and back Henderson's next scheme, the establishment of a public seminary. Henderson and the exclusivist rump of the Society continued to be reviled in the *Tasmanian* and *Colonial Times*. By March Henderson had wearied of Van Diemen's Land, and departed for the more congenial climate of New South Wales. He had little better success there with his grandiose plans.

Bereft of its founding stimulus, the Van Diemen's Land Society declined. Enthusiasm was temporarily injected in May 1830, when Captain Matthew Friend, fellow of the Royal Society, presented the group with a set of proposals for co-operative work with a number of British institutions. Either ignorant of the history of the beleaguered Society or carried away by commissions given him variously by the Royal Society, the Medico-Botanical Society, the Geological Society, the Zoological Society, and the British Museum, Friend spoke of his astonishment at finding such a flourishing organization already in existence.[32] He then proceeded to lecture his colonial brethren on the type of information and specimens sought by European naturalists (platypuses, skeletons and reproductive organs of marsupials, heights and mineral composition of mountains, etc.) and admonished them in true Baconian fashion to 'Avoid theories unless you have ample materials and shun hypotheses at all times'. There was no disgrace in mere collecting, he continued; even the old and distinguished scientific societies of Europe were doing no more than collecting facts for analysis by future generations.

That evening there were signs of renewed vitality in the Van Diemen's Land

Society. Papers were read, new members balloted (among them Friend and Thomas Lempriere) and Friend indicated that the Earl of Stanhope, Davis Gilbert, Everard Home, J. G. Children and N. Vigors, all distinguished British naturalists, would accept honorary membership to the Society. The Van Diemen's Land Society met regularly until at least August, but the Society had run its course.[33] Antipathy towards it was sufficient for Friend to attract the wrath of the radical newspapers. The *Colonial Times* mocked him for his attempts to revitalize the 'Botany Bay Aristocratical Institution'; the *Tasmanian* even took issue with Friend's grammar.[34] The Society faded from existence, having lasted a shorter period than its New South Wales predecessor, the Philosophical Society of Australasia.

The demise of both societies is attributable to the same cause. As had been the case with the Philosophical Society, membership of the Van Diemen's Land Society was bound up with the centre of power in the colony. Although Governor Arthur displayed little concern for the Society, many in his colonial administration were caught up in the events. Weighed down by vying political interests, the Society had little chance of surviving. The Van Diemen's Land Society was trapped in the dilemma that plagued all early colonial science: without the patronage of powerful figures in the colonies, science had little opportunity for growth; with that patronage science ran the almost inevitable risk of being subject to factionalism and a quick death. Political factionalism always overwhelmed the common interest in science. Scientific societies could not survive, much less become successful, until a sufficiently large group of individuals with limited connection to, and interest in, political factions developed in the separate colonies.[35]

In the years after the brief existence of the Van Diemen's Land Society, natural history followed the pattern set in New South Wales in the late 1820s. Its activity transferred from societies to individuals. Substantive societies were again established in Van Diemen's Land in the late 1830s and 1840s and it was this resurgence that ensured the colony's place as the leading scientific centre in Australia during this period.

The hiatus in the formal structuring of natural history saw the Mechanics' Institute movement increasingly dominated by the middle stratum of society rather than by the political élite. The lecture series continued to be the primary activity of the institute and its success varied from year to year. There was sufficient scientific awareness in the colony for Adam Turnbull's suggestion, that the Earth was no older than the Biblical time of Adam and Eve, to be disputed by James Ross and reported by the *Hobart Town Courier*.[36] Turnbull, trained as a surgeon, later abandoned medicine and his career in the colonial administration of the colony to become a Presbyterian minister. The Mechanics' Institute was liberal enough to elect R. L. Murray, emancipist, to its committee of management in 1834.[37]

Other societies

In the outposts of the colony occasional bursts of enthusiasm resulted in the formation of rudimentary and short-lived philosophical societies. A Tasmanian Society flourished briefly in Launceston in 1831–32. The officers of the penal administration at Port Arthur formed a similar organization in 1834, an example that James Ross extolled to the rest of the colony.[38] Members of the small Port Arthur Society were reported to be collecting and sketching the natural productions of the surrounding district, organizing a museum and attempting to analyze mineral ores. The term

'Philosophical Society' may have been overly formal for this group before the late 1830s. One of the individuals most closely involved, Thomas Lempriere, confided to his diary the receipt of a copy of Swainson's *Zoology*, and his intention to sketch local birds, but the Society escaped mention.[39] A third group, centred in the middle of the island at Bothwell, established a Literary Society in 1834. After a slow beginning in 1836, the Bothwell Literary Society metamorphosed into a true literary and scientific society, although it maintained its original name.[40]

Despite the existence of these societies, throughout the early and mid-1830s the substance of natural history in Van Diemen's Land was vested in individuals. Thomas Lempriere, stationed in the various penal settlements of the colony; Robert Lawrence, landowner near Cressy; Joseph Milligan, Van Diemen's Land Company surgeon in Surry Hills; and Ronald C. Gunn, successively assistant superintendent of convicts, superintendent of convicts and police magistrate in Launceston, and police magistrate at Circular Head, all found time from their respective employment to advance natural history.

Robert Lawrence

European scientists had a standing need for information on the natural productions of Australia and Van Diemen's Land. During the 1820s William J. Hooker, professor of botany at the University of Glasgow, began to establish a worldwide network of botanical collectors. Despite his best attempts, Hooker initially failed to unearth a suitable correspondent in Van Diemen's Land. As early as 1823 Hooker commenced a desultory and unsatisfactory correspondence with Launceston merchant Thomas Scott. In 1829, Hooker again communicated with Scott and the letter was brought to the notice of Robert Lawrence, who was to serve Hooker to better purpose.[41]

Lawrence was a complete naturalist, one day committing details of botanical specimens in his diary, the next, the dissection of a platypus, the mineralogical analysis of water samples or the manufacture of a pneumatic apparatus for an experiment on gases.[42] As he acknowledged in his introductory letter to Hooker, Lawrence's initial competence in natural history was limited, but he was anxious to learn. Hooker might not satisfy Lawrence's want of someone in the colony to guide his study, but if Hooker would provide Lawrence with books on botany, especially Robert Brown's *Prodromus Florae Novae Hollandiae*, then he could be assured of a regular supply of new or rare plant specimens.[43] Lawrence's botanical education had been based mainly on borrowed books such as Humphrey Davy's *Elements of Agricultural Chemistry*, James E. Smith's *An Introduction to Physiological and Systematical Botany*, and Gilbert White's classic *The Natural History and Antiquities of Selborne*. In 1831, to supplement this reading, Lawrence received copies of Brown's *Prodromus* and Hooker's *Botanical Miscellany* from Hooker, and in turn despatched plant specimens to Glasgow. Typical of many of the early Hooker correspondents, Lawrence also opened a botanical exchange with Stewart Murray, superintendent of the Glasgow Botanical Gardens. While Hooker received herbarium specimens in exchange for species identifications, herbarium paper and botanical books, Murray swapped European seeds and bulbs for Tasmanian seeds.

In 1832 a letter from Lawrence to Hooker introduced a kindred spirit, Ronald Campbell Gunn, 'a gentleman who has lately acquired a passionate taste for the science of Botany, and who has become an enthusiastic collector'.[44] Gunn had arrived in the colony two years earlier, aged twenty-two, and became assistant superintendent of convicts in Launceston. Other letters to Hooker throughout 1832 and 1833 high-lighted the problems of the tiro naturalist in the distant colony of Van Diemen's Land: the uncertainty of correspondence with Europe and the concomitant loss of books or specimens; the pressure of work reducing time for botany; and even the unavailability of the most elementary books on botany. Yet there was recompense for the continual frustrations: the friendship of fellow naturalists such as Ronald Gunn; the wide, untrammelled field for collecting specimens; and Hooker's kind letters.

Ronald Gunn

In October 1833 the twenty-six-year-old, newly married Lawrence died. But the candle of botanical correspondence, guttering weakly when passed from Thomas Scott to Robert Lawrence now burned bright in Gunn's hands.[45] Ronald Gunn's first letters to Hooker reiterated Lawrence's concerns—his slender knowledge of botany and his inadequacy as a correspondent. Gunn initially had access to Lawrence's small scientific library but shortly before he died Lawrence had moved to an estate some distance from Launceston and the library was lost to Gunn. Echoing Lawrence, Gunn asked for a copy of Brown's *Prodromus* and anything that Allan Cunningham, then returned to England, had published on Australian botany. Again, like Lawrence, Gunn's botanical learning led him away from the Linnaean botanical system to the natural affinity system of the de Jussieus and Brown.

The enthusiasm of novice naturalists in Van Diemen's Land was kept alive in the mid-1830s by the steady but relatively infrequent communications from overseas naturalists. More haphazard stimuli were the occasional reconnaissances made of the colony by visitors with some knowledge of natural history. These ranged from official exploratory and scientific voyages, complete with recognized naturalists aboard (Dumont d'Urville's *l'Astrolabe* and *la Zélée*, and James Ross's *Erebus* and *Terror* expedition), to visits by individuals. The Quaker, James Backhouse, who arrived in the aptly named barque *Science*, visited Van Diemen's Land between 1832 and 1834 investigating penal conditions and the treatment of Aborigines. Trained as a nurs-eryman, he was sufficiently interested in botany to join Gunn on at least one botanical collecting trip.[46] In 1834 the *Hobart Town Almanack* included 'Some Remarks on the Roots and other Indigenous Esculents of Van Diemen's Land', and the 1835 *Almanack* printed 'Index Plantarum, or an attempt towards a popular description of some of the most common and remarkable indigenous plants of Van Diemen's Land'. Both were written by Backhouse.[47]

The correspondence with overseas botanists was, however, vastly more important in maintaining Gunn's enthusiasm for natural history than these visits.

For Gunn, along with other isolated naturalists, the letters from established natu-ralists such as Hooker formed their only real connection with the mainstream of natural history. Colonial naturalists depended on such communications for both species identifications and direction of their studies. In March 1835 Gunn could request 'The *Best* Work in Natural History in General'. Hooker replied,

> There is no really good one. The fact is that Natural History is now become so extended a branch of Science that no one dares venture as in the days of Linnaeus to grasp the whole. Nay, discoveries are so continually pouring in upon us that there is not one that even approaches to perfection. No man can study fully and satisfactorily any branch of science without having recourse to an immense library . . . If I were a Naturalist & going

to a distance from Europe I should like with me in preference to all other Books on Natural History the 'Nouveau Dictionnaire des sciences Naturelles'.

As Hooker acknowledged, however, *Nouveau Dictionnaire* was expensive and entailed sixty volumes of text and many more of plates. Hooker's advice for Gunn was to

> Make use of such works as you can command & trust to your friends in England, among whom you must reckon *me*, to give you the best information they can with respect to a large portion of what you will collect.[48]

The interchange of letters between Gunn and Hooker over the next decade document the relationship between an increasingly sophisticated colonial botanist and his established European mentor. Such correspondence comprised a loose-knit natural history society and was a substitute for many of the intellectual and social functions of formal societies. Gunn acknowledged this in commencing a letter, 'I am induced to write to you . . . from the want of any one nearer with whom to exchange thoughts, opinions, &c.'.[49] In addition to the botanical, Gunn's letters often contained details of both his official work and his personal life.[50] Hooker responded readily to Gunn's letters including fulsome praise, 'You were surely born a Naturalist . . . for not only are your notes on the habits of the Birds well drawn; but you possess a faculty of preparing and preserving the skins of animals which I have rarely seen equalled . . .'.[51] Hooker's letters to Gunn could run to twenty-two pages of longhand.

Barring Hooker, the support the local men of science received from British naturalists was often niggardly. Over the years, Gunn despatched specimens to Robert Brown, John Lindley, J. E. Gray, William Swainson and Richard Owen. Much to Gunn's dissatisfaction few responded as quickly or as generously as Hooker. In March 1835 Gunn informed Hooker that he had received not a single letter of thanks from Lindley and would send him no more specimens. These accusations of ingratitude, at least in Lindley's case, were groundless. Lindley had written to Gunn in April 1834, both acknowledging the collections and forwarding books. Lindley despatched other books through Hooker in 1836. The 1834 letter was held up in the Colonial Office but eventually was received by Gunn in September 1836. Gunn accepted Lindley's explanation of the delay and intended to resume the correspondence but it was two years before he again forwarded specimens to Lindley.[52] Despite their sometimes uneasy relationship, Gunn and Lindley remained in communication until at least 1843.

Men such as Hooker, Owen and Lindley maintained extensive networks of correspondents and often were unable to find the time to reply immediately. Colonial naturalists, such as Gunn, generally had few correspondents and were quick to perceive unintended slights. The established naturalists in England, who had daily intercourse with other naturalists, were unaware of how much isolated collectors depended on them for stimulus.

The recipients of Gunn's specimens also had financial problems. Richard Owen, Hunterian Professor of anatomy at the College of Surgeons, London, was anxious to make some return to Gunn, but the College of Surgeons relied on donations and had money neither to buy books for exchanges, nor even to pay the costs of shipping specimens.[53] By comparison with William Hooker, Lindley and Owen's response seemed penurious to Gunn but others' proved even worse. Gunn asked Hooker to forward bird skins to William Swainson in exchange for books on ornithology. Hooker's reply cautioning Gunn about Swainson, who was known not to be generous with exchanges, was ignored. Gunn persisted and then became angry when he did not receive what he thought was his due. J. E. Gray of the British Museum also received specimens without making a return to Gunn. Gray was particularly unscrupulous, for he sold some of the specimens to John Gould. Many of the consignments sent to England had been purchased with Gunn's own money and he thought the British Museum should be able to reward him liberally.[54] Robert Brown was similarly reticent about making a return for Gunn's specimens, but in his admiration of the competence and detail of Brown's earlier work on Australian plants Gunn was willing to make allowances for Brown's parsimony. Joseph Hooker was not inclined to leniency with Brown, informing Gunn in 1853 that Brown's duplicity and secretiveness was such that botanists would puzzle over whether or not Brown had actually advanced botany.[55]

Hooker's continual and generous support compensated for some of the problems faced by Gunn and the other colonial neophyte naturalists. His frequent shipments to Gunn included books that spanned the whole gamut of science, from ornithology, physics and medicine, to the *Library of Useful Knowledge* and much of the *Naturalist's Library*. One box alone brought books costing some £30, a considerable sum for the times.[56] Gunn offered to pay for these books but there is no indication that Hooker accepted payment.[57] Hooker's support manifested itself in other ways. Early in his correspondence with Lawrence and Gunn, Hooker suggested that both should write reports of their excursions for inclusion in one of the various publications he edited. Hooker published one report of Lawrence's in Volume 1 of his *Journal of Botany*.[58] Gunn also found his name before the public when Hooker published 'Contributions toward a flora of Van Diemen's Land from collections sent by R. W. Lawrence, and Ronald Gunn, Esqrs, and by Dr Scott' in the *Journal of Botany*.[59] Another early expression of gratitude by Hooker for the steady flow of plant specimens to England came when he named the species, *Ranunculus gunnianus*, for Gunn. Other species and the genus *Gunnia* (later invalidated by Ferdinand Mueller) were eventually to honour Gunn's name in the botanical literature.

From 1830 to 1836 it was generally the lot of the naturalist of Van Diemen's Land to work alone. Articles of natural history in the local press failed to arouse public interest.[60] A loose network of geographically separate Vandemonian naturalists did, however, help ameliorate the isolation. Gunn, for instance, established communication with Dr Joseph Milligan, medical officer of the Van Diemen's Land Company at Hampshire Hills. Milligan made local plant collections for Gunn, some of which were forwarded to Hooker.

John Lhotsky

One of the itinerant scientific entrepreneurs to visit the colony during the mid- to late 1830s was Czech naturalist–adventurer John Lhotsky. After obtaining a degree from the University of Jena in 1819, Lhotsky commenced a turbulent career. Before quitting Europe for Brazil in 1830, his political polemics had brought him to the attention of the authorities. Arriving in Sydney in May 1832, Lhotsky unsuccessfully applied for the posts of colonial botanist and colonial zoologist, positions which had been vacant since the deaths of Charles Fraser and William Holmes. Lhotsky supported himself instead through lectures, articles in the local newspapers, and the sale of natural history specimens.[61] During 1834–35 Lhotsky explored sections of the

Australian Alps and prepared his serial work, *A Journey from Sydney to the Australian Alps*.

Fleeing from unpaid debts in New South Wales, Lhotsky arrived in Van Diemen's Land on 14 October 1836. Within days of his arrival, he raffled off a drawing of the Australian Alps to boost his finances.[62] As in New South Wales, he survived by giving lectures and writing newspaper articles.[63] Lieutenant-Colonel Kenneth Snodgrass (Bourke's understudy in New South Wales until seconded as the stopgap governor of Van Diemen's Land between the departure of Arthur and the arrival of John Franklin) granted Lhotsky rations and convict servants for his collecting excursions. In January 1837, according to Lhotsky, Surveyor-General George Frankland recommended his appointment as colonial naturalist but Snodgrass preferred to leave any such decision to Franklin.[64] Lhotsky eventually received limited official sanction in February 1837 when Franklin employed him for several months to report on the production of coal from the Tasman Peninsula mines. By May Franklin had decided that the government could dispense with Lhotsky's services. He lingered on in Van Diemen's Land for almost another year before embarking for London on 1 April 1838. Before he departed, he offered a collection of mineralogical, zoological, and botanical specimens to the government for £120, but the proposal was declined.[65] The collection was put up for public sale in November, and was eventually purchased by the Mechanics' Institute.[66]

Although Lhotsky has received charitable treatment in recent years, the Van Diemen's Land press was seldom sympathetic.[67] These attacks were in part attributable to the rancorous nature of the local press but Lhotsky continually alienated those whose patronage he needed to secure the public offices to which he aspired. He successfully and successively managed to irritate the scientific community of New South Wales, Van Diemen's Land and England.

Ronald Gunn heard rumours of Lhotsky long before he came to Van Diemen's Land. In sending Hooker a copy of Lhotsky's *A Journey from Sydney to the Australian Alps*, Gunn noted that Lhotsky was reputed to be 'a German Adventurer like Dr de Dassel professing to know everything, but really quite ignorant, & assisted by others in his compilations'.[68] Gunn avoided Lhotsky, apparently never meeting him, but on 'the best Authority' cautioned Hooker that Lhotsky 'was utterly devoid of good moral principle'.[69] Gunn concluded that Van Diemen's Land would be well rid of Lhotsky. Most damning of all, 'Short & Lhotsky have made Naturalists at a sad discount out here'. Others joined in the damnation. George Frankland, who had ostensibly recommended Lhotsky for the position of colonial naturalist, wrote to J. E. Calder that Lhotsky's final lecture might yet turn a profit by the sale of the apples and peaches thrown at him; a somewhat ironic comment on Vandemonian society given that the lecture was entitled 'Science, Education and Civilization'. Frankland continued that, during the lecture, unbeknown to Lhotsky, arrangements had been made to have two devils rise suddenly on either side of the lectern, thrusting burning torches towards him. This was calculated to induce Lhotsky to step backwards on to a hidden trap door which would give way, removing him from the theatre 'amidst the plaudits of an admiring and discerning Public'. Much to Frankland's great disappointment, the plot miscarried and Lhotsky ran off the stage before the devils could make their appearance.[70]

In 1836 the pulse of natural history in the colony again began to quicken. In February of that year (although it went unrecorded by the naturalists of the colony)

HMS *Beagle* called at Hobart with the then unknown Charles Darwin aboard.[71] That same month Ronald Gunn was appointed police magistrate at Circular Head on the far north-western coast of Van Diemen's Land. Gunn's diary entry of his arrival at Circular Head records 'the place however altogether looks bleak and miserable. I however anticipate much time for my natural history pursuits'.[72] The post at Circular Head did indeed provide Gunn with sufficient freedom to prepare a manuscript journal, 'The Circular Head Scientific Journal', although the 'Journal' is really no more than the private correspondence of two friends, Gunn and James Grant, who shared similar interests in natural history.[73] Before leaving Launceston, Gunn had made the acquaintance of Grant, who had recently arrived in Launceston to practise medicine and had a particular interest in ornithology.

CHAPTER FOUR

a renaissance of natural history

VAN DIEMEN'S LAND, 1837–43

In his isolated eyrie at Circular Head, Ronald Gunn was informed by Hooker of an event integral to the resurgence of natural history in Van Diemen's Land: John Franklin was to be sent out to Van Diemen's Land as the replacement for Lieutenant Governor George Arthur. Hooker wrote of his friend Franklin, 'If you remain in Van Diemen's Land you will be delighted in him'.[1]

In reply Gunn was critical of the recalled Arthur. In previous correspondence he had referred to Arthur's 'well known encouragement to Science' but now concluded, 'To Science he was unfavourable and less is known of the Nat Hist of V.D.L. in it— than in England'.[2] Grudgingly Gunn admitted that Arthur had at least allowed Van Diemen's Land to achieve 'an almost unexampled degree of prosperity', but Gunn was displeased by Arthur's almost total lack of interest in natural history.

Governor Franklin

Franklin reached Hobart on 6 January 1837 and Gunn soon informed Hooker that 'there is little doubt but a man of his character will please'.[3] However, much of the goodwill towards Franklin was the result of Arthur's unpopularity rather than Franklin's perceived merit.

The colony that Franklin came to govern in 1837 was still a brutal convict society. Unlike New South Wales where the winds of change were already building in strength to sweep aside the infamies of 'Botany Bay', a similar transition was not to occur in Van Diemen's Land until the 1850s. The colony was still small with a population of approximately 42,000. Slightly more than half (24,000) was free. It was a predominantly urban society divided between Hobart (24,000) and Launceston (6,000), with the remainder of the population scattered among the smaller towns or stations. This scant population led to a closed incestuous society.

When Arthur sailed for England he left a legacy of colonial protégés, all with vested interest in maintaining Arthur's policies. Matthew Forster, married to Arthur's niece, retained his position as chief police magistrate. The colonial secretary, John Montagu, who was to give Franklin many problems and eventually secure his replacement, was also related to Arthur by marriage. As well as Arthur's protégés Franklin inherited Arthur's bitter enemies who sought to use Franklin in their battles against the Arthurite camp, and a number of unresolved disputes which were to bedevil his administration.

The man now sent to govern this unruly colony was already known by name to many. His life seemed modelled on heroic endeavour: he fought under Nelson at Copenhagen; served as a midshipman on HMS *Investigator* from 1801 to 1804 under Matthew Flinders during exploratory voyages around the coastline of Australia; befriended Robert Brown; participated in the Battle of Trafalgar; befriended Joseph Banks; and won fame as an Arctic explorer on two voyages. Elected a fellow of the Royal Society in 1822, Franklin also won the gold medal of the Geographical Society of Paris in 1828 for his Arctic exploration. Yet for all his achievements Franklin lacked experience in the administrative role he was now to undertake, and the dour Franklin's administration was to be characterized by naïvety.

On his arrival in Van Diemen's Land, Franklin set in motion a number of natural history initiatives. At his instigation the executive council petitioned Glenelg, secretary of state for the colonies, for the employment of a colonial collector; but unimpressed with this proposal to spend public money, Glenelg rejected it out of hand. The pursuit of government patronage for science was not abandoned by the rebuff, for in November 1839 a petition directed to Franklin from the scientific men of the colony solicited the governor's influence in obtaining the appointment of a colonial naturalist.[4] The individual to be appointed had already been designated, at least by Franklin and his wife. Jane Franklin wrote to her husband from New South Wales in June 1839, 'I hope you will not relax in your endeavour to procure Dr Hobson the Colonial Naturalist's place. Cannot you write to Herschell [sic], Swainson, Murchison, Buckland +c. about it'.[5] The impulse that gave rise to the request for a colonial naturalist also contributed to the formation of the 'Natural History Society of Van Diemen's Land'. The idea of the Natural History Society was canvassed within a year of Franklin's arrival in Hobart. Gunn travelled south to Hobart to meet the Franklins in 1837 and was suitably impressed.

> Sir John & Lady Franklin are sincerely desirous of forwarding the Cause of Natural History in this Colony. A Nat. Hist. Socy. has been Established and Lady Franklin is about purchasing a piece of ground out of her private income for a Collection of our indigenous Plants a thing most urgently wanted.[6]

The Society, however, appears to have been shortlived.

John Gould

In September 1838 a figure destined to assume immense stature by the middle of the century came to the resurgent natural history community of Van Diemen's Land. John Gould was already known and lionized for two previous serial illustrated publications. He now turned to the fauna of Australia for his next works. His decision to personally voyage to the raw antipodes was made easier by the fact that two brothers-in-law lived in New South Wales. Gould's was no solitary quest. He brought with him his talented artist wife Elizabeth, his eldest son, John Gilbert, a zoological collector who was immediately despatched to Swan River, and assorted servants. Gould captivated the Franklins and his extended stay in the colony was spent at Government House. A second son, Franklin, was born to the Goulds while in Van Diemen's Land. Gould accompanied Jane Franklin and Ronald Gunn on various collecting excursions, including an abortive attempt to reach Port Davey. Seduced by the convivial atmosphere of Hobart, Gould lingered in Van Diemen's Land for much of the time he spent in Australia. By the time Gould departed for England he had made fast friends of local naturalists Thomas Ewing and Ronald Gunn. Gunn later supplied Gould with mammal and ornithological specimens, zoological information, and acted as distribution agent in Van Diemen's Land for Gould's works (in return for a ten per cent commission).[7]

The Mechanics' Institute had suffered in the years before Franklin's arrival and was virtually dormant. There was even talk of the formation of a new institution or a literary and scientific society.[8] On Franklin's arrival the Institute installed him as its patron and the Institute began to revive. In 1837 the organization again presented numerous lectures and ambitiously promised an even better programme for the coming year. During previous seasons a hodge-podge of subjects was presented, but after 1837 the Institute was confident that its resources would allow a series of elementary lectures to be conducted, systematically covering various disciplines. It was a promise the Mechanics' Institute made several times over the coming decade but seldom redeemed. In addition to the renewed vigour of the lecture series, the nucleus of a small museum (Lhotsky's collection of geological and mineralogical specimens) had been purchased and further donations were solicited. Although the annual reports for the late 1830s contained impressive claims for new membership, as many dropped out each year as joined, resulting in a membership list that never grew dramatically.

The committee of management of the Institute held out some hope for a government grant. In 1837 the Institute addressed a petition to Franklin requesting government funds, citing as a precedent the £200 per annum provided by the New South Wales legislative council to the Sydney Mechanics' School of Arts from 1835 onwards. During 1838, the legislative council of Van Diemen's Land recommended a grant-in-aid of £150 per annum for the Mechanics' Institute, but the grant required the assent of the secretary of state for the colonies and the approval was not given until early 1841. The Mechanics' Institute might have expected greater governmental support. In 1839 Jane Franklin wrote to her husband from Sydney indicating that the government of the senior colony was to give the Mechanics' School of Arts £4,000 for a building. New South Wales Governor Gipps would have contributed more had not the School of Arts adopted exclusivist rules.[9] Limited government funding was eventually gained by the Van Diemen's Land Mechanics' Institute but the provision of a building was a perennial problem.

John Lillie

The revitalization of the Mechanics' Institute is partly attributable to Franklin's generosity with public money but more so to the arrival of a new group of individuals in the colony. Some, such as Franklin's private secretary, Alexander Maconochie, had already found their way into the Institute. In the long term the most important of these men was to be the Reverend John Lillie. Lillie developed into a spokesman for the relationship between natural history and society. In 1839 Lillie replaced Pedder as president of the Mechanics' Institute and his leadership further strengthened the organization. Indicative of Lillie's impact was his vigorous 'Opening Lecture' of June 1839 delivered at the Theatre Royal before Lieutenant-Governor Franklin and an audience estimated at over 500. The oration was characteristic of Lillie's role as an exponent of science and was a model for Lillie's later public discourses. The lecture centred on a defence of science from accusations made against it in the early nineteenth century. To those who saw contradictions in the teachings of religion and scientific knowledge, Lillie offered the Paleyite argument of design. To those who questioned the usefulness of science, he answered that 'The intention of science . . . is to *confer* power. It teaches man the laws which govern nature for the purpose of giving him command over her'. No Lillie exposition was complete without a sermon on the advantages of science as rational amusement and he completed the lecture by advancing the argument that science not only strengthened and invigorated the intellect but developed a simplicity of character and love of truth in its practitioners.[10]

By 1839 the Mechanics' Institute was run by the emerging middle class of Vandemonian society. With the exception of Joseph Hone, the gentlemen officers of the Institute seldom, if ever, attended its meetings. The committee of management, which met regularly to conduct the business of the Institute, was dominated by the bourgeoisie and there is little evidence that mechanics had gained any power. The 1839 lecture series, the organization's most public offering, still had only minor relevance to the needs of mechanics.[11] Even so, not everyone approved of the lowering of the tone of the Institute and John Franklin regretfully wrote to his wife, 'His [Lillie's] being President of the Mechanic's Institution will tend to bring him much with the middle order of our Society'.[12] In the Franklin years the Mechanics' Institute gained a new maturity. This came in part through the influx of enthusiastic new members, in part from Lillie's influence, particularly his concern with instruction of the young 'as a source of rational amusement', and from Franklin's perceived sympathy for science. Sadly James Ross, that ardent supporter of mechanics' institutes, died in 1839.

Tasmanian Society I

Attempts to organize a natural history society after the advent of Franklin's governorship did not fully coalesce until Ronald Gunn's move from Circular Head to Hobart in October 1838. Repeated requests made to Franklin by English naturalists anxious for information of and specimens from Van Diemen's Land were frequently cited by the participants as the impetus for the founding of the Tasmanian Society.[13] Preoccupied with governing the colony, Franklin hit upon the same scheme that had occurred to Henderson almost a decade earlier. He saw the formation of a natural history society as the way to facilitate some response to these requests. But the question of just who founded the Tasmanian Society later proved a source of controversy, producing an argument between members John Gell and John Lillie. Gell repudiated Lillie's claim to have been the founder, noting that he had heard it on good authority that Edward Bedford, a surgeon in Hobart, was the man responsible. Lillie emphatically replied that he, in the company of fellow naturalists Ronald Gunn and Edmund Hobson, had begun making excursions around the environs of Hobart, and that when he and Gunn mentioned their excursions to Jane Franklin, she seized upon the idea of a society and proposed that the meetings take place at Government House under the governor's auspices.[14] Whatever the merits of Lillie's argument, Bedford certainly played an early part in the Society. A paper he apparently wrote for a meeting of the Society (or one of its predecessors) was dated 23 March 1838.[15] Franklin's role in the Society was never to be more than that of a patron. He provided a meeting place at Government House (later, at the suggestion of his wife, dinner before discussion became part of the ritual), the prestige of the governorship and money (the expenses of the *Tasmanian Journal* were paid out of his pocket). However, it can be fairly concluded that Ronald Gunn, with the help of his friend Edmund Hobson, was primarily responsible for the formation of the Society. Both men were contributors to the meetings and all attempts to organize a society failed before Gunn moved from Circular Head to Hobart.

The Society seems to have been formally established on 17 October 1839 at a meeting attended by Bedford, Ewing, Franklin, Gunn, Hobson, Lillie and Turnbull. The minutes of that meeting, the earliest extant, document the adoption of a rule providing for fortnightly meetings. A rented room was to be set aside for a museum, and a police constable stationed at Bothwell was to be paid one shilling and ninepence for each bird preparation carried out for the museum. Thomas Ewing undertook to write to John Gould, then in New South Wales, asking him to communicate the results of his ornithological work to the Society.[16] The initial emphasis on ornithology, Ewing's field of interest, in the Society reveals his considerable influence.

By November 1839 the Society was well-established. At the first working meeting of 5 November 1839, attended by Franklin, Gunn, Hobson, Lillie and Turnbull, Hobson was the centre of attention when he read a paper on the blood of *Ornithorhynchus paradoxus*, the platypus, and used a microscope to demonstrate the difference in the shape of red blood cells in oviparous (man) and viviparous (goanna) blood. On the basis of blood morphology, Hobson incorrectly argued that monotremes were viviparous.[17] At a subsequent meeting on 30 December 1839 this issue, of immense interest both in Australia and overseas, was reopened. Edward Bedford explained he had questioned Aborigines about platypus eggs and was told they produced live young which they hid in their holes. Bedford, however, noted that there was some doubt as to whether the Aborigines had correctly understood the question.

A fortnight after the 5 November meeting, Ronald Gunn delivered a paper describing a walk between Hobart and the Huon River, and the plant species characteristic of the terrain.[18] At the last meeting for 1839 on 30 December, Gunn again read a paper and exhibited specimens, this time on the edible plants of Van Diemen's Land. Of perhaps greater interest was discussion of various discovery expeditions. Dumont d'Urville, commander of the French exploratory vessels *l'Astrolabe* and *la Zélée*, then riding at anchor in the Derwent, and Charles Jaquinot, his second-in-command, attended the meeting, and both were elected honorary members.[19] Franklin read a letter from John Herschel concerning the British expedition of Captain James Ross, which was about to embark on a voyage to make terrestrial magnetic observations and carry out maritime exploration of the Antarctic. The expedition was expected to call at Hobart in April 1840.

A further letter was read from Robert Brown introducing the microscopist Dr William Valentine who was on his way to Van Diemen's Land. The letter also indicated Brown's desire to establish a botanical correspondence with Ronald Gunn. Gunn later wrote to Hooker, 'The *great* Robt Brown has requested me through Sir John Franklin, to correspond with him . . .'. Gunn added Brown to his carefully chosen list of correspondents.[20] In anticipation of his arrival Valentine was immediately elected a member of the Society, as was Dr Pugh of Launceston.[21]

Gunn and Hobson dominated the early meetings of the Society delivering papers and exhibiting specimens, but for the most part the Society progressed slowly. The 27 January 1840 meeting was attended by only Gunn and Hobson, and after 10 February, with Franklin absent from Hobart and Hobson and Bedford ill, the meetings were suspended until May.[22]

When the Tasmanian Society reconvened on 18 May the pace of proceedings increased. Cotton delivered a paper on the steam engine and its utilization in the colony. The request for ornithological observations made to John Gould produced a paper on the bush turkey of New South Wales.[23] Three new members were elected: John Phillip Gell, Dr Agnew of Port Phillip, and Captain Parkes.[24] By June the Society was occupied with discussion of its greatest claim to scientific legitimacy: the publication of the Society's *Proceedings*. Preparations for the journal had been under way for months and Lillie, in his role as spokesman for natural history in the colony, read part of the 'Introductory Essay' he was preparing for the journal.[25]

The heyday of the Tasmanian Society commenced in August when James Ross's *Erebus* and *Terror* expedition arrived. The vessels remained in Hobart until 12 November when they departed south towards the Antarctic. Their three months in Hobart were a stimulating time for the small scientific community. Attendances at meetings of the Tasmanian Society reached a peak and included the officers and scientific complement of the two vessels, among them Captain Ross, Captain Crozier of the *Terror*, Dr McCormick (surgeon and nominal zoologist aboard the *Erebus*), Assistant Surgeon Lyall of the *Terror*, and Assistant Surgeon Joseph Hooker of the *Erebus*. Lillie again read his 'Introductory Essay'.[26] To John Franklin, burdened daily with the administrative chores of government, the arrival of the Ross expedition was a welcome anodyne. As a former Arctic explorer and a personal friend of Ross, Franklin could commiserate with the trials and exult in the triumphs of the expedition. In nine days 200 convict labourers built an observatory for magnetic observations and Lieutenant Henry Kay, nephew to Franklin, left the discovery vessels at Hobart to take charge of it. At monthly intervals (the so-called 'term days'), in conjunction with other observatories around the world, simultaneous magnetic observations were taken every two-and-a-half minutes over a twenty-four-hour period. For such labour-intensive work Franklin enrolled members of the Tasmanian Society: Gell, Henslowe and Turnbull. Franklin himself worked twelve-hour stints. The chance to participate in the experiments and forget the problems of government even for a few hours brought about a sea change in Franklin, and one of his subordinates noted

> He was quite warmed with enthusiasm and spoke with such delight about the experiments and subsequent calculations made by the Commanding Officers of the Erebus and Terror that he never looked to such advantage before.[27]

When the *Erebus* and *Terror* sailed south, Franklin watched their departure with regret.

Joseph Hooker

While the vessels were still in Hobart, society fêted the ships' officers, although not all were interested in dancing and dining at Government House. Joseph Hooker, second son of Gunn's long-time botanical correspondent, William J. Hooker, preferred to spend his time collecting specimens in the company of Ronald Gunn. Through his long-standing correspondence with Hooker senior, Gunn knew of Joseph and his interest in natural history long before his father wrote to announce that his son was sailing on the *Erebus* as assistant surgeon and botanist.[28]

Joseph Hooker retained an interest in zoology while aboard the *Erebus* but he was now following in his father's botanical footsteps. This is hardly surprising given his father's network of botanical acquaintances, which included all the foremost botanists of Europe. It was this network of powerful friends that gained Joseph Hooker the berth of assistant surgeon and, more importantly, botanist, aboard *Erebus*. Robert

McCormick, surgeon, appointed zoologist to the *Erebus*, lacked Joseph Hooker's enthusiasm and ambition, and so confined his activities to the collection of ornithological and geological specimens.[29] Accordingly Hooker became the *de facto* naturalist for the voyage. Despite the lengthy sea journey, during which he read the recently published *Voyage of the Beagle* by Charles Darwin, Hobart held little appeal for Joseph Hooker. John Franklin wrote to William Hooker describing Joseph's zeal. 'He would always be at his work and in this respect reminded me often of our mutual friend Dr Richardson.'[30] This enthusiasm sometimes conflicted with the strong religious disposition of the Franklins. Joseph confided to his father, 'I got specimens after service on Sunday although Lady Franklin did not like it and very properly but I thought it excusable as being my only chance at gathering Anopterus galdulosus'.[31]

During Joseph Hooker's time in Van Diemen's Land he and Ronald Gunn established a warm and enduring friendship. In his 'Introductory Essay' to the *Flora of Tasmania* (1860), Joseph Hooker described his time in Hobart:

> we either studied together in the field or in his library; or when he could not accompany me himself, he directed one of his servants, who was an experienced plant collector, to accompany me and take charge of my specimens. I can recall no happier weeks of my various wanderings over the globe, than those spent with Mr Gunn, collecting in the Tasmanian mountains or forests, or studying our plants in his library . . .[32]

While in Hobart, Joseph Hooker intimated to Gunn that he intended to write a monograph on the eucalypts.[33] It was to be part of an extended series of publications dealing with the flora of Tasmania which Hooker published over the next two decades.[34] Not all of Joseph Hooker's publications were well received. Volume I, number 1 of the *Tasmanian Journal of Natural Science* contained an article attributed to Hooker, 'On the Examination of some Fossil Wood from Macquarie Harbour, Tasmania'. Hooker later indicated that the paper had not been intended for publication and had appeared without his consent. Ronald Gunn had added sufficient conjecture to the original notes to make it 'unintelligible'. Hooker's dismay at seeing the paper in print may have been partly due to Robert Brown's reaction; the latter labelled it 'a very careless production'.[35] The *Erebus* and *Terror* sailed, first for the Antarctic and then home to Britain, in November 1840.

Tasmanian Society II

In February of 1840 Gunn succeeded Henry Elliot as private secretary to Governor John Franklin and was therefore able to resign his official posts. Gunn's tenure as private secretary was brief and his posting was never more than a temporary measure while Franklin awaited the arrival of Francis Henslowe. By December 1840 Gunn was eager for Henslowe's arrival which would allow him to accept an offer to manage the estates of W. E. Lawrence on the northern half of the island. Gunn's relief in giving up the position was obvious. Jane Franklin informed Gunn's friend, Edmund Hobson '. . . his health & spirits are improved by having got rid of the care and drudgery of his office'.[36] Shortly after Gunn's move north, his long-time correspondent, William J. Hooker, was appointed director of Kew Gardens.

When Gunn took up the management of Lawrence's estates, Francis Henslowe became secretary to the Tasmanian Society. He brought to the position a somewhat more bureaucratic mind than Gunn's, and the Tasmanian Society acquired a formal minutebook to replace the scraps of paper on which Gunn had recorded the minutes.[37]

The cover of the minutebook was graced with a drawing of a platypus and the Society's motto 'All things queer and opposite'. With neither Gunn nor Hobson now resident in Hobart (Hobson had emigrated to Port Phillip), the Tasmanian Society began to lose its momentum and meetings were reduced from fortnightly to monthly intervals. The 3 March 1841 meeting heard scientific papers and saw additional corresponding members elected, but much of the time of the Society was taken up with the mechanics of the impending publication of the *Tasmanian Journal*. At this meeting Franklin defended the use of the newly established office of government printer to issue the *Journal*, which had been called into question by complaints from Edward Abbott, owner of the *Hobart Town Courier*, and John Hall, proprietor of the *Advertiser*.[38] The circumstances which led the government printer, James Barnard, to compete with private printers in the production of the *Tasmanian Journal* were later described by Ronald Gunn. Gunn had applied to Elliston, the proprietor of the *Hobart Town Gazette*, to have the *Journal* printed but Elliston had neither the press nor quality of typeface the Tasmanian Society required. In the colony the government printer alone had the necessary type. With neatness and accuracy deemed of paramount importance for a scientific publication, there was no other choice but to use Barnard.[39] At the following monthly meeting (7 April), James Barnard was elected a member of the Society.

In contrast to the formal minutes of the Society during 1841 are entries in the diaries of G. W. T. Boyes, colonial auditor and member of the Society. Boyes makes no mention of the Society in his entries for 3 March and 6 May, although he was recorded in the minutes as having attended meetings of the Society on both days. Entries in his diary for 4 June, 4 August and 3 November do chronicle meetings of the Society but, with the exception of 4 August, make no comment on their content. At the latter meeting, in addition to observing that both Jane Franklin and John Franklin's niece, Sophia Carcroft, were present, Boyes added the laconic comment that Bradbury read a paper on New Zealand 'so poorly that he sent Sir John to sleep who snored like a hog'.[40] Clearly, some of the meetings of the Society were less than stimulating. Just as clearly, a number of the members of the Tasmanian Society had little expertise or interest in natural history. G. W. T. Boyes was one of these social members; others included George Bagot, Franklin's aide-de-camp, the self-admitted unscientific Francis Henslowe, and James Barnard. Barnard had no illusions of his scientific competence. He wrote to Gunn of the unanimous election of his 'unscientific self' to membership in the Society.[41] The timing of Barnard's election and his agreement to print the *Tasmanian Journal* are unlikely to have been coincidental. In contrast to its inception, the Tasmanian Society had now become a club not strictly based on science. In fact, as was becoming increasingly evident, the Tasmanian Society was proving as exclusive as its predecessor, the Van Diemen's Land Society.[42]

Although occasionally attacked in the more radical colonial press on charges of exclusivism, there is no direct evidence that the Society was exclusive. There is little doubt, however, that many of its founders saw the Society as an exclusive scientific club and were decidedly anti-emancipist. Francis Henslowe, secretary of the Society in 1842, discussing the creation of a later competitor, the Royal Society of Van Diemen's Land, dismissed it as a 'Frankenstein' body which included convicts.[43] John Gell, Henslowe's successor as secretary of the Society, was a diehard exclusivist. Lamenting the problems of the Tasmanian Society in 1843–44, he wrote to Gunn 'How is it that people will never let well enough alone. The Tasmanian Society was an autocracy, and flourished until we came to the nonsense of voting and titles +& all that'.[44] The following year Gell noted that he had not attended the Queen's birthday celebrations in the colony since Governor Eardley-Wilmot had not excluded 'improper persons', specifically the newspaper proprietor and emancipist Robert Murray. Gell, in a state of high moral indignation, continued 'But the daughters of Van Diemen's Land, to the shame of their fathers be it said, are come to that pitch that they will sooner dance with a Convict than not dance at all'.[45] Even Ronald Gunn, while not manifestly exclusivist, was a leader in the movement to continue transportation of convicts to Tasmania as a source of cheap labour for landowners in the 1850s.[46] With the exception of Adam Turnbull, individuals who had taken a stand for a non-exclusive Van Diemen's Land Society a decade before, men such as James Ross, John Burnett and Charles Swanston, played no part in the Tasmanian Society.[47]

Bothwell Literary Society

A smaller society, both in terms of membership and its impact on Tasmanian science, the Bothwell Literary Society clearly illustrates the tensions created by the emancipists' claim to social respectability. Despite its name the Bothwell Literary Society was more properly a traditional 'philosophic society' incorporating both literary and scientific elements. The Society existed as early as June 1834 but only met in a desultory fashion.[48] By May 1836 it had begun its metamorphosis from a circulating library into a philosophical society, and its activities included the organization of a museum.[49] That winter in Bothwell the Society inaugurated a lecture series at the schoolroom: 22 June, 'The Atmosphere—its component parts and peculiar properties' (J. Garrett); 29 June, 'The advantage of reading history in preference to works of fiction by its communication of truth' (Barr); 21 July, 'Botany' (J. Sharland); 28 July, 'Optics' (J. P. Moss); and 18 August, 'The infinite variety which characterizes the material creation' (J. Garrett). These lectures attracted a wide audience. Mrs Williams confided to her diary

> Attended the Lecture on Optics delivered last night by Mr Moss and was much pleased; I think it the best we have yet heard. He had taken great trouble in preparing paintings which were fastened to the wall to assist his explanation of the effects of light . . . I liked the lecture for I felt that it added to my store of knowledge, and on an interesting subject of which I before was very ignorant . . . It is really astonishing to see such things in so young a settlement: It is most pleasing, and I trust and pray that all knowledge will be sought by us all that it may inlarge our minds, improving our understanding, and lead us to adore and love the Wonderful Being into whose glorious Works knowledge enables us to look.[50]

The annual report for 1836 of the invigorated Bothwell Society indicated that £25 had been raised to purchase an airpump and a magic lantern for demonstration lectures. When this equipment arrived from England the following year, however, the magic lantern was found to be defective, rendering the accompanying astronomical slides useless. The influence of the local Presbyterian minister, Reverend James Garrett, on the Society is obvious from the annual report of 1836:

> It is only *by connecting* the discoveries of Literature and Science with the discoveries of revelation and making the former subservient to the latter and reducing the whole to a practical bearing on our moral destinies that the grand results of literary and scientific knowledge are to be gained.[51]

The Bothwell Literary Society resembled nothing so much as a provincial mechanics' institute under another name. Perhaps this is not surprising given that Garrett, the mainstay of the Society, had been educated at the University of Glasgow, a city which was an early home to the mechanics' institute movement.

The following year the Society petitioned newly arrived Lieutenant-Governor John Franklin to become its patron.[52] The lecture series of 1837 was devoted particularly to natural history and natural philosophy and, significantly, at the instigation of Phineas Moss, the Society undertook to form a class in natural philosophy. For threepence a week the intricacies of physics and mechanics could be explored every Wednesday evening.[53] All this, in a town so remote that the Society's annual report for 1837 noted 'It is with considerable regret that your Committee would observe that the course of Lectures was interrupted by the alarm occasioned by Bushrangers . . .'.[54]

The Society continued its lecture series over the next several years. In 1840, in the aftermath of a long-running dispute over the dual occupation by both Anglicans and Presbyterians of the only church in Bothwell, Reverend Garrett resigned his ministry. At the 8 June 1841 meeting of the Bothwell Literary Society, Garrett also resigned as its secretary. The newly arrived Episcopalian minister, the Reverend Thomas Wigmore, was elected secretary in Garrett's place, although Garrett continued to attend meetings.

The Bothwell Literary Society now entered a period of riotous turbulence. In 1836 the *Hobart Town Courier* had hoped that the Society, remote from party feeling in the colony, would flourish.[55] Unhappily this was not to be. At the 17 August 1841 meeting H. M. Cockerill, an emancipist, was admitted as a member; but three weeks later, at the annual meeting, Major Schaw, police magistrate in Bothwell, moved that irregularities in Cockerill's admission invalidated his membership. The motion was seconded by Police Constable Redmond. Dr Hall, supported by Garrett, objected to the exclusivist motion rescinding Cockerill's membership, but it was nevertheless carried.[56] Hall and Garrett immediately moved that Cockerill be readmitted to the Society but the meeting adjourned without a vote. A week later the meeting was reconvened with a liberal majority present. Cockerill was again elected a member but Reverend Wigmore was most displeased with this result and he subjected the supporters of Cockerill to considerable verbal abuse.[57] The Society met next on 7 October but Wigmore continued to be abusive, indicating with 'great violence of manner' that he had attended the meeting only to disrupt it, issuing threats to all present and refusing to fulfil his duties as secretary. A vote taken to dismiss Wigmore from the Society had no effect. Eventually McDowell, the chairman, requested the police constable to remove Wigmore from the meeting, but Wigmore's fellow exclusivist, Redmond, declined to act.[58] The following day Reverend Wigmore and Police Magistrate Schaw broke into the library of the Society to emphasize their contempt for its actions. The capacity of the free–emancipist debate to rupture communities was evident: a former minister, the local medical officer and a number of prominent citizens of Bothwell had taken one side, while the current minister and many of the local colonial officers provided stern opposition.

The dispute now moved into the newspapers. The 22 October *Hobart Town Courier* published a letter from the pseudonymous 'Vindex' purporting to report what went on at the meeting of 'The Illiterate Society of Low Fellow'. Most of those present, with the exception of Wigmore, came under criticism from 'Vindex'. A second report, disputing the facts of 'Vindex', was also printed.[59] The *Hobart Town Courier* terminated the controversy on 29 October when it published a letter under the signatures of ten members of the Society repudiating 'Vindex's' report as 'a tissue of malicious falsehoods from beginning to end and a fit emanation from the despicable individuals of the quadruple alliance who sat in congress to concoct it'.[60] The quadruple alliance was presumably the police trio, Schaw, Redmond and Robinson, together with Wigmore.

The emancipist–free dispute dismembered the Bothwell Literary Society and it lay dormant for two years until the Reverend John Robertson attempted to reorganize it. Those who attended a meeting of the Society called for 15 August 1843 were of the pro-emancipist faction. Schaw, Redmond and Robinson were notably absent, but Reverend Wigmore chose to attend. When he attempted to put forward an innocuous motion the chairman, McDowell, refused to hear it on the grounds that Wigmore had previously been expelled from the organization.[61] Further meetings censored the minutes Wigmore had entered during the period of controversy and reasserted Wigmore's loss of membership.[62] It is somewhat ironic that emancipist Cockerill, the catalyst in the controversy, had dropped out of the Society by 1844.[63] The Society soon decided to dispose of its philosophic apparatus, and reverted to a purely literary body.[64]

The end of the five-year heyday of the Bothwell Literary Society as a philosophic organization paralleled the faltering of the Tasmanian Society. Initiatives already set in motion, particularly the *Tasmanian Journal of Natural Science*, continued in 1842 but how often the Society met is open to question. A trend that did continue was the growth of its membership. In August 1841 the Society included eleven resident members and thirty corresponding members, but by the end of 1842 the numbers had grown to thirty-three resident members and thirty-nine corresponding members. Although an appreciable increase in membership had occurred, the figures are somewhat misleading. Resident membership in 1841 was generally limited to those who lived in or near Hobart; resident members in 1842 included all those who lived in Van Diemen's Land.[65]

By 1842 the focus of the Tasmanian Society had been transferred almost exclusively to the *Tasmanian Journal of Natural Science*. The first four parts were issued in 1842 and bound with the fifth part into Volume I.[66] The vast majority of contributions were original scientific papers written by colonial naturalists, or at least naturalists temporarily resident in the colony.

In a related enterprise, the Society's *de facto* patroness, Jane Franklin, arranged for construction to commence on a building to house a museum. The museum was originally destined to be part of a college. Until the college opened, however, Jane Franklin proposed investing custody of the building in the Tasmanian Society. When that option was stalled by legal difficulties, the building was vested in trustees drawn from the ranks of the Tasmanian Society. Caught up in the political machinations of the colony in the 1840s, the proposed college never opened and the museum, left in limbo after the recall of Franklin and his wife, was neglected after 1843.

Franklins farewelled

Political events had now begun to overtake natural history. Franklin's initial period as governor had progressed well enough, despite the necessity of implementing decisions with which he often did not agree, made half a world away. There was also continual pressure from the Colonial Office to reduce local expenditure, a situation made critical after 1840 when the boom years of Van Diemen's Land gave way to a severe recession. The change of administration from Arthur to Franklin had thrown up problems, the most significant of which were Franklin's difficulties with the leader of the Arthurite faction, Colonial Secretary John Montagu. The problem was temporarily alleviated in February 1839 when Montagu took leave and departed for England. But he returned in March 1841 and was immediately reinstated as colonial secretary. Typical of the colonies during this period, the relationship between governor and colonial secretary, and the power wielded by each, waxed and waned depending on the incumbents.

Franklin's naïvety and inexperience increased the political effectiveness of the colonial secretary. Montagu was clever, mercenary, and never reluctant to wield his power.[67] By 1842 Montagu had been dismissed for questioning the accuracy of Franklin's memory. G. W. T. Boyes was temporarily appointed colonial secretary in his place. Montagu sailed for England and by lobbying his contacts in the Colonial Office eventually brought about John Franklin's recall.

The year began successfully enough for natural history. The Tasmanian Society met on 2 January 1843 to elect Captain Beard, commander of the visiting French vessel *le Rhin* a corresponding member. Additional members elected included Renaud and Verreaux, respectively first lieutenant and naturalist of *le Rhin*, and J. B. Jukes.[68] The subsequent meeting, held four months later on 17 May, heard a paper sent by Jukes and undertook balloting for other members including the new colonial secretary, John Bicheno, and P. Fraser, the colonial treasurer. The election of these individuals continued the expansion of the membership, a number of whom tended to be scientifically naïve. Of the thirty-six resident members many lacked any particular interest in science. The Society had changed drastically from the small coterie of active naturalists brought together by Gunn and Hobson.

By July dissension was starting to wrack the organization. Bedford sent in his resignation to the 5 July meeting when Franklin informed him that discussion of a note by Turnbull, which Franklin considered an unfit subject for the drawing room, was not to be resumed. Two days later Boyes recorded in his diary that Henslowe had called a meeting to discuss Turnbull's note and Bedford's resignation. Boyes declined to attend the meeting, pleading the pressure of work.[69] The following meeting, 2 August, reinstated Bedford but Turnbull submitted his resignation. Whatever the importance of the episode, it was soon to be lost when on 17 August John Eardley-Wilmot stepped ashore to replace Franklin as lieutenant-governor of Van Diemen's Land. Franklin did not receive official notification of his replacement until three days later but must have known unofficially of his recall from at least the beginning of July when papers announcing Eardley-Wilmot's appointment were landed in Hobart. In August the Tasmanian Society sent a delegation to the bishop of Hobart, F. R. Nixon, requesting him to assume the vice-presidency of the Society, and an address was drawn up for presentation to the departing Franklin. Indicative of the dissension in Van Diemen's Land was the fact that, even within his select scientific society, Franklin felt it necessary in a draft reply to the address to acknowledge that some, or even all, of the members may have disagreed with the policies of his administration.[70] This evidence of divisiveness was deleted from the final address.

With Eardley-Wilmot's arrival, Franklin retired to New Norfolk until transport could be arranged for his party to return to England. This was not until 3 November.[71] In the months before his departure, Franklin was to witness the apparent disintegration of the Tasmanian Society. Events came quickly, and it appears that the Society was undermined by one of its own disaffected members. As protocol dictated, the Society solicited Eardley-Wilmot to assume the presidency vacated by Franklin. Eardley-Wilmot accepted the office on 3 October and nominated Saturday 14 October, at Government House, as the time and place to meet the Society in his new role. To the surprise of the members, they found a sizeable contingent of non-members present at the meeting. Their worthy president immediately proceeded to propose a reorganization of the Society and presented a plan whereby the thirty-six members would be increased to fifty, who in turn would ballot for between 200 and 300 further members. Each member of the enlarged body would pay a £2 entrance fee and a £1 annual subscription, and a secretary to be paid £200–300 per annum was to be appointed. Finally, the Government Garden, until then the responsibility of the colonial administration, was to be turned over to the Society along with an annual grant of £400 for its maintenance.[72]

Members of the Tasmanian Society, after their initial shock, saw the imminent disintegration of their organization at hand and rallied to its defence. Bedford questioned the entrance fee; Gell proposed that the changes be printed and distributed to the members of the Society for consideration; and Ewing declared he would not be a member of the changed Society, for he was not prepared to see the organization overwhelmed by new members and its character changed completely. To add to the confusion, W. Champ, who was not a member of the Tasmanian Society, announced he had heard nothing about changing it and that furthermore he did not wish to belong to the Tasmanian Society and had come to form a horticultural society.

Finally Belcher declared that many of the members of the Tasmanian Society had no desire to assume responsibility for the Government Garden. Rather than become a horticultural society, they wished to maintain the wide scientific aims of their original charter. Thereupon Eardley-Wilmot, impatient with such obstructionism, adjourned the Society *sine die* and immediately set about forming a new organization. Members of the Tasmanian Society, with the exception of Barnard, Boyes, Cotton, Lillie and Milligan, left the meeting. The lieutenant-governor, with Barnard, Boyes *et al.*, plus Allport, Champ, Chapman, Dobson, Fraser, Hone, Howe, J. Kerr, R. Kerr, MacDowell, Perry, Poytner and Swanston, remained to inaugurate the Van Diemen's Land Botanical and Horticultural Society.

Van Diemen's Land Botanical and Horticultural Society

Eardley-Wilmot had received instructions from the secretary of state for the colonies stipulating that the governor's residences, which included the Government Garden, would henceforth be funded from the governor's salary. Eardley-Wilmot conceived the idea of divesting himself of the Government Garden by constituting a Van Diemen's Land Botanical and Horticultural Society to undertake its management. Eardley-Wilmot's initial proposal evolved into a Royal Society of Van Diemen's Land for Horticulture, Botany and the Advancement of Science, and the idea was submitted to the secretary of state for his approval in a despatch dated 15 September 1843, a month before the meeting at Government House.[73]

There already existed a Hobart Town Horticultural Society which would have seemed a ready vehicle for Eardley-Wilmot's proposal, especially as Charles Swanston, a firm supporter of Eardley-Wilmot in the events which followed, was its president. That Eardley-Wilmot chose not to follow this course may have been due to the influence of one person, the Reverend John Lillie. In the aftermath of the 14 October meeting, Lillie resigned from the Tasmanian Society and noted that his enthusiasm for the Society had ended in 1841 due to

> the appointment of a certain person as Secretary, Editor, etc who though they doubt-lessly take abundant credit to themselves as guardians + representatives of Literature and Science in the colony have not been able to get that credit from anyone else.[74]

The individual indirectly referred to by Lillie was John Gell. Lillie's immediate election to the council of Eardley-Wilmot's new society and his subsequent appointment as a vice-president would seem to confirm his role in establishing the new organization at the cost of the older Tasmanian Society.[75] Ronald Gunn, sequestered in Launceston away from the immediate events, was less annoyed at the turn of events than the Hobart members of the Tasmanian Society. He wrote to William Hooker that Eardley-Wilmot had 'established a Horticultural & Botanical Society at Hobart Town but I doubt very much its success.—There are no men in the Colony who give up time to these things'. Gunn also summed up Franklin's tenure as governor. 'He may not have been a brilliant Governor, but he was certainly a good man & influenced by the best and purest motives.'[76] That same day Gunn began seeking ways to reactivate the Tasmanian Society. He proposed to Gell that they have Franklin resume the presidency, that the *Tasmanian Journal* be printed in England if Eardley-Wilmot refused the services of the government printer (Gunn favoured this course for it allowed articles to be reviewed by prominent English naturalists), that articles for publication be vetted by a local committee to eliminate unsuitable material, and that Ewing should become secretary.

Despite Gunn's optimism, the Tasmanian Society suffered a further setback. The Hobart members met on 29 January 1844 and heard a new proposal put by Barnard and Cotton to amalgamate with Eardley-Wilmot's Society. The meeting agreed to the union and this vote for amalgamation was communicated to the Botanical and Horticultural Society, only to be spurned.[77] The bishop of Tasmania, absent from the meeting, was so annoyed that the Society had contemplated taking such a step in his absence that he promptly resigned the vice-presidency. Gell himself wished to resign as secretary and suggested that Gunn should organize the Tasmanian Society from the northern side of the island.

> Here it is impossible to carry on ... The suicide has been committed, it needs no Coroner's jury to tell us that. They are all afraid of the Governor, anxious not to displease him. So there is the end of our philosophy.[78]

On 30 April the northern members of the Tasmanian Society met and heard the news from Gell that the Society in Hobart had 'virtually ceased to exist'. The gathering resolved that if the Hobart members did not intend to meet, they would claim Launceston as the headquarters of the Society. If Gell resigned, Gunn was to be appointed in his place.[79] By May the Tasmanian Society in Hobart was well and truly dead. The final meeting called by Bishop Nixon to hear his resignation attracted only two other members. Even the proposal that Gunn replace Gell as secretary could not be ratified, for the meeting had not been formally constituted. Gell indicated to Gunn that as the sole remaining officer of the Society he would call a meeting of Society members in Launceston, who could immediately accept his resignation and appoint Gunn in his place.[80]

Armed with Gell's resignation, Gunn set about resurrecting the Tasmanian Society and within two weeks a meeting was called in Launceston. Following Gell's suggestion, his resignation was presented, accepted, and Gunn appointed in his place. The meeting also decided to ask John Franklin to resume the presidency. At this gathering of northern Tasmanian Society members only four individuals were present (Lieutenant W. Breton, R. B. Davies, C. Friend and Gunn), but true to the traditions of the Society's early years, mineralogical and palaeontological specimens were exhibited and discussed.[81] The Society continued to meet monthly in its northern home and successive meetings elected new members, heard papers and discussed specimens. Those particularly active were Gunn, Breton, Friend, Grant, Pugh and Henty. During the following years, the Society forged strong ties with the growing community of naturalists across Bass Strait in Port Phillip. By 1846 the organization again had thirty-four members on its books, only eighteen of whom had belonged to the Society in 1842.[82] As could be expected, a much higher proportion of the resident members was now domiciled in the northern half of the island, but almost half still resided in Hobart. Absent from the 1846 membership list were John Lillie and Adam Turnbull.

By late 1844 Gunn must have held some hope that the Tasmanian Society would, on the strength of its journal, eventually supplant Eardley-Wilmot's upstart Royal Society (the society received royal sanction in September 1844). John Gell had written from Hobart that the southern members of the Tasmanian Society had come to regret the move of the society north and that the Royal Society was a failure.[83] Similarly, James Barnard communicated the news that, '*Here* [Hobart] *everything drags*'. Barnard was pleased to enrol himself a citizen of Gunn's new 'republic'.[84] But the resurrection did not occur. After 1843 the Tasmanian Society functioned as only a wan shadow of its former self, and that it continued to exist at all was almost entirely due to Ronald Gunn. Its existence was dependent on one thing, the continued publication of the *Tasmanian Journal of Natural Science*. The task was immense. As Gunn confided to Edmund Hobson in 1847, it was a costly exercise carried out at his own expense. If he could find no financial support for the *Tasmanian Journal* soon, Gunn supposed that he would be forced to give up the venture.[85]

The Tasmanian Society remained Launceston-based, but Launceston did not support a large enough community of naturalists to make the Society viable. The small band continued to meet and hear papers until at least May 1848, and the *Tasmanian Journal* continued to appear irregularly. But the dearth of naturalists in Launceston was most apparent in the increased proportion of papers published from outside Launceston or even beyond Tasmania.

Various proposals were made between 1843 and 1848 for the amalgamation of the Tasmanian Society with the Royal Society. After the rebuff of the Tasmanian Society's proposal of January 1844 the next initiative did not eventuate until the close of 1846. With the departure of Eardley-Wilmot and his replacement by the caretaker government of Charles La Trobe, the Tasmanian Society and the Royal Society now competed on more equal terms. La Trobe sought a reconciliation of the two societies as did his colonial secretary, James Bicheno, who held membership in both. At a special council meeting of the Royal Society held in January 1847, with Bicheno in the chair, the secretary of the Royal Society was instructed to communicate with the secretary of the Tasmanian Society to determine under what conditions such a union could be effected.[86] Lillie, secretary of the Royal Society, wrote to Gunn about an amalgamation and tentatively proposed union under the name of the Royal Tasmanian Society for the encouragement of Botany, Horticulture and other Science.[87]

Gunn, in polling the members of his Society about the union, tapped a wellspring of vitriol. William Valentine was not 'desirous of uniting with a society of swindlers and sinking into a mere club of market gardeners'.[88] Francis Henslowe asked 'Has it [the Royal Society] done anything more than undersell the Market Gardens of Hobart Town by devoting a portion of this £400 to the cultivation of Cabbages?'.[89] Edmund Hobson, from across Bass Strait, was even more vehement.

> Let us have nothing to do with the unclean beasts (I mean the Roys) . . . Never let us amalgamate with such impotence. Glory and honour are just now rewarding your exertion. I shall cease to do even the little I have done if you allow such an unholy alliance.[90]

Not all the Tasmanian Society members were so stridently opposed. James Agnew welcomed the union but wanted 'Horticulture' dropped from the name.[91] Nevertheless, Gunn's poll favoured rejection and this time it was the minutes of the Royal Society (4 March 1847) that recorded the Tasmanian Society as having vetoed the union.

As late as 1848 attempts to effect a formal union continued, notably through financial pressure from Lieutenant-Governor Denison and a scheme devised by William Henty, secretary of the Launceston Horticultural Society. This involved the Royal Society becoming an umbrella organization for local societies: the Launceston and Hobart Horticultural societies, the Tasmanian Society, and the Midlands Society.

Much of the bitterness of the members of the Tasmanian Society was over the issue of government patronage. Having had his recommendation for a colonial collector rejected early in his administration, Franklin was loath to seek similar funds for the Tasmanian Society and chose the indirect method of sending Glenelg's successor, John Russell, two copies of the first issue of the Society's publication, the *Tasmanian Journal of Natural Science*. Franklin's accompanying despatch was an indirect plea for a government grant for the Society.[92] The ploy was successful. Francis Henslowe, one-time private secretary to Franklin, later indicated that part of his duties had been to forward copies of the *Tasmanian Journal* to the secretary of state for the colonies and leading European scientists. The enthusiastic reception of the *Journal* had the effect that 'the Secretary of State spontaneously proposed that from the Public Fund a sum of £400 be granted to assist the *Tasmanian Society* . . .'.[93] This intention of funding and encouraging the Tasmanian Society was expressed by Russell's successor, Stanley, to Franklin's successor, Eardley-Wilmot. Finding that the Tasmanian Society would not bend to his will, Eardley-Wilmot created his new Botanical and Horticultural Society and diverted the annual £400 subsidy to it. Loyalist members of the Tasmanian Society were almost unanimous in believing this to be a misappropriation of funds and were vituperative in voicing their dissatisfaction. Thus Henslowe wrote of the malicious contrivances of Franklin's enemies; and Valentine, of swindlers establishing a society with the stolen property of the Tasmanian Society.[94] Attempts to secure a portion of this funding (reduced to £200 in 1845) for the Tasmanian Society were unsuccessful, and it was left with only the rental income of £75 from its custody of Jane Franklin's Ancanthe estate.

Although the last number of the *Tasmanian Journal* (Vol. III, No. VI) was dated January 1849, Gunn may have contemplated further publication. A letter from Bicheno in early February 1849 conveyed the lieutenant-governor's approval for the *Tasmanian Journal* to again be printed by the government printer.[95] Volumes II and III of the journal had come from the presses of Launceston printer Henry Dowling. But the Tasmanian Society was functionally dead after 16 August, 1848. That day Ronald Gunn was admitted into the Royal Society of Tasmania under a newly enacted rule that sanctioned the admittance of Tasmanian Society members without recourse to balloting. Within a year, holdouts from the Tasmanian Society such as Thomas Ewing and Matthew Friend had also joined the Royal Society.

With the accession of the active members of the Tasmanian Society into the Royal Society of Tasmania, and the appointment of an energetic secretary in the person of Joseph Milligan, the Royal Society of Tasmania could legitimately claim to be a scientific society. After 1848 the Royal Society of Tasmania expanded rapidly and became the focus for science in the colony.

Mechanics' Institute II

The imbroglio over the Tasmanian Society in 1843 had little affect on the Mechanics' Institute. The only observable consequence was that Lillie, after he resigned from the Tasmanian Society, briefly began to attend committee of management meetings.[96]

With the exception of the Reverend John Lillie, members of the exclusive Tasmanian Society had held themselves aloof from the Mechanics' Institute. Despite the Tasmanian Society's concentration of talent, few gave lectures at the Institute. The Mechanics' Institute was public and catered if not for mechanics, then at least for the aspiring middle class. It represented not so much a competitor to the Tasmanian Society as an alternative. The Mechanics' Institute maintained a museum, an honorary curator (in 1842, Henry Allnutt; subsequently, the Reverend W. R. Wade) and a library. Before 1848, the Tasmanian Society and, to a lesser extent, the Royal Society of Tasmania, were never really more than clubs; scientific in the case of the Tasmanian Society, horticultural in the case of the Royal Society. While members of both societies were naturalists of varying competence, they worked for their own pleasure, ambition and knowledge. It was they who were to win scientific honours (such as Ronald Gunn's election to fellowship in the Royal Society and Linnean Society), it was they who were involved in publishing papers.

The Mechanics' Institute brought natural history and science to the people of Tasmania, holding lectures both on applied science ('On mechanics', 'On the practical application of electrical sciences') and less utilitarian subjects ('On the anatomy and physiology of animals', 'On chemistry'). A preparation laboratory and apparatus room were accommodated next to the lecture hall, there was a growing museum, and the library contained a substantial number of works on natural history. Perhaps most importantly, classes had been inaugurated. Although a proposed class in chemistry lapsed through lack of interest, Professor Rennie's class in natural history averaged an attendance of fourteen who paid one-and-a-half guineas for the three-month course. These initiatives were premature: the museum went unvisited and the classes soon lapsed until the 1850s.

In 1842 a second Mechanics' Institute opened in Launceston and looked forward to every success. A series of lectures was promised from reverends Price and Garrett, Matthew Friend, Dr Paton and Ronald Gunn. Price's 'Introductory Lecture' was received by a crowded audience and Friend's dissertation on 'Astronomy' was heard by almost 150. Gunn's lecture did not eventuate and he became estranged from the Institute.[97] The Launceston Mechanics' Institute had its difficulties. It had trouble retaining individuals on its committee of management, because many did not pay their subscriptions. Lieutenant-Governor Franklin accepted the position of patron but declined to provide any public funds. The scarcity of books in its library led to under-utilization, and a curious dispute arose among members on teetotalism which caused a split in the membership.[98] Like its Hobart counterpart, the Launceston Mechanics' Institute was dominated by clerics, particularly Charles Price and John West, and focused much of its attention on rational amusement for the middle classes. In its *Rules* for 1844 the phrase 'the voluntary association of mechanics', included in the original 1842 *Rules*, was dropped. The fourth annual report expressed surprise that the Institute was so poorly patronized by mechanics and the operative classes. A suggestion was made that 'this lack could be remedied if master tradesmen would point out the advantage of the Institute to their workmen'.

After the initial enthusiasm, interest in the Launceston Mechanics' Institute waned. Audiences attending lectures in 1846 were so reduced that the committee did not ask for further lecturers. Later years proved more successful, but like many of its counterparts the Launceston Mechanics' Institute never realized its early promise.

There were many similarities between the course of science in Van Diemen's Land and in New South Wales during the 1820s and 1830s. In the 1820s both colonies saw exclusive scientific clubs set up to accommodate small groups of 'gentlemen'. Both societies were quickly riven by the social tensions inherent in the inadvertent social experiment taking place in the colonies as they began to change from convict to free societies. Both colonies were briefly governed by scientifically inclined governors, Brisbane in New South Wales from 1821 to 1825, and Franklin in Van Diemen's Land from 1837 to 1843. The tenure of these governors was cut short by ambitious colonial secretaries who, given wide latitude by their weak superiors, brought about each governor's recall. Science flourished under each governor's patronage then lapsed until the 1850s when vice-regal patronage was again restored. By then it was too late. The mantle of scientific leadership in the Australian colonies had passed to Victoria.

CHAPTER FIVE

Australia Felix

PORT PHILLIP DISTRICT, 1840–54

On 5 November 1839, a scant four years after the Port Phillip district had been settled from Van Diemen's Land, the Union Benefit Society called a meeting to consider the formation of a mechanics' institute.[1] The outcome of that assembly was the inauguration of the Mechanics' School of Arts of Australia Felix, an event reported with much satisfaction by the *Port Phillip Gazette*. Nine months earlier the *Gazette*'s editor had republished an extract from the *South Australian Gazette*, informing his readers of the inception of a Natural History Society of South Australia and noting the precocity of that infant colony in establishing such a society.[2]

The foundation of the Melbourne Mechanics' School of Arts marked a transition for natural history, and indeed science, in a region which was to become first the colony, then later the state of Victoria. It heralded the end of the era of the heroic, the passage of natural history from the mythic to the prosaic. Henceforth the Australian hero–explorer–naturalist would focus his attention on areas beyond the boundaries of the future colony. In the Port Phillip district, natural history became the domain of the settler: the labourer, mechanic, squatter, physician and professional naturalist.

The eventide of an era had descended. The course of natural history in Victoria over the previous forty-year period—from late on the morning of 10 December 1797, when the longboat of George Bass turned the corner of Cape Howe, until 1839—had been the realm of the discoverer. Men whose names figure prominently in the historical record of early Australia—George Bass, Nicolas Baudin, Matthew Flinders, Hume and Hovell, and Thomas Mitchell—had already played out their part. Many of these men were natural historians in their own right; other explorers secured naturalists, such as George Caley, Robert Brown, Quoy and Gaimard, to accompany their expeditions.

After the permanent settlement of Port Phillip in 1835, the area had initially remained the precinct of itinerant naturalists. From Circular Head, Van Diemen's Land, botanist Ronald Gunn crossed Bass Strait in March 1836 to collect specimens from Port Phillip, Western Port and Port Fairy. Some of the plant species from this voyage were eventually described in George Bentham's *Flora Australiensis*. Over the next decade Gunn corresponded with a number of resident collectors in the Port Phillip district including Miss Roadknight, a collector in Geelong who sent sufficient specimens for Gunn to publish his observations on the Geelong flora in 1842 and, most importantly, John Robertson, who reaped a rich harvest of plants for Gunn in the south-west of the region (the River Glenelg, Wando Vale, and Portland).[3] An overstraiter who emigrated from Van Diemen's Land to the Portland area in 1840,

Robertson had made Gunn's acquaintance before leaving the island. In late 1843 Gunn informed William Hooker that he had amassed some 300 plants from the Portland area which were ready for despatch to Kew Gardens. Six months later a second shipment of 600–700 Portland specimens followed.[4] As a practised botanist, Gunn refuted the complaint of previous naturalists who had superficially examined the flora of Port Phillip and complained that it did not differ appreciably from that of New South Wales. Gunn found the plants of the region were many and varied, with notable dissimilarities to the flora of Van Diemen's Land and Sydney.

A second short-term visitor was the naturalist and Quaker missionary James Backhouse who toured the Australian colonies in the 1830s. During his six years in the colonies Backhouse found time for only one week's visit to Port Phillip in November 1837. Scattered throughout Backhouse's notes on the area are comments on natural history including descriptions of the geology of the area and lists of the birds (Backhouse made the almost obligatory reference to the tinkling note of the bellbird).[5] Backhouse sent collections to England and is known to have given a herbarium of Australian species to the Kew Gardens.

By 1839, after four years of settlement, Melbourne had grown into a town; a change not to everyone's liking. The picturesque wilderness that once rang with the call of the bellbird had been soiled with the reality of commerce. The stench of tanners and soap boilers now dominated the once-pristine banks of the Yarra.[6] The census of March 1841 recorded the population of Port Phillip as 11,738, of whom the great majority (8,274) were male.[7] This growth in population increasingly included educated individuals—from England, overland from Sydney, and across Bass Strait from Van Diemen's Land—who set about recreating, in the wilderness of Port Phillip, the civilization they had left behind.

Botanic Gardens

One obvious example of this civilizing trend was the establishment of the Botanic Gardens. The call for such gardens had little to do with any perceived need for botanic gardens proper, with an emphasis on botanical research and acclimatization, or even for a government domain. Yet in late 1841 the *Port Phillip Gazette*, with much gratification, declared that Governor Gipps had approved the establishment of a public domain in Port Phillip for the purpose of cultivating indigenous and exotic plants. There followed a period of political procrastination with neither the government in Sydney nor the local administration accepting financial responsibility for the gardens, despite the municipal council of Melbourne pointedly observing that there was considerable financial support directed towards the Sydney Botanic Gardens and that Port Phillip could expect the same. With neither body willing to provide the necessary funds, the proposal lapsed until 1845 when the *Gazette* proposed that the government provide money to lay out the grounds while a private subscription be undertaken to fund the salary of a curator. Catering to the growing resentment in Port Phillip over the niggardly behaviour of the Sydney administration the *Gazette*, in language calculated to appeal to its audience, asserted 'when the Government reflects on the large sums that have at one period or another been drained from this Province, we hardly think it will refuse a small grant of money to set on foot an undertaking which is loudly called for'.[8] Although ostensibly only the Botanic Gardens were under discussion, the issue was a stalking-horse for many Port Phillip grievances.

1 Flowers by Thomas Lempriere. Previously unpublished. *By courtesy of the Dixson Galleries, State Library of New South Wales.*

2 'The Franklin Museum'. From the R. Gunn Papers *by courtesy of the Mitchell Library, State Library of New South Wales.*

3 'Captain Cook's Tablet at Cape Solander, Botany Bay, New South Wales', by John Lhotsky. The memorial was erected by the Philosophical Society of Australasia. Previously unpublished. *By courtesy of the Mitchell Library, State Library of New South Wales.*

4 'Common Insectivorous Birds found in Victoria' by John Cotton and John Gould. *By courtesy of the Department of Agriculture, Melbourne.*

5 'John Cotton: 1801–1849' by Maie Casey, from Allan McEvey's *John Cotton's Birds of the Port Phillip District of New South Wales, 1843–1849,* 1974. By courtesy of Allan McEvey.

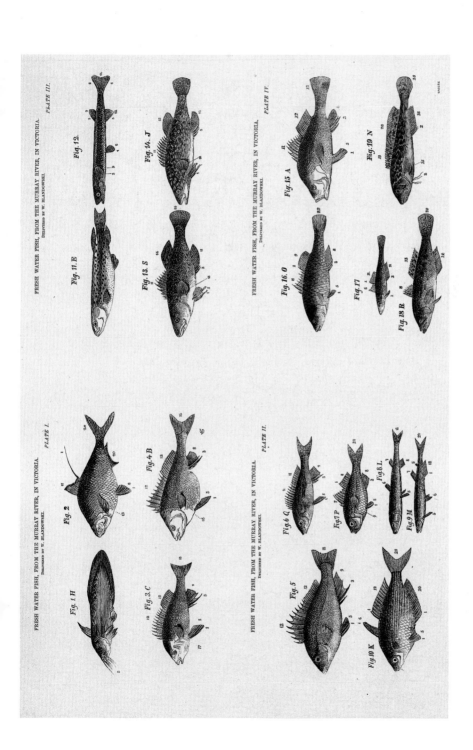

6 'Freshwater Fish from the Murray River in Victoria' by William Blandowski. From the *Transactions* of the Philosophical Institute of Victoria. Previously unpublished.

E-COD!!

Great excitement of Mr. E——d W-ls-n (we decline to give the gentleman's name) on
the arrival of a Murray River Cod at the Victorian Club.

7 'E-Cod!!', *Melbourne Punch* 21 May 1857.

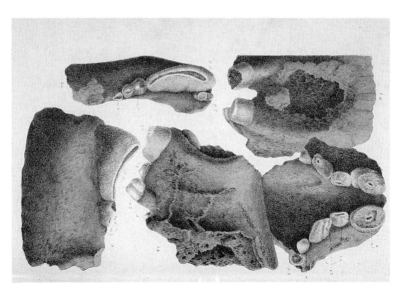

8 'Thylacoleo carnifex' from Frederick McCoy's *Prodromus of the Palaeontology of Victoria*, 1874–82.

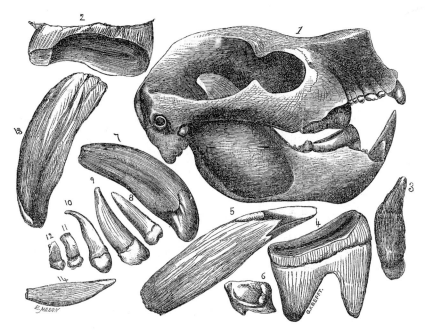

9 'Thylacoleo carnifex' by Gerard Krefft, *Sydney Mail*.

10 'Diprotodon!!', *Sydney Punch* 26 June 1874.

THE MUSEUM.

(A Hue and Cry.)

Stop, thief !   Stop, thief !
Who'd have yielded belief,
Had he only been told of this theft I wonder.
Shell, bird, fish, and beast,
From the greatest to least,
Are all carried off in this act of plunder.

Professor Mc Coy,
Like the late Rob Roy,
Asks no right but the power to take and retain,
If he gets them away,
'Twill be many a day,
E're our specimens we shall set eyes on again.

Messrs. Wilson and Hearne
Make haste to return,
Those things at the theft of which you've assisted,
Or new chum Irving
Will say you're deserving,
To be 'mong her Majesty's thieves enlisted

Don't strive, ye professors,
To be the possessors,
Of what is'nt yours, and remember that prison
Is the regular goal,
Of each larcenous soul,
Who prigs (as the adage runs) what isn't his'n.

11 'The Museum (A Hue and Cry)', *Melbourne Punch* 7 August 1856.

12 'The Successful Foray; or, the Professor's Return' and 'The Raid of the Museum', *Melbourne Punch* 14 August 1856.

The battle for funds to establish botanic gardens in Port Phillip was won in 1845–46 when £750 was allotted by the legislative council in Sydney. With money available, the problem of siting the Botanic Gardens, already a contentious issue, returned and was delegated to a committee chaired by La Trobe. The site eventually chosen was that which has been continuously occupied by the Botanic Gardens ever since. By December of 1845 negotiations between the town council and Superintendent La Trobe had agreed on a committee of management for the Gardens, consisting of the mayor of Melbourne, three members appointed by the council and three members nominated by La Trobe. The initial committee was eventually made up of Mayor James Simpson, William Thompson, sub-treasurer of Port Phillip, D. C. McArthur, manager of the Bank of Australasia, and Drs Godfrey Howitt and Edmund Hobson. Howitt, curator of entomology and botany at the Mechanics' School of Arts, was the only botanist on the committee. John Arthur, appointed first superintendent of the Gardens in early 1846, was faced with the daunting task of developing the Botanic Gardens. The allotted site was too extensive to be worked immediately, so Arthur concentrated on building up a smaller, five-acre section. His development was spartan, and in line with his horticultural training concentrated on the introduction of exotic trees and flowers rather than botanical research. Arthur's brief tenure of the position terminated in January 1849 with his death. If little botanical research had been accomplished, other important steps had been taken: the Gardens had been located, partial clearing of the site undertaken, a superintendent's cottage, seed and tool rooms constructed, and most importantly, successive appropriations steered through the legislative council.

Daniel Bunce

The choice of Arthur's successor was controversial. John Dallochy was appointed in preference to Daniel Bunce. Dallochy, although experienced in botanic gardens in England, including a stint with William Hooker at Kew, had limited knowledge of Australian species. Bunce, also trained as a gardener, possessed some fifteen years 'experience with Australian plants'.[9] In 1837, while resident in Van Diemen's Land, Bunce had commenced a monthly serial, *Manual of Practical Gardening*, which described when and what fruits and vegetables to plant and included short sections devoted to native plants.[10] On emigrating to Port Phillip, Bunce sought to establish himself as a dealer in seeds and plant specimens, in addition to running a nursery. He also participated in the abortive second transcontinental expedition of Ludwig Leichhardt (1846–47).[11] On the expedition's return, the capricious Leichhardt praised Bunce privately, but before entering the bush on his third and fatal expedition wrote to W. Macarthur 'I did not take Mr Bunce, because I had opportunity of ascertaining that he bore a very bad character in Port Philipps . . .'.[12] Leichhardt's inconsistency saved Bunce from a probable early death in the bush.[13]

One of Bunce's contributions to botany, *Hortus Victoriensis*, aroused hostility.[14] In the preface to the volume Bunce indicated that not only did he hope to cater for the growing taste of Victorians for botany, but also that the pamphlet might lead to the publication of a more comprehensive work, a *Hortus Australiensis*. Not everyone thought him qualified. From Van Diemen's Land Ronald Gunn denounced *Hortus Victoriensis* as a plagiarism of the list of Tasmanian plants compiled by James Backhouse and printed in the 1835 *Hobart Town Almanack*.[15] Gunn added that many of the supposed plants described in the book were

> palpable fabrications of names—names which exist in no botanical work whatever . . .
> Further, not only does the author of this new Hortus Victoriensis omit almost every
> well-known plant growing in the neighbourhood of Melbourne and Geelong and in the
> colony of Victoria generally, but we may safely assert that his catalogue contains
> numerous genera which have never yet been seen at Port Phillip and some not on any
> part of the continent of New Holland.

So confident was Gunn that most of the species listed in the catalogue were fictitious that he offered to pay Bunce £100 if he could produce specimens of one hundred of the listed species which had been collected from Victoria. Not everyone was as critical of Bunce's work. The *Illustrated Australian Magazine*, in reviewing Bunce's *Australian Manual of Horticulture*, recommended it to the notice of its readers, although complaining about the 'clap-trap' it contained.[16]

Mechanics' School of Arts

The establishment of the Mechanics' School of Arts in 1839 was another example of the trend towards civilization. Unlike the philosophical societies formed earlier in New South Wales and Van Diemen's Land, mechanics' institutes were never intended to be organizations devoted to the collection of natural history specimens for despatch to England. Accordingly, mechanics' institutes were not seen as adjuncts to the natural history and science of distant England but rather were directed towards the needs of their adopted home in the colonies, and were to be of ideological and practical value in Australia itself. If scientific societies had as their charter an attempt to reduce the chaos of nature to order, mechanics' institutes took as their warrant the taming of the wilderness in men's hearts. The *Port Phillip Gazette* suggested that one effect of a mechanics' institute would be that

> The diffusion of useful knowledge thus sent through the minds of the people would
> raise the tone of morality to a high standard, and impart to the understanding of the
> operative classes a zest after mental and practical improvements which could not fail of
> contributing largely to the general progress of the district.[17]

The Melbourne Mechanics' School of Arts intended transmitting the results of science to squatter, mechanic and labourer alike, for their mental and moral edification. As befitted a colony barely four years old, science was yoked to the service of mankind.

This visionary organization, with its writ for improving men's minds, was not without its own problems. The *Gazette* reported the proposal of a pre-determined slate of officers at the inaugural meeting. After long and heated discussion over such high-handed behaviour, the election of officers was postponed. The furore was, however, a minor hiccup in the domination of the Mechanics' School of Arts, first by the social élite of the colony and later by the petty bourgeoisie. Although initiated by mechanics, as had happened in Hobart and Sydney, the Melbourne Mechanics' School of Arts was soon taken over by those in Melbourne with cultural aspirations. The eventual difference between events in Melbourne and Hobart was that Vandemonian naturalists found more socially acceptable alternatives in the Van Diemen's Land Society in 1829 and the Tasmanian Society in the 1830s, and thus abandoned the Van

Diemen's Land Mechanics' Institute. Naturalists in Melbourne, on the other hand, appropriated the Melbourne Mechanics' School of Arts as their organizational vehicle. If the Mechanics' School of Arts did not fulfil its promise of inaugurating working-class scientific education in Melbourne, it did provide a rudimentary focus around which natural history could evolve.

In 1839 these events were still in the future, and a measure of success was not quickly achieved by the Mechanics' School of Arts. After the initial contretemps surrounding its birth, officers were eventually elected. Superintendent Charles La Trobe was elected as patron of the School of Arts, Captain Lonsdale as president, eight vice-presidents, thirty-two members of a committee of management, a librarian, and two curators for the museum (Drs Holland and Wilkie). The organizational honours taken care of, the School lapsed into inactivity prompting the *Port Phillip Gazette* to complain in February 1840 that nothing had come of the institute.[18] The pastorally dominated Port Phillip district was dedicated to the pursuit of business and the accumulation of wealth which left little time for scientific or moral enlightenment. The lethargy of the School was overcome in May 1840 when secretary T. Osborne advertised that he would receive donations of books for the library and specimens for the museum. The following month, its membership now over one hundred, the School's promised lecture series was inaugurated with a discourse on geology delivered by Dr Augustus Greeves. The *Gazette* published a lengthy review of the lecture, noting that the good doctor, in his learned discussion of the formation of the earth, had even-handedly arbitrated in the long-running feud between the Wernerians (who postulated the primacy of water as a geological mechanism) and the Huttonians (who advocated the dominance of heat) by declaring that it had now been proven that heat and water had an equal share in causing changes to the surface of the earth.[19] Although he had been in the colony but a short while, Greeves illustrated his lecture with local examples and prophetically noted that lodes of precious metals were often encountered in geological conditions similar to Australia. Not all the readers of the *Gazette* were willing to allow Greeves to take liberties with geological theory, and before a week passed a correspondent of the *Gazette* queried 'By whom, when, and how?' had the Huttonian theory been compromised.[20] Greeves' equal treatment of the Huttonian–Wernerian theories was almost a decade behind European thought, in which geological gradualism had gained a decisive edge with the publication of the first volume of Charles Lyell's *Principles of Geology*.

Other lectures were less contentious. Mr Sewell spoke on 'Heat', Mr Wilmot 'On the state of science', and Osborne discussed 'Phrenology'. In order that ladies could attend, the lectures were restricted to moonlit nights.[21]

The apparent success of the Mechanics' School of Arts inaugural lecture series was marred by the organization's inability to secure a permanent home. A land grant, solicited through the offices of La Trobe, was rejected by Governor Gipps in distant Sydney, although he did authorize a monetary grant of £300. However, members of the committee of management personally guaranteed a mortgage, a site was purchased, plans were drawn up, and by late 1842 a two-storey brick building was occupied. Although few mechanics or tradesmen served on the committee of management or as officers during this early period, the financial resources of those who did occupy these positions allowed the Mechanics' School of Arts if not to thrive, at least to survive its numerous crises. However, its fraught financial circumstances forced it to rent a portion of its building to such diverse organizations as the municipal council, the Baptist Society, and the Philharmonic Society. Indignation towards Governor Gipps over the lack of governmental support for the School of Arts caused it to lose its patron in 1841. La Trobe resigned, indicating that his position as patron was untenable given the unwarranted hostility towards his official superior by the membership of the School.[22]

By 1844 the Port Phillip district of the colony of New South Wales had been settled for ten years. Melbourne had begun the population increase that was eventually to see it out-distance its older intercolonial rivals in the 1850s. The city sagged beneath the growth. Streets were clogged with vehicles of every description, and the wooden buildings so prevalent in the town's first years were gradually replaced by brick and stone. Three steamers plied the Yarra and another regularly made the journey across Port Phillip Bay to Geelong. A larger steam-driven vessel, the *Shamrock*, made the voyage between Melbourne, Launceston and Sydney every three weeks.[23]

The same industry that changed the physical face of Melbourne in the 1840s also saw the Melbourne Mechanics' Institute (the organization had now adopted the title of 'The Melbourne Mechanics' Institute and School of Arts') develop as the focus for natural history. By 1843 the Institute had been captured by a scientific coterie who virtually turned it into a scientific club. The library and reading room of the Mechanics' Institute were the facilities used most frequently by the general membership, and produced the major expenses and brought in the greatest revenue (the reading room had a £1 subscription fee). Yet the officers of the Mechanics' Institute directed the organization towards their own interests in natural history. The annual report of 1844 considered the museum of greater significance than the library, parochially regarding it as pre-eminent in the Australian colonies.[24] The several thousand specimens housed by the museum now included Aboriginal skeletons, fossil bones from Mount Macedon identified by Richard Owen and Edmund Hobson, fossils from Van Diemen's Land, undescribed species of insects collected by Blakewell, Howitt and Gilbert, and mineral ores from England. While the annual report made passing reference to the promotion and encouragement of art and literature, the body of the report dropped art and literature when the new officers deplored the necessity of renting space to the municipal council 'within the sacred precincts of science'.[25]

Whereas one or two curators had served in the lean years, the curatorship had now increased to seven: zoology and comparative anatomy, ornithology, conchology, entomology and botany, geology, Aborigines, and fine arts. The honorary curatorial positions were created to fit the interests of those who ran the Institute, as witnessed by the curious grouping of entomology and botany. The roll of officers of the Institute and the expanded curatorial list gave notice that a new group of individuals had taken power. Edmund Hobson, Godfrey Howitt, Augustus Greeves and George Gilbert now dominated the proceedings of the Institute, but were no more mechanics than their predecessors. Indeed, the first three were physicians, and the fourth an itinerant scholar.

Despite their pre-eminence locally, members of the Melbourne Mechanics' Institute also sought the recognition and prestige of membership of the only established scientific society in the Australian colonies, the Tasmanian Society of Ronald Gunn. Hobson had been a foundation member, and later Port Phillip's corresponding members of the Society included Charles La Trobe, Godfrey Howitt and William Westgarth.

Hobson and Cotton

A comparison of two men, Edmund Hobson of Melbourne, physician, and John Cotton of the Goulburn River, pastoralist, indicates the heterogeneity of practitioners of natural history in the Port Phillip district of the 1840s.

Edmund Charles Hobson was born in Parramatta, New South Wales, in 1814. His family moved to Hobart shortly after, and Hobson went on to study medicine with the Van Diemen's Land colonial surgeon, Dr James Scott. Hobson then embarked for Europe, completing his medical degree in Germany. In late 1838, while in England, he became acquainted with three of the foremost comparative anatomists of England: Robert Grant (professor of comparative anatomy and zoology, University of London), Robert Jameson (Regius Professor of natural history, University of Edinburgh), and Richard Owen (Hunterian Professor of the Royal College of Surgeons).[26] When he returned to Hobart in 1839 Hobson quickly became associated with the small but strong natural history community that thrived under Franklin's patronage. Robert Grant sought to have Hobson appointed as naturalist to the colony of Van Diemen's Land. Governor John Franklin supported the proposal, but it was rejected by the secretary of state for the colonies.[27] Despite this setback, Hobson was active in helping to found the Tasmanian Society and later published extensively in the Society's journal.

Hobson's acquaintance with Port Phillip began in April 1839 when he accompanied Jane Franklin on a journey overland from Melbourne to Sydney. Hobson's diary of this journey records his introduction to the Port Phillip district flora and fauna and reflects the typical concerns of a naturalist of the period, particularly the emphasis on specimen collection.[28] In the middle of 1840 Hobson moved to the Port Phillip district where his brother had a station near Arthur's Seat. During his first few years in Melbourne, Hobson retained his allegiance to the Tasmanian Society and had little to do with the Melbourne Mechanics' Institute. By 1843, however, Hobson was part of the Howitt–Gilbert group that took control of the Institute. Along with fellow naturalist Godfrey Howitt, he was appointed to the committee of management of the Botanic Gardens in December 1845.

Hobson's career as a naturalist was almost fully documented in the *Tasmanian Journal of Natural Science*; hardly surprising given his friendship with Ronald Gunn, his part in the foundation of the Tasmanian Society, and the journal's status as the sole scientific outlet in the colonies. After Hobson's departure for Port Phillip, he and Gunn maintained a close correspondence, exchanging books and specimens. Despite separation by the chill waters of Bass Strait, each remained the other's warmest scientific friend (Hobson collected Port Phillip plants for Gunn, while Gunn reciprocated with Tasmanian fossils and mammals. Many of these specimens were eventually transmitted to Hooker or Owen). The initial number of the *Tasmanian Journal*, issued in August 1841, had as its lead scientific article, 'On the Callorynchus Australis' by Edmund Hobson, an investigation of the comparative anatomy and ecology of the species.[29] A second article followed in the next issue, when Hobson entered the controversy over the taxonomic position of the platypus with his 'Observations on the blood of the Ornithorhynchus paradoxus'.[30] The research for the two articles was conducted while Hobson was still resident in Tasmania, but they were not published until after he had moved to Melbourne and had become a corresponding member of the Society.[31]

The *Tasmanian Journal of Natural Science* continued to be the only viable colonial outlet for the publication of natural history throughout the 1840s, and continued as Hobson's preferred medium for scientific communications after his move to Melbourne. Volume II of the journal, issued in parts from 1842 to 1846, included an extract of a February 1844 letter from Hobson to Ronald Gunn entitled 'On some Fossil Bones discovered at Mount Macedon, Port Phillip'.[32] Hobson wrote a series of letters concerning Victorian fossils over the next few years, documenting the geology of the surrounding area and continuing to unravel the fossil species. Along with his letters, Hobson sent illustrations sketched by his wife and engraved on stone by his fellow curator at the Mechanics' Institute, George Gilbert. In later years Hobson's communications often took the form of letters to Ronald Gunn, which were subsequently printed in the *Tasmanian Journal*.[33]

Hobson also maintained a regular correspondence with his European mentors, and a steady supply of animals and fossils was despatched to England. The flow of specimens to Europe was rewarded, typically, in the form of books and journals.

Hobson's communications continued in the third volume of the *Tasmanian Journal*, and were devoted mainly to the dentition of *Diprotodon australis*.[34] Hobson's habit of writing his findings in letters which Gunn then abstracted and published in the *Tasmanian Journal* allowed for editorial abuse. In 1847 Gunn informed Hobson that he had rewritten one of Hobson's letters for publication; he then continued, 'I also *fabricated* an extract from an imaginary letter of yours so as to introduce the two species of Wombat'.[35]

In March 1848 Gunn had the sad duty of communicating to the Tasmanian Society the news that one of its founding members had died earlier that month. A final posthumous gift to the Society, a fossil of a trilobite from the Yarra, was forwarded by Hobson's wife.[36]

In contrast to the colonial-born, European-educated Hobson, John Cotton was born near London in 1802, educated at Oxford for the law and acquired a genteel interest in natural history and painting. He combined these pursuits in 1835 when he published *The Resident Song Birds of Great Britain* with seventeen colour plates. A year later an expanded version, *The Song Birds of Great Britain* with thirty-three plates appeared.[37]

Shortly after his arrival in 1843, John Cotton set about establishing himself as a pastoralist in Australia Felix. He took up two properties on the Goulburn River, and a year later acquired a third bringing his total holdings to more than 50,000 acres. Cotton continued to reside at his Goulburn River property until his death in 1849.

During his six years in Australia, John Cotton corresponded almost monthly with his elder brother, William, in Britain. These and other letters written to his cousin, Robert Hudson, record his development as a naturalist.

Many of John Cotton's early letters to his brother are devoted to the concerns of a pastoralist's life: the price of wool, drought, the condition of his land and the commercial and political affairs of Australia Felix.[38] Throughout his early letters, however, there also ran a thread of comment on natural history; of the birds of the region, the constant promise to send animal curiosities and his intention to complete sketches of flowers and birds.

By August 1844 life on an upland station had begun to pall, and Cotton sought refuge in art and natural history. He informed brother William of his interest in natural history, 'which you know I have taken up as a kind of hobby. You also know that I am not well grounded in these matters but merely feel a deep interest and love for the science'.[39]

John Cotton and his brother discussed various contemporary publications in their letters, ranging from books dealing with art to natural history; George Bennett's *Wanderings in NSW, Batavia, Pedir Coast, Singapore and China*, Strzelecki's *Travels in New South Wales and Van Diemen's Land*, and Robert Chambers' *The Vestiges of Creation*, all came under consideration.[40] Of equal interest were ornithological works. Cotton dismissed John Lewin's *Birds of New Holland*, originally published in 1808 but reissued in 1828 and 1838 under the title *A Natural History of the Birds of New South Wales*, as unimpressive. As usual Cotton considered the book overpriced but if William could obtain a copy at a reasonable cost, it might prove useful.[41] Gould's *Birds of Australia*, from which his brother occasionally sent extracts, Cotton thought to be splendidly illustrated, but again too costly and doomed to be found only in the libraries of the wealthy or in institutions. Cotton's opinion was that Gould would have made more money if he had published it in a cheaper edition.

It was perhaps the thought that there was still money to be made from a cheap, illustrated volume on the birds of Australia that set Cotton to painting in earnest. He had already contemplated a small volume, a three-year diary of first impressions of a settler in Australia interspersed with natural history notes, but had been forestalled in that venture by Richard Howitt's *Impressions of Australia Felix* (Richard Howitt was the brother of Godfrey Howitt and uncle of Alfred Howitt).[42] Commencing in early 1846 Cotton began sending his brother sketches and paintings of the Australian flora and fauna.[43] By August of 1848 he wrote that 'A very interesting work might be made of the fauna of Australia and a very pretty sum of money by any person or persons who might be capable of getting up such a work'.[44] In December that year he continued 'as I have now made upward of 100 drawings of birds in this district I think that something might be made of them by bringing them before the public in the shape of a small volume'.[45] Cotton envisaged that the book would contain about fifty coloured plates and appear under the title 'Ornithological sketches by a resident of Port Phillip, NSW'. Robert Hudson discussed the proposal with various publishers but to no avail. Everyone was agreed that illustrated natural history works did not pay and in any case John Gould, the entrepreneurial naturalist and publisher of illustrated bird folios, had pre-empted the subject.[46] From a field already well-trodden by Gould, and without his flair, there was no money to be made.[47]

The financial pitfalls associated with natural history were confirmed by Cotton's abortive speculation in bird skins. Cotton's son, William, had been placed with George Gilbert, something of a naturalist himself and secretary of the Mechanics' Institute, for drawing lessons. Gilbert convinced John Cotton to begin a collection of local insects and Cotton's desire for profit was inflamed when Hudson informed him that such collections were much sought after in London.[48] In December of 1847 he sent Hudson a large shipment of bird skins and a case of insects to be offered for sale. A second shipment followed a year later. Although John Cotton wrote confidently of the money to be made, those receiving the specimens found them difficult to sell. Hudson offered them to leading naturalists and natural history dealers, but was put off. One dealer thought the specimens not worth the price of cleaning, another replied that there were thousands of the same sort to be had in London for a shilling. An offer of threepence per skin was finally received.[49]

Before he died in 1849, John Cotton was already dabbling in the technology that was to partially replace natural history art. Cotton, George Gilbert and Frank Gilbert, the tutor of Cotton's children, all began investigating the potential of the recently invented daguerreotype.[50] The technique was not yet adequate for natural history for the technology was still too limited and Cotton's first crude attempts were centred on portraits of his family.[51] But that same year Ronald Gunn wrote to William Hooker at Kew indicating that he intended to send Hooker 'portraits' of all the important trees in Tasmania and queried Hooker about the most suitable apparatus, daguerreotype or photographic, for such work. With the lengthy exposure times required, Gunn realized that he would need an almost unnaturally still day to take his tree portraits.[52]

Edmund Hobson and John Cotton represent two of the diverging paths of natural history in the Australian colonies in the middle of the nineteenth century. Hobson was on the way to becoming a professional scientist. Two factors, his residence in Tasmania and Port Phillip and his early death, prevented him from achieving that status. Neither the relatively mature colony of Tasmania nor the newly settled Port Phillip district could yet support professional science, but the signs were there. Hobson had undergone specialized training with Jameson and Grant, sought a paid position as colonial naturalist in Tasmania, maintained an extensive correspondence with metropolitan scientists, had a network of scientific friends in the colonies and contributed a number of scientific papers to the *Tasmanian Journal of Natural Science*. Indications are that, given the choice, Hobson would have earned his living as a naturalist.

John Cotton, on the other hand, approached natural history as an amateur. In his particular field of interest, ornithology, Cotton adopted a system of taxonomic classification that had been briefly popular during the 1820s, the quinary system developed first by William S. Macleay and adapted for ornithology by Swainson and Vigors. In 1832 he attended a lecture series given by Vigors and faithfully copied a diagram of the quinary system, with copious notes.[53] He continued to use the system in his own works despite the ridicule it suffered in England during the 1830s. Aside from his zoological and botanical paintings, Cotton's major contribution to natural history was his catalogue of birds of the Goulburn River district, published in the *Tasmanian Journal of Natural Science* in 1849.[54] Given the option, John Cotton might have chosen to be other than a pastoralist, but probably would not have elected to become a professional naturalist.[55] For Cotton, natural history was never more than an amusement; for Hobson natural history was an avocation.

Other contemporaries

Hobson and Cotton did not exist in a cultural vacuum. By the mid-1840s a small band of men interested in natural history had formed in Port Phillip, and many were associated with the Melbourne Mechanics' Institute. Superintendent Charles La Trobe, 'a man of a thousand occupations; a botanist, a geologist, a hunter of beetles and butterflies . . .', stood at their head socially.[56] Godfrey Howitt, surgeon, exchanged botanical and entomological specimens with European naturalists, and served as a curator of the Mechanics' Institute.[57] Augustus Greeves, surgeon and editor of the *Port Phillip Magazine*, was also active in the Institute. William Westgarth, corresponding member and contributor to the Tasmanian Society, maintained an active interest in natural history.[58] George Gilbert, secretary of the Mechanics' Institute, was also joint editor of the *Port Phillip Magazine*, a journal which sought to encompass scientific, literary, agricultural and economic news.[59] Almost all these individuals had some claim to gentlemen's status, either through marriage (Gilbert and La Trobe) or profession (Cotton, Hobson, La Trobe, Greeves, Westgarth and Howitt).[60] For some at least, their scientific club was compensation for their inability to obtain membership of the more prestigious Melbourne Club. Science was a form of social legitimacy. To these men, G. Haydon's *Five Years in Australia Felix* must have come as a shock. In this 1846 publication Haydon claimed that although no better region than Australia Felix existed for the advancement of science, the population was too enamoured with chasing money to engage in scientific activities.[61]

Bunyip controversy

The issue that most excited the interest of Port Phillip naturalists in 1847 was the fabulous bunyip. In January of 1847 Athol Fletcher discovered an oddly shaped skull on the banks of the Murrumbidgee and was assured by local Aborigines that it came from a bunyip. Fletcher loaned the skull to Edward Curr who forwarded it to Gunn in Tasmania. After examining it himself and obtaining a second opinion from his Tasmanian scientific confidant James Grant, Gunn returned the skull to Port Phillip, where it became the centre of attention. After consideration of the issue La Trobe would not rule out the chance that Australia still held unknown monstrous animals.[62] Gilbert, after discussing the find with Hobson, thought it would be wise to withhold any description of the skull from the *Tasmanian Journal* for Hobson had raised the possibility that it was merely a deformed foetal skull.[63] Hobson's unease had also been noted by La Trobe. Across Bass Strait, Gunn was wary of the skull's legitimacy and considered that it might be from a foetal camel. He earnestly solicited Hobson's opinion for Hobson was 'the only one who can clear up the doubt'.[64] James Grant examined the skull and cautiously characterized it as originating from a foetal animal, although one unlike any he had seen.[65] Gunn, after rejecting lithographs of the skull executed by John Skinner Prout, had Gilbert prepare others from James Grant's sketches and published them along with Grant's analysis in the *Tasmanian Journal of Natural Science*.

The following issue of the *Journal* also contained a letter from William Sharp Macleay about the 'bunyip' skull, reprinted from the *Sydney Morning Herald*.[66] The skull had been sent to Macleay by Curr, and he concluded that it was that of a misshapen foetal horse. Hobson sent a drawing of it to Richard Owen who confirmed that it was a hydrocephalic skull of a foal or calf.[67] The incident indicated that Australian natural history was coming of age. Australian naturalists, although most were European-born and almost all were European-trained, had shown themselves capable of deciding issues without recourse to Europe.

Natural history in the colony of Victoria

Two events colour the historical fabric of Victoria in the years 1850–60. Although occurring at the outset of the decade, each helped set the tone for the following years and their all-pervading influence directed the development of natural history in the colony. The first event, long awaited by the residents of Australia Felix, was the announcement of the separation of the colony of Victoria from New South Wales. The separation had been agreed to in 1847 by the secretary of state for the colonies but the wheels of government ground slowly for the residents of Australia who were swept along by the separationist tide. 'Its here. At last', trumpeted the newspapers in November 1850.

Just as in Van Diemen's Land two-and-a-half decades earlier, the separation of Victoria from New South Wales produced a headlong rush to duplicate facilities and institutions. It also introduced an element of intercolonial rivalry, strengthened by the announcement of the second major event of the decade. As fateful as separation, it was given public cry in 1851 when the *Argus* proclaimed in its 26 July issue, 'Eureka! We have gold—gold in abundance'.[68]

Gold

The discovery of gold, first in New South Wales, then in Victoria, was felt to be long overdue. In the sixteenth and seventeenth centuries the Dutch and Spanish had explored the Pacific for gold. They sought it in the unknown southern land more on the basis of mythology than from firm evidence that gold abounded. If called on to justify their belief that gold must exist in Terra Australis, their answer was that the southern land was located in roughly the same latitude as Peru and Chile from which gold, in the best colonial fashion, had been looted during the previous centuries.

In the 1840s European geology provided a somewhat more scientific basis for the search for gold in Australia. Roderick Murchison, partially on the basis of a comparison of specimens from the Ural Mountains of Russia (which he saw himself) and the mountainous spine of eastern Australia (from specimens and maps supplied to him by Strzelecki), speculated on the presence of gold in Australia.[69] In the colonies, the Reverend William B. Clarke carried out field work in the Blue Mountains in the years after 1841 and became convinced of the existence of gold in the quartzites and schists of the mountains of New South Wales.[70] In later years, Clarke and Murchison were to carry on a protracted and acrimonious dispute over who had originally predicted the discovery.

Claims of gold finds in Australia were relatively few, sporadic and generally unfounded before the late 1840s. William Clarke found meagre specimens in 1841 in New South Wales and displayed a sample of gold to Governor Gipps but was cautioned, 'Put it away, or we shall have our throats cut'.[71] In the colony of New South Wales, still tied to its convict past, the discovery of gold was expected to excite ambition for wealth. A brief flurry of excitement arose in 1849 when gold was reportedly located in the Victorian Pyrenees (north-west of Ballarat) by a shepherd who brought samples to Melbourne. The exaggerated report that found its way to London was that a lode had been located that far exceeded the mines of California in its richness.[72] La Trobe responded to the putative lode by despatching a government team to investigate it and later wrote to his Tasmanian friend, Ronald Gunn, describing the find.[73]

Although these early discoveries did not fulfil their promise, the contagion of gold fever was widespread. The December 1847 discovery of gold in California drew its share of dreamers and adventurers from Australia. The colonies were ripe for Hargraves' February 1851 announcement of an abundance of gold in a remote valley of New South Wales, but Victoria was not to be outdone. It was not only a case of pride, which existed in good measure in the newly separated colony, but also of necessity. People deserted Melbourne by any available means for Sydney and the New South

Wales goldfields and there was concern that Melbourne would soon be depopulated. It was no idle fear. The Melbourne Mechanics' Institute, for example, lost a significant number of its members to the lure of gold. Drastic measures were needed and in June 1851 a meeting called at the Mechanics' Institute established a gold reward committee to offer a premium of £200 to anyone locating a goldfield within 200 miles of Melbourne. The race was on. Victoria was not alone in this respect: Tasmania also felt the need for its own goldfield but could offer only a £20 reward for the discovery of gold anywhere on the island. In Victoria, gold was discovered in August 1851 at Ballarat. The discovery directly influenced the course of natural history in Victoria. It led to Governor La Trobe's October 1851 request to the Colonial Office for geological assistance, and the subsequent arrival of geologist Alfred R. C. Selwyn in December 1852. Selwyn's work resulted in the establishment of the Geological Survey of Victoria in 1856.[74]

A less direct influence was the increase in institutions, either wholly or partly concerned with natural history. This institutional development was partially the result of the rivalry with Sydney (and to a lesser extent with Hobart) but also of the simple pressure of population growth. Melbourne's population soared with the discovery of gold and the subsequent invasion of gold diggers. In the period from 1851 to 1854 the city's population trebled. The overall population of Victoria rose accordingly: 75,000 in 1850; 97,489 in 1851; 168,321 in 1852; 222,436 in 1853; and 283,942 in 1854. By 1854 Victoria's population surpassed that of New South Wales. The increase brought enough individuals with an interest or training in natural history to allow science to flourish as it never had in sparsely populated Hobart. In 1854 two scientific societies (the Philosophical Society of Victoria and the Victorian Institute for the Advancement of Science), the National Museum and the University of Melbourne were all established. The infrastructure for institutional natural history in Victoria was now in place.

A third influence of the goldfields concerned the type of immigrants. Some individuals, such as Alfred Selwyn and Frederick McCoy, had come to take up positions in the newly formed institutions, but others arrived to try their luck on the diggings and only later became involved in natural history: Ludwig Becker, fated to die on the Burke and Wills expedition; Robert Brough Smyth, who built a bureaucratic empire as secretary of mines; Ferdinand Mueller, sometime government botanist; and William Blandowski, zoologist of the National Museum—all ventured to Victoria without official positions and all came either to seek gold or to exploit the economic opportunities opened up by the gold rush.

The population increase which followed the discovery of gold was a catalyst for Victoria's overall development and the development of natural history was similarly accelerated. New South Wales and Tasmania had acquired an infrastructure for natural history—botanic gardens, museums and scientific societies—over a comparatively long period. The older colonies, however, were limited more than anything else by the lack of interested or knowledgeable individuals. Victoria, specifically Melbourne, found itself within a three- or four-year period housing a considerable community of individuals interested in natural history. These naturalists set about almost immediately to organize the formal accoutrements of natural history and their expertise quickly made itself evident. Unlike collectors in the older colonies, who had initially been content to despatch specimens to England for analysis and classification, the Victorian community was confident enough to attempt taxonomy and to tackle theory.[75]

Geological Society of Victoria

The initial focus of much of natural history during the early 1850s was on mineralogy and geology. This interest gave rise to the first specialist scientific society in the Australian colonies, the Geological Society of Victoria. The Society was established in October 1852 at the instigation of several individuals of some geological competence. Founding members included George Milner Stephens, called on to chair the meeting; Evan Hopkins, fellow of the Geological Society of London and manager of the Port Phillip Gold Company; J. Ritchie and J. Brown, also managers of a mining company; Alderman Hodgson; William S. Gibbons; and a German immigrant, William Blandowski.[76] Stephens elaborated to the meeting his belief that the greatest benefit of the Society to the colony would be the purchase of a collection of minerals for public use. As an example of how this would profit the colony, Stephens told an anecdote concerning miners who, versed only in the characteristics of gold, unknowingly threw away precious gemstones. With a mineral collection available for comparative purposes such mishaps would be less likely to occur. Fortuitously, such a collection was on display at the meeting that very evening, and Stephens urged its purchase, reading testimonials from others stressing its high quality.

Like all newly founded institutions, the Royal Geological Society of Victoria (as it intended to style itself, although it never gained royal patronage during its short life) had high-minded objectives: development of the mineral resources of the colony and advancement of geological science in Australia. More prosaically, in gold-mad Victoria, the Society would provide miners and gold buyers with data for evaluating the worth of precious metals.

A week after the first meeting of the Society, the *Argus* ran an article under the leader 'The Geological Society' which made prodigious claims for science.[77] In the colony of Victoria, where the pursuit of wealth had an unusually firm grasp on the public's mind, science should be cultivated as being conducive to the 'happiness and the development of the individual'. Science not only 'improves the race, and the selflessness of the human soul', but 'A man intellectually inclined, whatever other charges may be brought against him, is rarely morally bad or an indifferent citizen'. Geology was mentioned as an exemplar of science. 'Its magnificent appeals to the high moral principles are at once startling and conclusive.' What in fact was startling, if not conclusive, was the overblown rhetoric of the article which applauded the formation of the Geological Society

> in golden times such as the present—when the demon of avarice would appear to have seized upon the hearts of the masses searing them to every feeling but the desire of self-aggrandizement . . . the Society just formed is indeed one absolutely required to wean the mind from pursuits that must be utterly ruinous to the better feelings.

Little else was heard from the Geological Society until 1 January 1853 when the *Argus* reported that late the previous month a deputation of Society members had called upon the governor with two requests. First, in keeping with colonial protocol, they offered La Trobe the presidency of the Society. La Trobe readily agreed, pledging his full support for the Society. The group took him at his word and asked La Trobe to include in the forward estimates sufficient funds to purchase a cabinet of mineral specimens for the Society. La Trobe procrastinated, suggesting that the Society might be better served by proving its existence for at least six months before making demands on the public purse. He then chided the officers of his Society, suggesting that the colony had greater need of a broad-based society covering the gamut of natural history rather than the narrowly based Geological Society. The example La Trobe held up to them was the Royal Society of Van Diemen's Land. The meeting, the *Argus* noted, concluded after desultory conversation and the deputation of the Geological Society retired, smarting under La Trobe's exhortation to rely on their own devices.

Within a month the Geological Society again pursued public funding when William Westgarth raised the issue of a museum of economic geology in the legislative council.[78] Westgarth stressed that a museum of economic geology would be for the many, as opposed to a natural history museum, which would necessarily be limited to a highly educated few. Westgarth proposed that a Museum of Economic Geology might be organized for less than £3,000. After some debate the proposal was approved by the legislative council and forwarded to La Trobe. No membership lists of the Geological Society are available but Westgarth, if not a member, was certainly a sympathizer who had sent his apologies for not attending one of the early organizational meetings of the Society.[79]

The denouement of the Geological Society came in August 1853. At a meeting called on 19 August nine new members were admitted, including the New South Wales government examiner of coalfields, W. Keene and William Kerr, editor of the *Argus*. Curiously, Alfred Selwyn, the newly arrived geologist, appeared never to have joined the Society. At the meeting George Stephens' mineral collection, on loan to the Society until it could be sold, was discussed. This collection, mentioned at every previous meeting of the Society as the nucleus of a Museum of Economic Geology to be run by the Geological Society, had preoccupied most of the Society's time and energy. At every turn the collection was praised, usually by its owner, vice-president of the Society, George Stephens. The collection and its sale seem to have formed the *raison d'être* for the Geological Society.[80]

Forming a Museum

Although the Geological Society disappeared after August 1853, Westgarth's call for a Museum of Economic Geology saw £2,000 included in the estimates of 1854 for that purpose. During the legislative council debate on the motion Dr James Palmer, while supporting the resolution for a Museum of Economic Geology, indicated he would prefer a museum of a more general nature, a Museum of Natural History. Palmer could find no reason to elevate one branch of natural history over all others.

In September, on the initiative of Mark Nicholson, the legislative council set up a committee to consider 'the propriety of presenting an Address to His Excellency the Lieutenant Governor requesting him to place a sufficient sum of money upon the estimates for the ensuing year for the purpose of establishing a Museum of Natural History'.[81] After debate, the motion to recommend the establishment of a natural history museum to La Trobe was carried thirty-seven to seven.[82]

John Foster, the colonial secretary, suggested to Nicholson that if he and others of like mind formed themselves into a scientific society to press the idea of a Museum, the government would look favourably on the proposal. In the small social circle that dominated the colony, this was sufficient encouragement.

Andrew Clarke

The documentary evidence available reveals only a sketchy outline of the process of establishing a Museum of Natural History. It is apparent that Nicholson, while maintaining an interest in natural history, was supplanted by others of greater influence. One was Andrew Clarke, lieutenant in the Royal Engineers, recently appointed surveyor-general of Victoria, and soon to be selected as an official nominee to the legislative council. Clarke, a protégé of William Denison, governor of Tasmania, had served as private secretary to Denison from August 1849 until May 1853. In Tasmania, under the tutelage of Denison, Clarke saw intimate bonds forged between science, vice-regal patronage and a scientific society. Clarke sought to nurture a similar arrangement in Victoria and, given La Trobe's interest and connection with the Royal Society of Tasmania, could count on the governor's support.[83]

In his public capacity as surveyor-general, Clarke was able to promote the formation of the Museum, not in the Public Library or the Mechanics' Institute, as originally mooted, but in the rooms of the Crown Lands Building where the Assay Office, under Clarke's control, had its offices. The initial steps in the formation of this Museum seem to have taken place in an *ad hoc* fashion without any formal approval. William Blandowski, a former member of the Geological Society of Victoria, was appointed zoologist in April 1854, although he was recorded in the financial returns as a surveyor.

Paris Exhibition

Blandowski's appointment anticipated the formal inauguration of a Museum of Natural History, but a number of factors were converging to assure its implementation. Government interest, the recommendations of La Trobe and Foster that a scientific society be formed, and the activities of Andrew Clarke, all gave credibility to the idea of a Museum. The most immediate factor, however, was the Paris Exhibition, scheduled for 1855.

One of the most obvious landmarks of the Victorian era of English history was the London Crystal Palace Exhibition of 1851. Exhibitions appealed to the mid-nineteenth century mind, with their gaudiness, their display of huge collections, and the notion that they diffused knowledge to the working masses who thronged the exhibition halls. The 1851 London Exhibition, which had the Western world agog, had garnered only a weak presence from the Australian colonies for only Tasmania had been adequately represented.

The Paris Exhibition of 1855, drawing on the lessons of the London Exhibition and spurred by French nationalism, had greater expectations than its predecessor and the colonies were determined to play a role in it. Intercolonial rivalry was inevitable and it became known that New South Wales intended to be fully represented at the Paris Exhibition. The *Sydney Morning Herald* announced that no effort should be spared, 'when it appears only too likely that our position as the head and metropolis of the Australian group may be disputed and even wrested from us'.[84]

Melbourne Exhibition

The Melbourne *Argus* attempted to stimulate Victoria's participation in the Paris Exhibition suggesting it was an opportunity to establish a society both to take on the organization of the proposed Museum and to manage the collections chosen for exhibition in Paris. To encourage local interest, a Victorian committee was set up to oversee the preparation of exhibits for the Paris Exhibition and proposed holding a Victorian exhibition in Melbourne. Government funding was obtained to house the Melbourne event, by designing a building for conversion to offices after the close of the exhibition.[85] Displays for the Melbourne Exhibition were marshalled into six categories, including 'Natural History', 'Metals, minerals and mining', and 'Vegetable Productions'. [86]

The Exhibition was inaugurated on 17 October 1854 with a grand opening ceremony. Governor Hotham closed government offices for the day and most commercial enterprises followed suit, turning it into a general holiday. Inside the Exhibition hall Ferdinand Mueller offered a selection of colonial timber but the accolade for the most interesting display went to the Museum of Natural History for its wide-ranging collection of minerals, marine invertebrates, insects, mammals, birds and Aboriginal skulls.[87] In addition to institutional displays, many local naturalists contributed individually.[88]

CHAPTER SIX

societies and concerns

PORT PHILLIP DISTRICT, 1850–60

Victorian Institute for the Advancement of Science

The Mechanics' Institute, which had seemed both capable and likely to assume a leading role in natural history in Victoria after it had been taken over by the Hobson–Howitt–Gilbert group, lost its impetus in subsequent years and had become no more than an umbrella organization for various recreational activities. The thrust of the organization had reverted to a middle-class recreational institution preaching rational amusement. It failed to retain its mantle of leadership in natural history and even the Institute's principal facilities, the library and reading room, came under criticism.[1] Despite the carping of the *Argus*, the Mechanics' Institute was home to educational classes—chemistry, botany, the arts and languages—and almost weekly lectures.[2] Despite many of the lectures being given over to phrenology, mesmerism and spiritualism, and the poor attendance, the Mechanics' Institute still attempted to fulfil its function. Many had expected it to take the lead in the intellectual affairs of the colony, willing upon it a task for which it had neither the charter nor the capacity. In particular, the Institute was never designed to become the scientific club of well-bred naturalists it had briefly been in the 1840s.

Neither the Mechanics' Institute nor the Geological Society had satisfied the need for a broad-based society called for by La Trobe. William S. Gibbons, who had been involved with both, set about stimulating debate and canvassing support for a general scientific society. Much of the discussion was documented in the pages of the *Argus* which Gibbons often used as a forum.[3]

In May 1854, under the heading 'Intellectual Recreation', the *Argus* advocated the foundation of a literary or philosophical society, reiterating the well-worn and often-repeated moral arguments of rational amusement. Other Australian colonies had already taken the lead: Tasmania had its Royal Society of Van Diemen's Land; and New South Wales, its Australian Philosophical Society. While it was true that Melbourne had a Mechanics' Institute and others were forming in the suburban areas of Prahran, Emerald Hill and Collingwood, the mechanics' institutes were a 'slow-going middle class sort of concern'. A Victorian institute devoted to art, literature and philosophy was called for.[4]

The following day, also through the pages of the *Argus*, Gibbons proposed the formation of an association for the promotion of sciences and art to be modelled after the British Association for the Advancement of Science. In keeping with the exemplar, Gibbons envisaged the association as an umbrella under which various disciplines—meteorology, statistics, mineralogy or agriculture—would stand.[5] Gibbons asked for comment on his proposal and intimated that a list had been opened for those interested in membership.

Within a month, Gibbons had forty names of prospective members of his society and a circular had been distributed calling for a preliminary meeting of the Victorian Institute for the Advancement of Science to take place at the Mechanics' Institute on 15 June. That same day the *Argus* carried a leader entitled 'The National Institute of Victoria'.[6] Although supportive of the idea of a scientific society, the *Argus* cautioned the organizers against expecting too much. The society 'should be the grand intellectual, as the Government is the grand political organ for promoting the progress of the colony', but would need to receive a government grant if it were not to fall into the same disrepute as the Mechanics' Institute ('office-bearers without a function, curators without a museum, classrooms without classes, and a lecture hall without lectures').

Attended by seventy individuals, the inaugural meeting of 15 June agreed unanimously to the Institute's establishment. William Gibbons outlined a charter, noticeably different from one published earlier in the *Argus*, and organizational details. An executive council for the society, to which the government engineer, Captain Pasley, J. J. Moody, W. Gibbons, Dr Maund, F. Sinnett and A. Selwyn were nominated, was charged with drawing up a constitution.[7]

At 4 p.m. on Monday 31 July the first general meeting of the Victorian Institute took place at the Mechanics' Institute. The newly arrived lieutenant-governor, Charles Hotham, had graciously accepted the office of patron of the Institute. Gibbons moved the council's proposed operating rules and found unanimous acceptance. The council proposed a list of officers—Acting Chief Justice Redmond Barry as president, Surveyor-General Andrew Clarke as vice-president, Jacob Montefinore as treasurer, and William Gibbons as honorary secretary—which was adopted without change or challenge.[8]

The council itself was to be expanded and a prepared slate of names was presented to and accepted by the meeting, although not before C. Aplin, later to become a member of the Victorian Geological Survey, rose to voice a strident objection. Among those who came to the council this way was the government botanist, Ferdinand Mueller.

To introduce the Victorian Institute to the Melbourne public a conversazione was organized for 22 September at the Mechanics' Institute. On that date President Redmond Barry delivered a homily on the advantages that the Institute would confer, not only on science in Victoria, but on the wider community. Barry, well-versed in the ideology of the century, likened science to a vast treasury of facts, constantly augmented and capable of pretty display like a butterfly cabinet. Barry, however, called for more than just an immense dictionary of nature, empty of meaning and susceptible to that great nineteenth century horror, materialism; Barry wanted his treasury of knowledge to be subordinated to religion.

Ideological statements dispensed with, the public could view the exhibits arranged for the conversazione. Various displays were explained, and short public lectures on botany, chemistry, microscopy and electro-magnetism were delivered by Mueller, Maund, Gibbons and Sprague respectively.[9] Exhibits from the conversazione were subsequently moved to the Melbourne Exhibition.[10]

Less than a week after the conversazione monthly meetings of the Institute began in earnest. Despite an earlier suggestion of G. Guillame that the society should include all social classes, the Victorian Institute was élite, apparent from both the time set for the meetings, 4 p.m. on Thursdays, and the high cost of membership (a £2 entrance fee and a £4 annual subscription). Few tradesmen or clerks could attend meetings held during working hours and even fewer were likely to part with the sum of £4. In a promising start, however, two papers were read before this meeting 'Statistical Sanitary Processes' by W. Archer and Frederick Sinnett's 'Observations on the Country near Lake Torrens'. The latter paper provoked an examination of exploration in general. Ferdinand Mueller committed himself to bringing before the Institute the results of his botanical research in the Lake Torrens region, and a discussion arose on the problems encountered by exploratory expeditions venturing into the Australian interior.

Sinnett's paper was not the only stimulus to discussion of exploration that night. Another was an advertisement then appearing in Melbourne newspapers which announced the opening of a public subscription for funds to organize exploring expeditions devoted to the development of the resources of the colony, particularly those of gold and coal. The prospecting parties were to be sent out under the authority of the Philosophical Society of Victoria.

Philosophical Society of Victoria

The upstart Philosophical Society of Victoria, rival to the Victorian Institute for scientific acclaim in the colony, had its genesis in friction between Gibbons and Sigismund Wekey. During the debate in the *Argus* preceding the Institute's formation, Wekey had proposed that a philosophical and literary organization be established. On 17 June 1854, two days after the initial meeting of the Victorian Institute, the Philosophical Society began a series of initial meetings leading up to its formal inauguration on 12 August. This first meeting of 17 June was the antithesis of the well-attended and well-publicized initiation of the Victorian Institute. Present were Wekey, Dr W. E. Wilkie, Dr Ferdinand Mueller, Dr R. Eades, Dr S. Iffla, F. C. Christy, S. Hanaford and William Blandowski. As had Gibbons two days earlier, Wekey explained the objectives of the meeting in rhetorical flourishes appropriate to the occasion and spoke of the paramount importance of the founding of the Victorian Philosophical and Literary Society.[11] Mueller moved the formal establishment of the Society but amended the name to the Philosophical Society of Victoria. In subsequent meetings Wekey was elected honorary secretary (opposite Gibbons in the Victorian Institute) and he prepared a constitution for the Society which was accepted virtually unchanged.[12]

The question arises as to why men such as Ferdinand Mueller, heavily committed to the rival Victorian Institute, were also involved in the Philosophical Society of Victoria. The motivation for the formation of the Philosophical Society had been Wekey's disagreement with Gibbons on the type of society Gibbons wanted.[13] The Victorian Institute for the Advancement of Science took as its model the British Association for the Advancement of Science. Just as clearly the Philosophical Society of Victoria was to be based on the Royal Society. From its commencement the Philosophical Society saw its name as temporary and much time at council meetings was given to efforts to obtain the coveted royal charter. The Philosophical Society, which met in the offices of the embryonic Museum of Natural History and included

Museum zoologist William Blandowski, also took as its special responsibility the development of the Museum. As early as the formal inaugural meeting (12 August 1854) it solicited and received specimens. Given that the organizations had different charters, Mueller would have seen no reason not to contribute to both.

The nascent Philosophical Society was not averse to political manoeuvring and at the second of its preliminary meetings (24 June) it was resolved to send a delegation to seek Surveyor-General Andrew Clarke's membership and to solicit his advice on obtaining a royal charter.[14] The third meeting (15 July), on hearing that Clarke would be pleased to join the Society and had offered the use of the Museum for meetings, immediately and in his absence elected him first to membership, then to presidency of the Society. Clarke was never more than a figurehead as president. He owed his position as president to his control of the Museum, which the Society saw as its special responsibility, and to his access to the governor.

The Society's campaign for legitimacy was further advanced when Lieutenant-Governor Hotham became the patron. His private secretary, Captain J. H. Kay, FRS, was elected an honorary member.[15] In a further move for respectability Dr Godfrey Howitt, long-time curator of the museum of the Mechanics' Institute, was elected vice-president without having joined the Society.[16] The original members of the Society were content to place figureheads in the formal offices and to dominate the council which met regularly to plot the course of the Society. The inner circle of the council exercised complete control over the direction of the organization, and the monthly meetings were principally to hear papers by the members.

The first formal meeting of the Philosophical Society, at which President Clarke read his inaugural address, took place on 12 August. It was to be Clarke's only real contribution.[17] He called on his listeners to abandon 'the sublimity of deductive philosophy' for practical experimentation. Dr Ferdinand Mueller followed with a paper 'Definitions of Rare and Hitherto Undescribed Australian Plants, chiefly collected within the boundaries of the Colony of Victoria'.

The meeting of the Philosophical Society that took place the next month (10 September) was important not so much for the papers read, but for the attempt to meet one of the objectives of the Society, the development of the natural resources of the colony through exploration.[18] Wekey addressed the meeting proposing a committee be formed to strengthen the Society's intention to initiate exploratory expeditions. In a burst of enthusiasm, just a week later a special general meeting of the Society was called to hear the committee's report.[19] The gist of this report was that funds for any expedition would necessarily have to be raised by public subscription. The advertisements which appeared in the Melbourne newspapers, and which sparked discussion in the rival Victorian Institute, were the means to this end. Following discussion of the report Robert Brough Smyth read a paper on the 'Comparative value and durability of Building Materials used in Melbourne' and, at Wekey's instigation, Brough Smyth was elected an honorary secretary to share the burden of the duties with Wekey.

After this meeting the Philosophical Society began to draw public attention to itself. The *Argus* noticed the Society, its gatherings at the Museum of Natural History and the intention of renowned Irish botanist, William Harvey, then collecting in the Australian colonies, to read a paper on the algae of Australia at the October monthly meeting.[20] The Museum itself continued to develop and now included animal, mineral, and fossil specimens. Brough Smyth, its acting curator, had recently purchased Australian bird specimens for the collection.

The Philosophical Society's advertisement opening a public subscription for exploratory expeditions met with indifference, attributed by the Society to the downturn in economic activity in Victoria.[21] Seeking alternative sources of funds the Society approached the governor and the legislative council but was again rebuffed.[22] Through his private secretary, the governor regretted that public funds were already insufficient to meet outstanding expenditure. In any case, Hotham said, the numerous prospecting parties already scouring the length and breadth of the colony were sufficient to survey Victoria for gold, and coal fields located at Western Port were reportedly adequate to last a generation.[23] Hotham, perhaps deliberately, confused the goal of the Society's proposal, exploration *per se*, with the Society's justification for it: the survey of mineral resources.

Amalgamation

Thwarted in their effort to organize exploration by their inability to raise funds the Philosophical Society next entertained another contentious proposal: amalgamation with the Victorian Institute. On 9 January 1855 the council of the Philosophical Society met to consider an invitation from the Victorian Institute for such a union.[24] The plan of amalgamation to end the 'apparent if not real rivalry' was received coolly by the Philosophical Society and throughout the protracted negotiations over the marriage of the two institutions, lengthened by the antipathy between Wekey and Gibbons, the Victorian Institute was always the ardent suitor, the Philosophical Society a reluctant bride.[25] After one exchange of correspondence concerning a joint meeting, the Philosophical Society addressed a letter to the council of the Victorian Institute, since 'further correspondence with the Secretary Wm. Gibbons is deemed impracticable, from the tone advocated in his enclosed note'.[26] Wekey, for his part, did his best to thwart the amalgamation by reading to the Philosophical Society a statement comparing the two societies in which he pointed out that the Philosophical Society had £170 in its treasury while the Victorian Institute had only £68. Additionally Wekey emphasized the lack of papers read before the Victorian Institute.[27] Although Wekey dwelt upon the differences, analysis of the papers published in the respective *Transactions* of the two societies emphasizes the similarities.[28]

Wekey and Gibbons were fighting a losing battle. The colony could not yet support two scientific societies and a *de facto* amalgamation had already taken place by the cross membership of both officers and members in each society. A report on the procedure for the union was read at the May monthly meeting of the Philosophical Society and the initial meeting of the combined societies took place on 10 July 1855 under the hybrid name of the Philosophical Institute of Victoria.

Under the amalgamation scheme, all three honorary secretaries (Gibbons, Wekey and Brough Smyth) were to continue to serve. Minutes of the early council meetings, however, reveal that when Wekey was present, Gibbons was generally absent and vice versa. The 19 July council meeting decided, however, that three secretaries were unwieldy and unnecessary, and that all three were to resign and contest an election for a single position. This decision was taken despite the Victorian Institute having made it an essential condition of the amalgamation that Gibbons retain office as joint secretary.[29] The council attempted to avoid any sentiment of favouritism by appointing Blandowski secretary until the election could be held. Both Gibbons and Brough Smyth declined to stand in the election for honorary secretary, and Wekey was elected unopposed at the 2 August 1855 meeting. Seeking to maintain his involvement in the Institute, Gibbons nominated for the council that year but Wekey was able to frustrate even this appointment.[30] The following year Gibbons again tried for election to the council but was ignominiously defeated and subsequently faded from the history of the Institute.[31]

Wekey enjoyed the satisfaction of defeating his rival for only a short while. At the 19 June 1856 meeting of the Institute, Wekey resigned and Robert Brough Smyth was elected in his place. Even Wekey's departure caused controversy for it was discovered that he had taken office space for the Philosophical Institute in the Mechanics' Institute, but neglected to pay for it. The Mechanics' Institute sequestered the Philosophical Institute's books, and eventually sold them to pay for the back rent.[32]

National Museum

Three major concerns dominated the early years of scientific societies in Victoria. The first issue, exploration, was raised early but then forced into the background by lack of funds. Nevertheless, exploration was never far removed from the collective mind of the Philosophical Institute. A second concern, the acclimatization of animals, occupied attention briefly before a society formed to devote its entire attention to the issue. The third subject, the Museum of Natural History, dominated the years 1855–56.

The Museum was the pivotal interest of the Philosophical Society and its successor, the Philosophical Institute. It was the Society's particular interest and its members contributed many of the specimens. At the 28 February 1855 council meeting of the Society, Solomon Iffla put forward a motion that an application be made to the legislative council to formally transfer custody of the Museum of Natural History to the Philosophical Society.[33] When Wekey announced this motion at the following 13 March monthly meeting Andrew Clarke, making one of his infrequent appearances at the Society, informed the gathering that the legislative council already had the matter under consideration and there would be no point in pressing the issue until the council's deliberations were known.[34] After amalgamation of the two societies into the Philosophical Institute in July 1855, the Museum continued to attract attention. Concern over custody of the Museum arose from reports circulating in Melbourne that it was about to pass into the control of the recently founded University of Melbourne. One of the early initiatives of Frederick McCoy, foundation professor of natural science at the university, had been to organize the Museum there. At the 17 October 1855 meeting of the council of the Philosophical Institute a motion was passed calling on the secretary of the Institute to write to the private secretary of the governor enquiring when a deputation, made up of Iffla, Maund and A. K. Smith, might call on the governor 'to urge the impolicy of removing the Museum of Natural History to the University'.[35]

The next council meeting heard the governor's dismissive reply. Hotham would discuss the matter with Clarke.[36] The Institute, of which Clarke was president, could have expected Clarke to inform it of any decision taken about the Museum. However, no communication on the subject was recorded as being received. A year later the question of the removal of the Museum to the University was still unresolved. At the monthly meeting of 15 April 1856, Arthur Dobree gave notice of a petition to Acting-

Governor Edward Macarthur requesting that the Museum be entrusted to the Public Library rather than the University.

At the subsequent Philosophical Institute meeting a committee was appointed to present the Institute's belated petition to Acting-Governor Macarthur. Macarthur assured the delegation that locating the Museum at the University was only a temporary measure, and a building would be constructed to house what was now becoming known as the 'National Museum'.

Despite clear indications that the government had already decided on the fate of the Museum, the Philosophical Institute persisted. A second committee was convened on 19 June 1856 to oversee the enquiry into the fate of the Museum but to their dismay the committee learned that the National Museum had been closed, and specimens were being prepared for removal to the University 'in pursuance of instructions received'. The hapless Museum committee could suggest nothing beyond organizing a meeting to bring public pressure on the government.[37]

This meeting, called for 26 July at the Mechanics' Institute, achieved little. Even as preparations for the public meeting were being formulated, the Museum's collections were 'hastily removed' from the Assay Building to the University.

The reaction of the Philosophical Institute to the University's usurping of the Museum was timid. The issue quickly dropped from discussion, collections were presented to the University's custody and McCoy, at least partially responsible for the transfer, was re-elected to the council of the Institute.[38] Four years later, in a delightful piece of irony, McCoy, acting in his capacity as director of the National Museum, wrote to the president of the Philosophical Institute, offering the Institute any duplicate specimens that could be spared from the National Museum.[39]

The part played in the affair by the ostensible founder of the Museum, Andrew Clarke, is murky. Clearly McCoy could not have secured the specimens from the Assay Office without Clarke's consent and connivance. Previous discussion of the Museum's fate had always seen the matter referred back to Clarke by both Governor Hotham and Acting-Governor Macarthur, and the orders for packing the specimens prior to their late-night removal from the Assay Office could only have come from Clarke. Discussion at the Institute and in committee meetings also indicates that Clarke, despite his position as president, did not inform the Institute of the fate of the Museum. It would seem that Clarke favoured the transfer of the Museum to the University rather than to the Philosophical Institute.

The role played by McCoy in the transfer of the collection to the University was less nebulous than Clarke's. McCoy continually assured the Institute that the despatch of the specimens to the University was only a temporary measure and that the University and Museum collections would be maintained as separate entities.[40] McCoy himself was to be appointed the first director of the National Museum, a post he occupied for forty years.

Evidence of residual ill-feeling over the Museum surfaced in 1857. At the 15 July 1856 meeting of the Institute, McCoy had read a paper on 'Museums in Victoria'. The paper aggravated feeling between McCoy and Macadam, an opponent of the Museum's removal. Only part of McCoy's paper was included in the 1856 *Transactions of the Philosophical Institute* (published in 1857) and McCoy accused Macadam, honorary secretary of the Institute and editor of the *Transactions*, of wilfully obstructing publication of the paper. Much of the quarrel was characterized by pettiness on both sides, but the council of the Institute backed Macadam. McCoy thereupon published the paper in the *Argus* prior to its inclusion in the 1857 *Transactions*.[41]

McCoy's tenure as director resulted in a greater expansion of the Museum's collections than probably would have occurred otherwise. The letterbooks of the National Museum record McCoy's tireless lobbying of the Victorian government for funds and his strengthening of the collections through his contacts with European naturalists.[42] He also led the fight to retain Australian specimens in Australia insisting that at least some of the Cranbourne meteorite be preserved in Victoria, and requesting that bird specimens sent to John Gould be returned to the National Museum.[43] McCoy was also quick to take offence on behalf of the Museum. He wrote to the secretary of the Smithsonian Institution complaining that the National Museum had been left off the Smithsonian's 'Circular of Foreign Correspondents'.[44]

The Museum had been lost by the Philosophical Institute; any close relationship that had once existed between the Philosophical Society of Victoria and the Museum was severed. For the rest of the century the Museum was controlled by McCoy.

The ineffectual response of the Philosophical Institute to the Museum episode confirmed many Melbourne residents' view that scientific societies had little to offer Victoria in the 1850s. The *Melbourne Punch* found ample material for its satiric pen in caricaturing Philosophical Institute members as clubby, heavy-drinking and irrelevant.[45] The Museum imbroglio featured prominently in the satirical press.[46]

The battle to retain control of the Museum lost, the Philosophical Institute threw its energies into other facets of its charter, when it was not distracted by the petty quarrels which so roiled it. The absence of Gibbons and Wekey did not reduce internal friction, a point highlighted in 1857 in an obscure taxonomic paper.

In August 1857 Ferdinand Mueller read an 'Account of some New Australian Plants' to the Institute, in which he had

> the pleasant opportunity of attaching to several of them [plants] the names of members of the Philosophical Institute, not only as a token of personal respect, but also as an appreciation of their services rendered to this society, and as a slight acknowledgement of the disinterested manner in which they fostered and cultivated science in this country.[47]

Included in this gesture were the genera *Wilkiea* (David Wilkie, vice-president of the Institute), and *Eadesia* (Richard Eades, member of the Institute), and various species named for Charles Wilhelmi (assistant government botanist) and other botanists working in the Australian colonies. This flattery drew out the worst in another Institute member, William Blandowski, who had previously caused dissent in the Philosophical Institute.[48]

In September Blandowski read a paper to the society innocently entitled 'Recent Discoveries in Natural History on the Lower Murray', a preliminary report on Blandowski's recent explorations, originally prepared for and submitted to the Board of Public Lands.[49] Assisting Blandowski on the excursion had been another German-born naturalist, Gerard Krefft, who was later to head the Australian Museum in Sydney.[50] Part of the brief for the expedition had been to collect specimens for the National Museum, and according to Blandowski's report some 16,000 specimens were brought back. Blandowski antagonized many in the colonial administration when he abruptly abandoned the expedition in August, leaving Krefft to continue as best he could. On his return to Melbourne with much of the collected material, Blandowski refused to give up the specimens and sketches to the government, even under the threat of legal action. The *Illustrated Melbourne News*, noting that Blandowski may have been previously ill-used, correctly forecast that he would lose support if he continued to refuse to yield up the specimens.[51]

Some discussion followed the reading of Blandowski's paper. The council of the Institute indicated their intention to publish the report and voted £30 to fund engraving of the accompanying plates. A week later this decision was reversed, on the basis that the paper had originally been prepared as a government report and was therefore the property of the government.[52] At the next monthly meeting William Clarkson gave notice of a motion to repeal the council's rejection of the paper, but withdrew it when the council decided to go ahead with publication. By early March 1858 Blandowski's paper was ready for inclusion in the Institute's *Transactions*. It covered geography, geology and zoology, and it was in the latter section that Blandowski showed his truculence. Noting that only three species of fish had previously been recorded from the Murray, Blandowski proceeded to describe nineteen so-called species. Many were named after members of the Philosophical Institute: *Ceruna eadesii*, *C. nicholsonii*, *C. ifflaensis*, *C. wilkiensis*, *Kohna mackennae*, *Turruitja acheson*, *Jerrina dobreensis*, *Uteranka irvingii*, *Tilka wilsonia*, *Collundera muelleriana* and *Brosmius bleasdalli*. The descriptions Blandowski attached to some species caused problems: particularly *Ceruna eadesii*, 'A fish easily recognised by its low forehead, big belly and sharp spine', and *Brosmius bleasdalli*, 'a slimy, slippery fish. Lives in the mud . . .'!

On 5 March William Wilson, professor of mathematics at the University, read these descriptions from Blandowski's paper to a council meeting and moved that the four offending pages be removed from the forthcoming *Transactions*. The motion was carried unanimously. Blandowski, who did not attend the meeting, was requested to furnish a written explanation of the unscientific descriptions—in writing, for several members of the council objected to meeting him in person.[53] A week later Blandowski, first by letter, then in a personal appearance, pleaded innocence of any intention to insult. Ingenuously, he offered to provide taxonomic works which contained the descriptive terms he had used and offered to submit specimens of the fish in question. Blandowski retired from the meeting and the council continued to discuss the offending pages until Wilson moved that Blandowski be requested to resign from the Institute. The motion was lost, lacking the two-thirds majority necessary.[54] Wilson and Bleasdale, elected to the council less than two weeks earlier—as was Blandowski—announced their resignations and quit the meeting. Supporters of Blandowski subsequently attempted to defuse the issue by suggesting that Blandowski be required to rewrite the scientific descriptions.[55]

The issue continued to fester, and at the 24 March monthly meeting Secretary John Macadam indicated that a letter had been received from Bleasdale. After some heated discussion over the admissibility of the letter, it was read, although with the proviso that its contents not be included in the minutes.[56] Further discussion then took place until Blandowski requested that a committee of enquiry look into the issue. The strong feelings raised by the controversy were evident when the membership originally proposed for the committee was overturned, and another committee elected in its place.[57]

The subsequent monthly meeting heard the enquiry's report, but the minutes of the meeting give no indication of its content, recording that 'A lengthened discussion' ensued which involved most of the principals of the issue.[58] Eventually the committee's report was rejected. A motion was then made for the resignations of Bleasdale and Wilson not to be accepted, and was carried unanimously.

The outcome of the meeting was an uneasy truce. The aggressor and the aggrieved continued their membership in the Institute and Blandowski continued to read papers before it, but they must have been anticipated with much trepidation by the members![59]

Predictably, the *Melbourne Punch* took advantage of the controversy with a cartoon and doggerel.[60]

> Vot shall I say, vot shall I do
> I did describe ze vish quite true;
> I wish zat I could please you all,
> But not can make his belly small?
>
> Mein himmel—all vot I fish
> You look yourself upon ze vish
> You see ze spine, ze little pins
> Vot sticks out here upon his fins

Zoological Society

Another issue which held the attention of the Philosophical Institute during the mid- and late 1850s was the acclimatization of foreign organisms to the colony. This issue eventually produced a quasi-scientific society towards the end of the decade, the Zoological Society (and its 1861 successor, the Acclimatization Society of Victoria).

Whilst botanic gardens throughout the world had long had an interest in, and a charter for, the acclimatization of foreign plants to local conditions, the concept of exotic animal acclimatization was taken up with a vengeance in the 1850s. The surge of interest in exotic animal acclimatization in Australia from the mid-1850s on derived from Europe. In February 1854 the French Société Zoologique d'Acclimatation was founded; six years later, a British Society for the Acclimatization of Animals was born. This latter organization was partially the work of the one-time editor of the Melbourne *Argus*, Edward Wilson, who was closely involved with acclimatization in both Britain and Australia. That the Australian, particularly the Victorian, preoccupation with acclimatization was so nearly contemporaneous with the European interest is attributable to Wilson's alternating periods of residence in Victoria and England.

An early Victorian expression of interest in animal acclimatization occurred in 1856 at a legislative council session, when Dr Thomas Embling moved that a committee be appointed to report on the desirability of the introduction of the South American alpaca to Victoria.[61] The committee's report recommended the introduction of the alpaca as an alternative to sheep in mountainous regions.[62] The committee adopted a cavalier attitude to the minor detail that exportation of the alpaca was banned by the Peruvian government. The imperial mentality condoned flouting the laws 'of a community, small in number, and partly in an aboriginal state, which asserts a monopoly of one of the most valuable of animals found upon the earth . . .'. The report received an indifferent reception in the legislative council, but this did not end Embling's efforts to introduce the alpaca to Victoria.[63]

In April 1856 Ludwig Becker persuaded the Philosophical Institute to set up a committee of enquiry into the introduction of camels and other useful animals to the colony. The focus of this enquiry was on camels as a necessary adjunct to exploration. A formidable proponent of acclimatization, Edward Wilson, contributed two papers to the Philosophical Institute in 1857. The first concerned his work on the Murray cod. Wilson observed that the species was found only in those rivers that flowed north and west, never in those running south or east.[64] Believing there to be no reason why such a 'natural law' could not be violated, Wilson privately financed a scheme to transfer Murray cod from the tributaries of the Murray to tributaries of the Yarra. In justifying his meddling with nature, Wilson reiterated the rationalizations in which acclimatizers typically sought ideological refuge. Nature had lavishly produced a myriad of species but acted capriciously in their distribution. Surely part of man's task on the earth was to equalize this eccentric distribution? Nature 'properly and kindly left to man the interesting and agreeable task of supplementing her own efforts, of discovering by experiment and the action of his own intellect how far the gift itself may be multiplied, extended, and improved'. In response to Wilson's tirade the Philosophical Institute set up a Murray cod committee.

Wilson's second paper 'On the Introduction of the British Song Bird', suggested the introduction of skylarks and nightingales to Victoria. Wilson wanted to temper the harsh laugh of the kookaburra and the raucous shriek of the cockatoo with the song of the skylark on a spring morning, and that of the nightingale during a summer's evening. Firmly entrenched in the precepts of acclimatization was the concept of nature as an imperfect machine to be tinkered with by man. The mechanistic models that had dominated other sciences for centuries were finding their way into natural history. On receipt of Wilson's paper the Philosophical Institute promptly, and typically, set up a committee to consider the introduction of the British song bird.

Over the next several years the Philosophical Institute and its successor, the Royal Society of Victoria, heard other papers on acclimatization. Ferdinand Mueller read a paper 'On a General Introduction of Useful Plants into Victoria'.[65] In his 'Presidential Address' of 1859, Mueller returned to the theme of acclimatization and spoke of the Australian Alps made productive by the alpaca and the cashmere goat, and the desert interior of the continent providing a home to African game and the camel.[66] That same year P. Nisser contributed a paper on useful animals of South America that might be introduced to Victoria.[67] Although some limited active measures were taken by the British song bird committee, the Philosophical Institute was generally content to do little else than debate issues. The Institute's inactivity eventually led to the formation of other, more vigorous, groups.

On 6 October 1857, a group of enthusiasts met at St Patrick's Hall to form, in the words of Frederick McCoy, 'an Ornithological Society, having in view chiefly the rearing of the finer kinds of poultry and cage birds'.[68] At the meeting the scope of the society was enlarged to a Zoological Society 'for the purposes of science and for that of affording the Public the advantage of studying the habits of the animal creation in a properly arranged zoological garden'.[69] A committee of twelve was set up to manage the Society and to carry out its charter of collecting zoological specimens, holding exhibitions, encouraging the introduction of exotic species, and ambitiously, the domestication of indigenous animals and birds. In keeping with the group's original design, the first undertaking of the Society was to be the organization of bimonthly exhibitions of indigenous and imported poultry and birds.

The new Society received a less than enthusiastic greeting from some newspapers and journals. The *Illustrated Journal of Australia*, commented caustically,

> we fear that both they and the public will be disappointed for both titles are misnomers as the design of the promoters was merely to put up poultry shows to which the introduction of songbirds is now to be added. The assumption then, of the title of Zoological Society is an injury to science and an affront to those who otherwise have helped the movement.[70]

The sudden outbreak of activity in the area of acclimatization was in great measure attributable to the 1857 appointment of a legislative assembly committee to report on the importation of stock to the colony. When the committee recommended the introduction of exotic species (and £3,000 for that purpose), the Zoological Society had quickly been formed to shoulder the task of advancing acclimatization. For several months after its formation, however, the Society lay dormant. With its funds limited to membership subscriptions, the Society languished.

In 1858, however, the Zoological Society was brought dramatically to life. In January of that year the chief secretary of Victoria, William Haines, announced the intention of the government to contribute £3,000 and thirty acres at Richmond Paddock for the establishment of the Zoological Gardens. By April, in expectation of the promised grant, the Society had entered into a £700 contract for clearing, levelling and fencing the Gardens.

In addition to commencing preparation of the grounds for the Zoological Gardens, the Society undertook negotiations with Mr Billing, proprietor of a travelling menagerie, to appoint him managing keeper of the Zoological Gardens. Billing was to bring the animals in his care to the Gardens and the Society would maintain them with an option for eventual purchase. The committee conducting the negotiations forecast that the Gardens might open to the public by the middle of August 1858.[71]

At the end of May 1858 the membership of the Zoological Society was called together to hear a report on the financial status of the organization. As of that month the society had paid out £1,200. It had not received the promised grant and the income from subscriptions had been only £400. The need for government intervention was desperate. The gist of the report, forwarded to the colonial government, proposed handing over control of the Zoological Gardens to the government and dissolving the Society. The report further suggested that the Zoological Gardens become self-supporting and that a board of directors be appointed from the committee of the Zoological Society and the government's scientific body.[72]

Subsequently a committee of management composed of government officials and members of the Zoological Society took over direction of the Zoological Gardens. The *raison d'être* for the Zoological Society had evaporated, and the Society faded from existence. The insalubrious site of Richmond Paddock, having already absorbed hundreds of pounds, was abandoned, and temporary housing of the songbird aviary and other Society animals in the Botanic Gardens continued until the Zoological Gardens were moved to Royal Park in 1862.

Edward Wilson

In 1861 Edward Wilson, no longer editor but still proprietor of the *Argus*, had returned to the colony after a visit to Europe. Wilson's presence and influence in Melbourne helped return the acclimatization movement, which had increasingly drifted into the management of the Zoological Gardens, to its original purpose. On 25 February 1861 the provisional committee of the Acclimatization Society of Victoria met at the Melbourne Mechanics' Institute. The formation of the Acclimatization Society demarcated the Society's interests from those of the Zoological Gardens. One group sought to keep animals in cages, the other to liberate them to the colony at large. The difference was never to be distinct to the public and was to dog both organizations for much of their existence.

Exploration

During the lean years of the late 1850s, interest in exploratory expeditions was kept alive in the Philosophical Institute. Individuals associated with the Institute continued to carry out private explorations or to attach themselves to official expeditions but the organization's inability to despatch its own expeditions rankled. Clarke referred to this unsatisfactory state of affairs in his 'Anniversary Address' of 1856, reminding his listeners of their failure to enlist public support for mineral exploration when the benefits of such exploration were so obvious.[73] The apathy of the legislature and the indifference of the citizenry of Victoria could, Clarke felt, only be combatted by the Philosophical Institute's taking up the cudgels for exploration.

At the 11 November 1857 meeting a motion was passed forming a committee to advise on the practicability of an expedition to follow up on the initiatives of the lamented Ludwig Leichhardt, whose third and final expedition had disappeared without a trace while attempting to cross northern Australia in 1848. In particular, the proposal anticipated an east–west expedition from Curtis Bay on the east coast to Shark Bay on the north-west coast.[74] Discussion in the Institute centred around the benefits of the expedition to geography and the possibility of discovering Leichhardt's fate.

A bloated committee totalling thirty-three members was nominated to pursue the project, and held its first meeting three days later.[75] Mueller, a member of the committee, fuelled the enthusiasm for exploration when he read 'An Historical Review of the Explorations of Australia' to the Institute.[76] In his overview, Mueller recommended that any expedition the Institute might fit out should rely on horses rather than camels. Mueller advised that camels would balk if the expedition met with stony terrain and would require special handlers. Mueller also suggested a preliminary survey of the region directly north of the limits of the colony of Victoria.

Just under a month later a special general meeting of the Institute convened to hear the report of the exploration committee. Based on meetings and correspondence, the report had been drawn up by Wilkie, Mueller and Macadam. Enquiries made by the committee to Augustus Gregory, the noted explorer of northern Australia who Mueller had accompanied in 1855, brought a frustrating answer. The forbidding and barren nature of the country rendered the proposed east–west route dangerous. Even the shorter north–south route across the unknown interior was unlikely to succeed, but of the two choices it was the better. Gregory's recommendation was for a slow, incremental, nibbling away at the unknown.[77]

Although disappointed that they could not recommend the grand expedition they envisaged the committee could, and did, follow up Mueller's suggestion, and pushed for the immediate organization of an expedition to survey the country north from the Darling River towards the Victoria and Thompson Rivers, stressing that any implementation of such a survey needed to commence immediately to take advantage of the coming rainy season (1858). This reduced reconnaissance was expected to last about five months and cost an estimated £2,000. The committee followed Mueller's earlier recommendations and decided on a party of five men on horseback. The problem of funding this survey was met by the committee's suggestion that the Philosophical Institute petition the government for £2,500. In passing, the committee noted that a member of the Philosophical Institute, Thomas Belt, proposed to undertake a solitary expedition south from the Gulf of Carpentaria to Adelaide. [78]

Having finally chosen a leader just two months before the expedition was to leave Melbourne, the committee re-evaluated the proposed route. The agreed Cooper's Creek to Victoria River route was thrown into question in the middle of 1860. Various members of the committee suggested a variety of other routes.

A public meeting was also called to generate community support for exploration.[79] Chaired by Clarke, the well-attended meeting carried resolutions proposed by Wilkie and Mueller which emphasized the importance of the exploration of the interior of Australia and the need for a preliminary reconnaissance to open communication between the Darling and Victoria rivers. A third resolution was advanced specifying the duty of the public of Victoria to support the Philosophical Institute's scheme, but the *Argus* was silent on the outcome of the motion.[80] The fourth and final resolution deputized a committee to present to the governor the case for public funding of the expedition.

Throughout 1858 the exploration issue was kept alive in the Institute by discussion, papers related to exploration, and a series of reports from the exploration committee.[81] The third report of the committee, issued late in 1858, mentioned the birth of a rival committee. At a public meeting held at the Mechanics' Institute on 1 September under the chairmanship of William Stawell, late president of the Philosophical Institute, an exploration fund committee was established. The committee had obtained an anonymous offer of £1,000 on condition that it raise £2,000 from the public.[82] This new public committee pledged to work closely with the exploration committee of the Philosophical Institute. Well it might, for the active members of each were identical. By December 1858 the two had combined, but funds remained hard to come by and little of the wealth of the goldfields found its way into the exploration committee's coffers. The wealthiest of the Australian colonies could find only £900 for the fund in eleven months. Although the money was finally in hand by October 1859, further delays occurred. The camels that the committee had now agreed on as transport for the expedition were not expected to arrive before March of 1860. The optimistic schedule of 1858 was long forgotten.

On 23 January 1860 the Philosophical Institute of Victoria gained what it had so long waited for: the coveted royal charter. It officially became the Royal Society of Victoria. That same day the united exploration fund committee called a public meeting to report on its progress. The most significant news was that the Victorian parliament had voted a sum of £6,000 for exploration. The public meeting decided to entrust the exploration committee of the Philosophical Institute with management of the expedition in order to speed up preparations for the expedition. The need for haste was evidenced when the chairman of the meeting, John Hodgson, MLC, indicated that the exploratory party should leave in February, less than a month away, but these optimistic expectations were unrealized. By April, as Governor Henry Barkly noted to the Royal Society, the committee had dismissed the possibility of any expedition to take advantage of the winter, but stood ready to have one in place at Cooper's Creek by the following autumn to take advantage of next year's winter rains.[83]

Interest in the exploration party had steadily strengthened. Shortly after the expedition was first announced, suggestions for routes and equipment began to appear in the mail of the Philosophical Institute. As early as September 1858 individuals began applying for positions with the expedition. On 4 December 1858 Francis Marsh wrote to the committee suggesting that the reconnaissance might be cheaply organized by employing Chittagong Lascars from Calcutta at wages of £3 per month. Marsh, a sea captain, felt qualified to command the party. Other letters tackled the problem of providing water during the desert crossing. Joseph Clements devised a complex plan to supply the party with water by unreeling a hose from a cart as the party advanced. The hose was to be connected to a reservoir of water and pump set on the edge of each river the party reached. Another plan called for a device to trap rainwater, while a third sought to overcome the problem of muddy springs by a tube of gutta-percha capped with a ball.[84] Suggestions of a more practical nature arrived from Charles Ledger in London, who forwarded ten pounds of coca leaves along with notes on their medicinal use. Ledger had found the leaves particularly efficacious on his trips to South America to obtain alpacas for shipment to Australia. He believed the leaves to be an all-purpose anodyne, not only for thirst and hunger but for stomach pains, wounds, snakebites, contusion and a variety of other medical problems.[85] The ingredient of the leaves that gave them this miraculous curative power was, of course, cocaine. Others anxious to contribute to the success of the expedition sent all manner of goods from seeds to telescopes.

By the early months of 1860 the plans of the committee had begun to unravel. There had been no question of who would lead the expedition. Augustus Gregory was the natural choice and the man recommended by everyone consulted. Gregory's obvious reluctance and indeed persistent refusal of the position was a minor inconvenience. It was not until early 1860 that the committee finally accepted that Gregory was not going to participate. They next settled on Peter Warburton, an experienced explorer of the South Australian interior. Although the committee advertised the position of leader of the expedition and attracted numerous applicants, they had clearly wanted Warburton. However, Warburton declined the position, tactfully stating that he thought the Victorian Exploring Expedition should be led by a Victorian.[86] As the months passed in 1860, the committee refused to accept Warburton's decision and his name appeared on a list of candidates for the position at the 2 March committee meeting.[87] In the middle of March, the committee again delayed any decision on the leadership until Warburton had been made a formal offer, and as late as May there was a motion before the committee that Warburton be requested to accept the leadership. But by May another name, that of Robert O'Hara Burke, police superintendent of the Castlemaine district, began to be widely mooted as leader of the expedition. Burke found backers in the Reverend John Bleasdale and the government astronomer Neumeyer. It was not until a 20 June committee meeting that the leadership issue was finally settled, when Burke gathered ten votes while Warburton, who had never applied for the position and had specifically declined it, still received five votes.

Having finally chosen a leader just two months before the expedition was to leave Melbourne, the committee re-evaluated the proposed route. The agreed Cooper's Creek to Victoria River route was thrown into question in the middle of 1860. Various members of the committee suggested a variety of other routes. At meetings on both 17 and 20 July, Stawell, Neumeyer, Mueller and Wilkie supported the Cooper's Creek starting point, Embling suggested Shark's Bay, and Selwyn advised Port Augusta. Ligar, the surveyor-general, recommended King's Sound on the north-west shoulder of Australia, while a further option entertained was shipping the expedition to Blunder Bay, the outlet of the Victoria River, and then travelling south to Cooper's Creek. Wilkie, however, pointed out that the only reasonable starting point for a Victorian expedition was Cooper's Creek. On 23 July the route was again debated and a motion to send the camels to Cooper's Creek was carried by a majority of five.[88] Four days later the committee met to consider a starting date. It was set for less than a month later, 20 August.

So it was that despite committees devoted to the expedition having been in existence for over three years, a leader was not chosen until two months prior to departure, and the route finalized less than a month before the departure date. While there were other contributory factors—the problem of raising finance, and intercolonial rivalry—the delay in reaching these decisions, indeed the results of these decisions (Burke as leader, and the Cooper's Creek to the Victoria River route) can clearly be attributed to the organization of the expedition by a committee. The inability to make early decisions laid the groundwork for disaster. Either an extraordinary leader or extraordinary luck might still have allowed the expedition to succeed. The Victorian Exploring Expedition had neither.

Burke, once chosen, immediately commenced preparations. The unwieldy committee was finally pared down to a smaller group of five: McCoy, Neumeyer, Wilkie, Cadwell and Watson, with Macadam as secretary.[89] By 9 July Burke had submitted his list of expedition personnel, including Landells as second-in-command, Wills as astronomer and meteorologist, and Beckler as medical officer and naturalist. Beckler had previously undertaken botanical collecting and presented a testimonial from Mueller with his application. Royal Society member Ludwig Becker's name was raised by members of the committee, and it was decided that McCoy should examine both Beckler and Becker on their scientific knowledge. On 13 July McCoy reported back that Beckler was competent medically and botanically, but deficient in the required zoological, geological and artistic skills. Someone of Becker's abilities was needed, and he took his place in the party.[90] McCoy, Mueller, Neumeyer and Selwyn were appointed as a subcommittee to draw up scientific instructions for the expedition.[91]

On 16 August Burke requested that the financial arrangements for the expedition ensure that he could draw cheques on the treasurer of the Royal Society, a measure designed to eliminate the need for him to carry money. In acceding to this request the Royal Society gave Burke financial control which resulted in a series of dishonoured cheques flooding into the Royal Society later that year. Control of all other arrangements had also passed to Burke, as became evident when two members of the original party asked for an enquiry into their dismissal. The committee informed the two 'that the affairs of the Expedition were entirely in the hands of Mr Burke'.[92] The stage was set for the tragedy that followed. With the departure of the Victorian Exploring Expedition (later known as the Burke and Wills expedition) from Melbourne on 20 August 1860, the Royal Society of Victoria's active participation effectively ended. All that was left were financial problems, recriminations and rescue operations.

Burke was barely out of sight when the Royal Society of Victoria, and specifically its exploration committee, started its loss of innocence. On 30 August the chief secretary wrote to the secretary of the exploration committee pointing out that the funds allotted by the government for horses and stores already had been overdrawn by £500.[93] Less than a month later a report on the financial condition of the committee indicated that there were only sufficient funds to meet the expedition's expenses until 1 January 1861, an impossibly short time for it to accomplish its work. All the committee could do was preach economy to Burke by mail, and apply for another £6,000 to be placed on the estimates of the following year.[94] The return of dishonoured cheques, the resignations of Landells and Beckler, and the news that Stuart had nearly crossed the continent to win the coveted honour, followed one upon another. News of the death of Ludwig Becker, long-time member of the Philosophical Institute and the Royal Society, was merely the prelude to later news of the deaths of Burke, Wills and Gray. The age of innocence for natural history was over.

CHAPTER SEVEN

the issue of progressive development
INTERCOLONIAL, 1860-70

The débâcle of the Victorian Exploring Expedition, organized and run under the auspices of the newly proclaimed Royal Society of Victoria, ended the innocence of colonial scientific clubs. Attendance at meetings and dinners in the civilized precincts of Sydney, Hobart, or Melbourne was a far cry from accepting responsibility for the death of men—through starvation, thirst, or exhaustion—in the interior of the country. The ensuing decade, the 1860s, witnessed a similar loss of innocence in the tradition of natural history itself. In 1858, when papers written by Alfred Wallace and Charles Darwin were presented to a meeting of the Linnean Society of London, and the following year when Darwin's *On the Origin of Species* was published, the issue of progressive development was brought to the fore. While it could still be ridiculed, as it had for most of the century, evolutionary theory could no longer be completely ignored.

In 1844 the initially anonymous publication in Britain of the controversial *The Vestiges of Creation* had focused attention on the debate over progressive development.[1] A consensus quickly emerged, however, among British natural historians that *Vestiges* was a mishmash of natural history containing an abundance of errors. Charles Darwin privately characterized the book as admirable in style, inexact in its geology, and doubtful in zoology. *Vestiges* failed to gain acceptance as a scientific work for it lacked a mechanism through which it might work. Despite derision, the book was sufficiently well-written to be extremely popular; it went through four editions in England in six months. *Vestiges* effectively introduced to the popular imagination the concept of removing God one step from the natural world, particularly in relation to the creation of plants and animals. No longer was it necessary for God to have individually and specifically created each separate species as it appeared in the geological record. *Vestiges* helped popularize the notion that God stipulated natural laws, which in turn set in motion and controlled the progressive development of plant and animal species. Primitive organisms progressed by small incremental changes to more advanced types.[2] The mistakes of fact in *Vestiges*, which drew such critical attack from individuals committed to special creation, made little impact on the popular audience.

The debate over *Vestiges* found echoes in the Australian colonies where reception of the book was mixed. Those who belonged to the central kernel of Australian natural science were wholly unsympathetic to the ideas advanced in *Vestiges*. Those on the periphery of science, who worked in the hinterlands—either physically or metaphorically—often adopted a different view. The Goulburn River pastoralist, John Cotton, commented that *Vestiges* was 'a work of deep interest but the author's views are visionary and I do not suppose they will be adopted by right-thinking men'.[3] The book made little impact in the colonies and Cotton's prognosis of the acceptance of *Vestiges* was accurate. William Sharp Macleay, one of the leading colonial scientists, read the volume and his views reflected those of his British colleagues. He wrote derisively of '. . . *Vestiges of Creation*, a work which I recollect telling you at the time as *more* incorrect as to facts and therefore valueless, however attractive it may be in style'.[4]

Between the publication of *Vestiges* and Darwin's *Origin* the idea of the evolution of species was occasionally brought to the attention of the colonial public. In 1850–51, the *Australasian*, in seeking to provide reading material for the 'upper classes of colonist', reprinted articles from British journals including 'The Natural History of Man' and 'Geology versus Development'. Although almost all were critical of evolutionary ideas, these articles at least kept the debate before the public.[5]

The simultaneous acceptance of *Vestiges* by the public, and its disparagement by natural historians anticipated the reception of Darwin's *On the Origin of Species* on its publication in 1859. Particularly in the Australian colonies, acceptance of or opposition to the Darwinian hypothesis was often relative to the distance of an individual's vocation from the dispute. The general public tended to accept Darwin's ideas most readily; there was more erratic approval among naturalists who were not specifically taxonomists (geologists, comparative anatomists, collectors and general naturalists); and taxonomists and palaeontologists were most resistant to it.[6] Darwin himself had greater hopes for his theories being accepted by intelligent laymen than by professional scientists with their preconceived ideas of fixed species.[7]

Major figures involved in systematic taxonomy in Australia at this time included Ferdinand Mueller and Frederick McCoy in Melbourne, and Gerard Krefft, William Macleay and the Reverend William Branwhite Clarke in Sydney. Others, including Charles Moore, director of the Sydney Botanic Gardens, Simon Pittard, curator of the Australian Museum in Sydney, Ronald C. Gunn in Tasmania, and James Drummond of the Swan River colony, played little part in the reception of the theory in Australia. These men, although competent in their fields, were only marginally involved in theoretical taxonomy. They were users of classification schemes rather than devisers of them.[8]

The response to the Darwinian hypothesis by the majority of established workers, Mueller, McCoy and Macleay in particular, was outright condemnation. Macleay, in what may have been the earliest Australian response to *Origin*, wrote to Robert Lowe in May 1860, 'It is far easier for me to believe in the direct and constant government of the Creation of God, than that He should have created the world and left it to manage itself which is Darwin's theory in a few words'.[9] Macleay, along with many of his contemporaries, saw Darwin's theory as relegating God to the status of a non-interventionist observer after progenitors had been established. Maintaining that he daily saw evidence of direct intervention by the supreme being—the world abounded with monstrosities and malformed animals, which, he curiously reasoned, were due to the direct intervention of a supreme being—Macleay refused to accept an arms-length God. His superficial and often incorrect reading of *Origin* led Macleay into errors concerning Darwin's theory but his fundamental criticism was based on faith rather than fact. For all his disapproval of *Origin*, Macleay gracefully continued 'Nevertheless, Charles Darwin is an old friend of mine and I feel grateful to him for his work'.

The lines of battle over evolutionary theory were not yet so tightly drawn that men could not agree to disagree as gentlemen. Three years later, still conflating very different ideas about progressive development, Macleay wrote to William Clarke 'I am utterly opposed to Darwin's or rather Lamarck's theory'.[10]

Victorian reaction

Before 1859 Ferdinand Mueller corresponded with Darwin, but after the publication of *Origin*, Mueller wrote more in sorrow than in anger to Richard Owen, one of Darwin's principal detractors in Britain, of his steadfast belief in the immutability of species.

> I had . . . never cause to entertain any doubt, that we are surrounded by species clearly defined by nature, all perfect in their organization, all destined to fulfil by unalterable laws those designs for which the power of our creating God called them into existence . . . I have therefore no hesitation in affirming that nature in her eternal laws has created always well-defined unalterable species . . .[11]

Mueller was to maintain this opinion in the face of opposition from George Bentham during their uneasy collaboration in the preparation of *Flora Australiensis*. When Bentham informed Mueller of his conversion, Mueller dogmatically replied, 'species are permanent and immutable'.[12] Before the heresy of evolution, Darwin had been much esteemed by Mueller, but the strain of serving opposing interests proved too heavy. A somewhat piqued Charles Darwin was later to ask the aid of the Reverend William Clarke in a botanical experiment, noting that Mueller was apparently too busy to help him.[13]

Mueller and Macleay saw Darwin's *Origin* as a misguided continuation of the approach of the deluded Lamarck and the anonymous author of *Vestiges*, a turbulence that natural history could weather. Another member of the anti-Darwin camp, Frederick McCoy, was more vehement in his denunciation. McCoy, a collaborator of strident Darwinian critic, Adam Sedgwick, took up the fight in Australia. His contribution to the *Catalogue of the Victorian Exhibition of 1861*, 'On the Ancient and Recent Natural History of Victoria', brooked no progressive development nonsense.[14] Even before the publication of *Origin*, McCoy ensured that students at the University of Melbourne left that institution with a suitable repugnance for ideas contained in *Vestiges*. A question set for the 1856 examination in geology demanded, 'Give some decisive palaeontological facts against the theory of "Progressive Development"'.[15]

McCoy expressed his distaste for the development hypothesis in other ways. When McCoy was offered Darwin's *Voyage of the Beagle* for the library of the National Museum by the Melbourne bookseller, F. Baillieu, it was returned with no explanation.[16] The National Museum's earliest requisition book, covering the years 1859–72, reveals that none of Darwin's books was among the many natural history books recorded as purchased.[17]

Another of McCoy's attacks on the Darwinian hypothesis was aimed at both the public and the scientific community and concerned the relationship between man and monkey—an issue which attracted fierce attention in both Britain and Australia. McCoy was convinced that if he could secure specimens of monkeys and gorillas for public display, it would be obvious to all that the human race could not be descended from such brutish creatures. In January 1861 McCoy received the donation of a monkey for the National Museum.[18] Eight months later he wrote to a specimen supplier in London, Edward Gerrard of the British Museum, seeking a reasonably priced stuffed gorilla.[19] The collection of gorilla specimens made by Paul du Chaillu in the late 1850s excited Europe when it arrived from Africa, and had no less an impact in Australia. McCoy's efforts to obtain one of the specimens involved an extended correspondence; he wrote to Richard Owen and J. E. Gray in his attempt to secure a gorilla, expanding his shopping list to include casts of gorilla and monkey skulls and a series of South American monkeys.[20] In early 1864 McCoy heard that his agents had failed him, the entire du Chaillu collection of gorilla skins and a skeleton having been bought at auction by a Dr Edward Crisp. McCoy wrote to Crisp informing him that should he wish to dispose of the specimens, he would find a buyer in the National Museum.[21] It was not until 1865 that a small collection of gorillas was purchased for the Museum.[22]

During this period McCoy found an ally at the University in his fight against the theory of natural selection, particularly the notion that man might have evolved from primates. In 1862 George Halford—on the recommendation of Richard Owen and James Paget—was appointed professor of anatomy, physiology and pathology. In July of 1863 McCoy received requests from Halford for the loan of Museum specimens of monkeys to illustrate lectures he was to deliver on the relationship between man and monkey. Despite the policy of the Museum's forbidding loans of specimens, a stuffed orang-outang, chimpanzee, and gibbon, and the skeleton of a monkey were provided to Halford.[23]

In a lecture delivered before the chancellor of the University and almost fifty gentlemen, Halford addressed the question of 'the terminal limbs of man and monkey', one small part of what Thomas Huxley had called 'the question of questions for mankind, whence our race has come'. In a very real sense this was what Darwin's hypothesis had been reduced to: was man a higher order of being than the brute animal? Was there a qualitative difference between man and monkey rather than just a quantitative difference? The question was often reframed to ask: was there a greater difference between man and gorilla than there was between gorilla and the other primates?[24]

The *Argus* left no doubt of the outcome of the Halford lecture; it was an unqualified success. Halford had roundly refuted the Huxley position, and shown conclusively that man was a different order of being from the ape.

> Gentlemen, (said Professor Halford) if any among you entered this theatre, dreaming that you had any descent from creatures like these (pointing to a group of stuffed apes), banish the cursed nightmare from your minds at once. Awake, or be forever lost. There can have been no gradual development from apes to man ... But (said Professor Halford) if we are to sneer because Professor Owen could not see the *hippocampus minor*, what are we to say to the shortsightedness of Thomas Henry Huxley, fellow of the Royal Society, whose work, for its tendencies, might have been written by a devil?[25]

Halford's description of Huxley's work as that of a devil was seized upon by newspapers and the *Melbourne Punch* alike. In an article entitled 'Punch Past and Present', *Punch* quietly mocked Victoria and its institutions, predicting that the University of Melbourne, although Halford had temporarily saved it, would soon go to the devil.[26] The whole question was reduced to a joke. 'One of the University Professors sends us the following:—What would you call a lecture on the Gorilla, if you were describing it? An 'arangue-outang, of course.'[27] By August 1863, *Punch*, and presumably much of the reading public of Melbourne, had had enough and called for an end, if not to the controversy, then at least to coverage of the issue in newspapers (although *Punch* itself was the greatest offender).[28]

When McCoy's long-awaited gorilla eventually arrived in Melbourne, its reception was mixed. Perhaps the *Melbourne Punch* spoke for the majority of people in the town when the much-talked-about gorilla went on display in the Museum at the University. In *Punch*'s view, either McCoy or du Chaillu had misinformed the public. The gorilla was not the ferocious brute described, but rather amiable. Halford, however, put the specimen to immediate use. On 24 July 1865 he delivered before the Royal Society of Victoria a paper 'On the skeleton of the Gorilla'. It was written solely to illustrate that man could not have evolved from the lower primates. Halford listed extensive differences between the skeletal structure of man and gorilla, but the majority of his exposition was simply a recitation of quotations from Richard Owen.[29]

The crucial argument for Halford, one that would only have been aired behind the closed doors of a scientific society during the Victorian era, was that male primates had a bone in their penis, while human males had none. Halford maintained, 'Now it is an universal law that no part of the body withers and dies out, unless from disease'. Halford apparently meant disuse rather than disease for he went on to ask how such a bone could disappear given that monkeys in the past made no less use of the organ than at present.[30]

Not everyone present at that Royal Society meeting was willing to endorse creationist dogma as readily as Halford and McCoy. Dr Thomas disagreed with Halford, and C. Aplin defended Huxley, suggesting Huxley's views on the man–gorilla comparison had been misrepresented. McCoy, the proceedings note, took up the cudgels for Halford, as did the Reverend Bleasdale. Halford closed the meeting by condemning Huxley's work.[31] Two days after Halford's paper had been delivered, Ferdinand Mueller informed Richard Owen of events in the antipodes, stating that both he and Halford were agreed that the gulf between man and gorilla was too great to substantiate the transmutationists' view.[32] Mueller also reaffirmed his abiding faith in the limits of species and their immutability.

The following year Robert Ellery, in summing up the papers delivered before the Royal Society during 1865, perhaps best described the attitude of most of the members of the Society to the man–monkey debate, 'I believe few of us will venture to ally ourselves to any particular side of the moot points'.[33] In his 'Victoria as a Field for Geologists', Thomas Harrison wrote 'I cannot see my way at all clearly as a developmentist . . .'.[34] Ellery's 'President's Address' of 1867 again returned to the theme when he referred to the 'somewhat animated controversy both inside and outside these walls, which took place about two years ago, concerning myological and other distinctions between man and apes'.[35] Ellery then closed ranks with the scientific élite of the Society by pointing out that the French zoologist, Professor Gratiolet, had come out against Huxley's views.

The controversy, as Ellery indicated, had extended beyond the bounds of the Royal Society in Melbourne. In 1863, soon after his arrival in Victoria, Halford had given the public lecture referred to earlier. He later published a rebuttal to Huxley's *Evidence as to Man's Place in Nature* under the confusing title *Not Like Man, Bimanous and Biped nor yet Quadrumanous but Cheiropodus* which was subtitled somewhat more informatively 'Observations on the dissection of two macaque monkeys'. The upshot of his arguments was that 'Professor Huxley has fallen into grievous error' by seeing the foot of the monkey as closely resembling the foot of man.[36] Halford maintained that there was little resemblance between the two and that it was doubtful that one could have developed from the other.

The esoteric debate on the resemblance between man and monkey, reduced to anatomical points too complex to allow the public access to the issue, was one of the primary battlegrounds, at least in Victoria, in the struggle for the acceptance of evolution. Some of the debate took place in the pages of the *Australian Medical Journal* through articles by Halford, and reviews of his pamphlets. The *Australian Medical Journal* was almost always supportive of Halford, especially in the period 1863–65.[37]

The focus of the debate by this time had shifted from Darwin to Huxley and he bore the brunt of the criticism directed against the evolutionists but seemed to relish his role as a target. Huxley continually staked out positions which seemed, to the public and naturalists alike, extreme. With his sharp, ready wit, Huxley needed no defenders in England but found one in Victoria in William Thompson. Thompson was fully prepared to use the letters section of the *Argus* and to issue pamphlets to promote Huxley's views. Thompson's pamphlet *Not Man, but Man-Like* was a mocking rebuttal to Halford's similarly titled pamphlet. Thompson satirically asked 'Did not Halford's lecture illustrate the theory it meant to refute?'. The printed version of Halford's lecture was considerably different from the lecture itself, indicating progressive development. Thompson characterized the original lecture as an animated sermon on natural theology and monkeys, designed to rebuke the infidel Huxley, while the pamphlet had been reduced to a scientific treatise. Thompson was no less severe in his personal criticism: 'the erudition of the professor of anatomy would appear to be as defective as his logic is fallacious'. Not content with mere invective, Thompson also tried to refute Halford's scientific arguments.

Both the *Age* and the *Argus* of 17 July 1863 published letters from the pseudonymous 'Opifer' which attacked Halford's rough treatment of Huxley. The mocking tone, combined with the anatomical detail included in these letters, suggest that Thompson adopted the pseudonym 'Opifer'. Halford was not put off. The following year he published *Lines of demarcation between Man, Gorilla & Macaque*, a comparative chart which outlined the differences between man and the primates.[38]

The evolution–creation debate continued to attract attention in the Royal Society of Victoria. Some sought a compromise. Thomas Harrison, who had earlier opposed the development argument, read a paper in 1868 which outlined a reconciliation between the religious and scientific viewpoints. Only an abstract of the paper was printed in the Society's *Transactions*, but the *Argus* printed more details.[39] Harrison apparently sought to graft the evolutionary views of Lamarck, Chambers (*Vestiges*) and Darwin to his own ideas, thus allowing God to continually supervise the development of species. He proposed that man might indeed have evolved from some lower animals, but only under the continual and direct guidance of God. The paper, which drew most of its supporting evidence from the Bible, was poorly received by the Society. At its conclusion Professor Wilson complained of its mixture of science and theology and suggested that the Bible had been written not for scientific instruction, but for moral and spiritual instruction.

Against the voices decrying the heresy of Darwinism there stood one of Australia's many eclectic clergymen, the Reverend William Branwhite Clarke. While not condoning Darwin's theories, Clarke argued that they should at least be given a fair hearing. Secure in the knowledge that ultimately the finite mind of man could never comprehend the infinite mind of God, Clarke maintained that theology could never be invalidated by science. Research and enquiry should therefore be carried out fearlessly.[40] As early as November 1861 Clarke had delivered a paper before the Philosophical Society of New South Wales (the immediate predecessor of the Royal Society of New South Wales) in which he quoted both *Vestiges* and that recent work of a 'great philosopher', *On the Origin of Species*. Clarke prefaced his comments to indicate that he passed no judgement on the validity of the theory of progressive development, but in fact part of the paper was devoted to undermining a piece of evidence cited by Darwin in support of his hypothesis—that there were no Palaeozoic or Secondary geological formations in oceanic islands, among which Darwin had included New Zealand.[41] Clarke was not averse to reading *Origin* and to corresponding with its author. An almost inevitable consequence of writing to Darwin was enrolment in his network of correspondents. Clarke was quickly sent a series of questions to which Darwin sought answers.[42]

Another member of the taxonomic workers, the most junior and least well-known, was Gerard Krefft who had arrived in Australia in 1852 from Germany. In June 1860 Krefft obtained the post of assistant curator at the Australian Museum, Sydney. Simon Pittard, curator of the Australian Museum, had given the Darwinian hypothesis a chilly reception. He delivered a lecture series critical of evolution in 1860, and employed Krefft's artistic abilities in adorning the Museum's walls with passages of the Scriptures.[43] There is no evidence that Krefft, at this early stage in his career, deviated from the creationist line, although in later years he was to become a supporter of Darwin. If Krefft did harbour any thoughts of evolutionary heresy in the 1860s, he kept them to himself.

In the Australian colonies, then, the initial reaction to the Darwinian hypothesis by most of the individuals whose work was directly affected was an equivocal silence or total repudiation. Aside from the taxonomic specialists, much of the opposition to the Darwinian hypothesis came from the distributors of vice-regal largesse on which so much of colonial science depended. Before copies of *Origin* arrived in Victoria, Governor Henry Barkly, in his 'Inaugural Address' of 1860 to the Royal Society, had referred to objections to the study of natural philosophy based on the mistaken 'apprehension that it leads to skepticism in matters of religious belief'.[44] Barkly was not wanting in the faith required and, coupling pragmatism with belief, suggested that 'any attempt to limit the scope of human inquiry must of necessity break down whilst the mere desire to restrict it savours of want of faith in the truth of Divine Revelation'. Apparently forgetting his own stricture, Barkly soon bitterly attacked the Darwinian hypothesis before the same audience. He opposed Darwin in an 1861 address when he railed against the gross and socially subversive theory of progressive development and its ingenious author. Two years later, after criticizing those whose imaginations indulged in the wildest fantasies, Barkly cautioned his members to hold to the inductive reasoning of Bacon, to accumulate facts before advancing theories which relied on slender evidence.[45] In many ways this comment is ironic, for Darwin, more than most of his contemporaries, is credited with gathering the detail necessary to support his theories.

New South Wales

Barkly's New South Wales counterpart, William Denison, did not bother reading *Origin* before criticizing it. In a letter to his sister he admitted that his ideas about the book were all derived from the *Quarterly Review* and from the 1860 lecture series on the principles of classification given by the curator of the Australian Museum, Simon Pittard. Pittard, Denison explained, had shown that natural selection was contrary to the way nature worked; further, Darwin could only speculate on hypotheses, while an omnipotent God could deal in logical impossibilities. Denison found it just as plausible that the human race could have derived from a turnip as from a monkey.[46]

Darwin often found support in unexpected places. Philip Gidley King, a shipmate of Darwin's from the *Beagle* days, wrote to tell him 'Your work "Origin of Species" has a prominent place in my Library and was read with much interest . . . I feel there is much truth in your deductions but the question is Where do they bear us to—or what is their limit'.[47] Like so many, King could see the logic in what Darwin wrote, but feared the consequences.

Mimicking a trend in Europe, *Origin* influenced political and social theory in Australia. Herbert Spencer's appropriation of evolutionary theory was matched by William Edward Hearn, professor of political economy at the University of Melbourne, whose 1864 book, *Plutology*, contains traces of what was to become known as social Darwinism.[48] Chapter XXI of Hearn's book, entitled 'Of the Industrial Evolution of Society', made a series of analogies between biology and social theory. Many of the analogies, however, dealt with the differentiation of a developing organism rather than the evolution of a species, for Hearn used the term 'evolution' to indicate a sequence of events which led from the simple to the complex. Despite this, Darwin's influence on Hearn is apparent. 'Even between individuals of the same species, either in the ordinary distribution of food, or still more in seasons of scarcity, the feeble as were are pushed aside, and trampled down by the stronger.' Hearn cited Darwin's *Origin* itself in a footnote.[49]

South Australia

In South Australia, one individual closely associated with classification and palaeontology rejected Darwinism while another, who was more peripheral to science, espoused it. The Reverend Julian Tenison Woods, one of Australia's many cleric–naturalists, was a firm member of the creationist network. He exchanged specimens with McCoy, was nominated for membership in the Royal Society of Victoria by Ferdinand Mueller and Reverend Bleasdale, and in 1864 published *Not Quite As Old As The Hills*, a pamphlet intended to rebut Darwin's theory of progressive development. Furthermore, his *Geological Observations In South Australia* (1862) indicated he had no time for those 'who when they discover a sequence in creation, do not trouble themselves to enquire why the Almighty chose such and such a plan . . .'.[50]

If Tenison Woods' reaction to the Darwinian hypothesis was predictable, that of Richard Hanson, second chief justice of South Australia, and first chancellor of the University of Adelaide, was much less so. After his arrival in Adelaide, Hanson was influential in the formation of a museum and various institutes and societies. Commencing in 1860 Hanson wrote and delivered a series of talks to the South Australian Institute and the Adelaide Philosophical Society. These lectures presented his audience not so much with Darwinism, but with the central tenets of positivism, although

Hanson used Darwin's hypothesis of natural selection as an example of positivism. The first talks of 29 August 1860 and May 1862 sought to separate theology from science and established themes that ran through all six lectures, which were subsequently published as pamphlets. Science and theology were to be kept isolated but significantly, the domain of theology was restricted while that of science was expanded. Theology had to accommodate science and where they clashed, for example in the case of scientific evidence against a universal deluge, theology had to give way.

Whatever the members of the Adelaide Philosophical Society made of all this, the committee of the South Australian Bible Society, of which Hanson was president, soon made obvious their reaction, particularly after the final lecture, 'Science and Theology'. Because of his outspoken and radical opinions Hanson was requested to resign his office. He refused, and at the next annual meeting of the Bible Society was deposed from office.[51]

Hanson chose to publish his controversial lectures, despite suggestions that examination of the issue should be restricted to a select coterie where reasoned discourse could take place. The concern was that the public either would not, or could not, trouble itself with the reasoning behind the discussion, and would remember only that the validity of the Bible had been called into question. Was discussion of *Origin* limited to philosophical societies then?

General reaction to *Origin*

Little mention of *Origin* appeared in newspapers. The *Sydney Morning Herald* indicated that the vexed question had been raised in an issue of the *Edinburgh Review* but, just as Hanson feared, most debate on progressive development seems to have taken place behind closed doors.[52] In 1863 the subject arose at a monthly meeting of the Philosophical Society of New South Wales during a dispute over the antiquity of man, occasioned by a paper on the Abbeville deposits of human artefacts.[53] At the meeting John Smith, professor of chemistry and experimental physics at the University of Sydney, a confirmed creationist and later a dabbler in theosophy, suggested that perhaps a few thousand years might be added to the conventional figure of 6,000 years for the antiquity of man. When the meeting was reported in the *Sydney Morning Herald*, it produced a number of letters to the editor. One, over the signature of William Keene, government examiner of the coalfields, rejected the accepted basis of geology, the gradualism of Charles Lyell, and plumped for catastrophism. Keene felt that the answer to those who sought to extend man's antiquity was catastrophic change, through which human artefacts could be abruptly buried under layers of sediment which would otherwise require hundreds of thousands of years of deposition.[54]

Despite little discussion of *Origin* in newspapers, catalogues of various libraries, public organizations as well as mechanics' institutes, indicate that many quickly obtained a copy.[55] Libraries that did not hold a copy of *Origin* often had the more readable *Man's Place in Nature* by Huxley and other books of avowedly Darwinian outlook.[56] Some institutions seemed to have had particularly good coverage of the controversy. The Ballarat Mechanics' Institute library listed in their 1864 catalogue: Darwin's *Origin*, Huxley's *Man's Place in Nature*, Lyell's *The Antiquity of Man*, Owen's *Palaeontology*, Chambers' *Vestiges of Creation*, and Hearn's *Plutology*. Significantly neither the National Museum library, nor the library of the University of Melbourne, both within the purview of Frederick McCoy, obtained copies of *Origin* before the late 1880s, although Hearn at the University must have had access to it.[57] Similarly, the Australian Museum library did not contain a copy of *Origin* until late in the 1870s.[58]

Origin was also in general circulation. Macleay, Clarke, and P. G. King in Sydney acquired copies soon after the initial publication, and William Archer in his *Tourist to the Antipodes (1876–77)* described the typical library of a station in the bush as including 'one or more of Darwin's works' among the standards tomes of Shakespeare, Macaulay and Mill.[59] The catalogues of the sales of private libraries indicate that many individuals owned copies of one or more of the Darwin or Huxley books. Many booksellers carried *Origin* for sale. Robertson of Melbourne, in his *Select Catalogue of Books* (1867), listed Darwin's *Origin* for seventeen shillings as well as volumes by Owen, and Huxley's *Man's Place in Nature*. According to his catalogue of 1873, George Slater stocked *Origin* and others, such as H. T. Dwight, had copies of Huxley's *Man's Place in Nature*, but no Darwin.

Despite the availability of the relevant literature, and the lectures either ridiculing or supporting the Darwinian hypothesis, the debate had little impact on the general public throughout the 1860s. The battle for hearts and minds was fought in the various philosophical and royal societies and in the universities where entrenched creationists preached their dogma to students of the natural sciences.

In 1869, however, the controversy moved into the public arena in Melbourne and again Darwin's English champion, Thomas Henry Huxley, was the cause. Huxley published a paper in late 1868 entitled *Protoplasm: The Physical Basis of Life*. As was often the case, Huxley made Darwin's ideas seem mild and conservative by comparison with his own. In *Protoplasm* Huxley put forward a purely mechanistic view of life which denied the philosophic concept of a 'vitality' inherent in all animate objects. Huxley proposed that under certain conditions the elements carbon, nitrogen, oxygen and hydrogen were sufficient to give rise to protoplasm, which formed the basis of all life. Huxley saw no discontinuities in the material world, thus denying the three great divisions inherent in much of natural history (and theology): the gulfs dividing the inorganic from the organic, the vegetable from the animal, and at the upper end of the scale, man from the rest of the animal kingdom.

Huxley's pamphlet was reprinted in Melbourne in mid-1869 and caused a furore. The pamphlet was available by late June when the *Melbourne Punch* printed its contribution to the debate:

The March of Intellect
Husband and Wife at table, opposite ends. Leg of Mutton &c. on table.
Husband to Wife: You see, my dear, when I eat the mutton now on my plate, I convert the dead protoplasm of the sheep into the living protoplasm of the man. D'ye see?
Wife: No, I don't quite see it yet.
Husband (whose notions on the subject are somewhat indistinct): Why, then, my dear, to make the matter plainer, I may say that the sheep becomes man—that is, what was sheep formerly is now man.
Wife: If you mean that you are a sheep, I can perfectly understand that.
(Husband collapses.)[60]

The example of the conversion of the dead protoplasm of mutton into living protoplasm of man had already appeared in Huxley's lecture and pamphlet, although not to the same effect.

Huxley's views drew a less light-hearted reaction from some of the clergy. The Reverend Higginson, in what he later described as an attempt to keep his congregation abreast with developments in science, delivered a sermon on 7 June 1869 which was severely critical of Huxley's protoplasmic theory. In response to the resulting sudden acclaim, Higginson graciously consented to repeat his sermon on 30 June as a public lecture which attracted 200 people to the Mechanics' Institute hall. The sermon consisted of a mixture of ridicule, personal abuse and wilful misrepresentation of the ideas of progressive development. The *Argus* noted, however, that Professor Halford who attended the meeting indicated that although he had previously disputed Huxley's theory of protoplasm, he now saw merit in it. Several people then chided Halford for supposed criticism of Higginson, and Halford concluded by suggesting that everyone should read the pamphlet in question.[61]

The *Age* presented a very different account of the lecture which was, if not pro-evolution, then certainly anti-Higginson. The newspaper commented on Higginson's ignorance of physiology and concluded that he had produced no arguments to refute Huxley's theory. The report also noted Halford's view that the theory of protoplasm was the only scientifically tenable thesis for man's place in nature. As the meeting ended, Halford's supporters suggested that he deliver a lecture on the subject himself.[62]

Over the next weeks Higginson and Halford debated the protoplasm issue via letters to the *Argus*, but the awaited lecture by Halford never eventuated.[63] The University of Melbourne refused Halford permission to treat the subject, on the grounds that it was a religious issue and therefore prohibited by university regulations.

In June 1869, shortly after the Melbourne publication of *Protoplasm*, Frederick McCoy delivered the first of two addresses on 'The Order & Plan of Creation' in a lecture series organized by the Early Closing Association.[64] The initial lecture presented a wide-ranging look at cosmogony, designed to dovetail Genesis with contemporary scientific knowledge. At the end of his three-hour oration, McCoy castigated Huxley and asserted that 'There was no authority, either in Scripture or science, for belief in the gradual transmutation from one species to another, or passage from a low creation into a higher one'. Finishing up to the cheers of the audience, McCoy accepted a vote of thanks. McCoy enjoyed a considerable reputation in Melbourne, and not only did he attract and hold for some hours an audience of almost 700, but the *Age* reported that McCoy dealt trenchantly with the Darwin and Huxley theories.[65]

Not all the clergy, however, adopted the obstructionist attitudes of Higginson. Just over a month after McCoy delivered his lecture to the Early Closing Association, the Reverend J. E. Bromby, principal of the Church of England Grammar School, addressed the same audience on 'Prehistoric Man'. In the most erudite and non-dogmatic discourse of the series, Bromby asserted that the Bible could only be held to be spiritual truth, not literal truth, and that Scripture was designed to teach neither history nor science. He illustrated this last point by citing the two differing accounts of creation found in Genesis. To the amazement of his audience and the discomfit of his fellow clerics, Bromby went on to discuss the progressive development of human beings, for Bromby was not one of those whose 'panic from time to time returns whenever science penetrates deeper into any of the arcana of nature—as geology did in the last age, and everything from positivism to protoplasm, does in this . . .'.[66]

Another entrant into the Darwin–Huxley debate was Charles Perry, Anglican bishop of Melbourne. On 20 September 1869 Perry lectured on 'Science and the Bible' and claimed that he had no less faith in the leading facts of geology than he did in the resurrection of Jesus Christ. It was only the absurd, arbitrary and unphilosophical hypotheses of Darwin and the author of that Perry found cause to dispute. Perry easily dismissed the author of *Protoplasm*, for clearly Huxley's objective was not so much to teach science as to spread infidelity. However, in an indication that the onus of proof now rested with theology rather than science, Perry emphasized that the Bible upheld geological facts rather than the reverse.[67]

In July 1870 the second of McCoy's lectures returned to the theme that Genesis could be directly translated into the framework that science had built up over the last century, an attempt at revealed science. McCoy produced a number of rebuttals of the theory of progressive development, including an updated version of the Paleyite argument for design, a dubious argument based on biogeography and the advocacy of vitalism. In his summation McCoy believed that he had shown that science was on the side of revelation, and that progressive development and Darwin's theories were just not tenable. The *Age*, in reporting McCoy's lecture, paid tribute to the expository powers of McCoy, 'A large amount of information was afforded even for those who dissent from some of his conclusions, and altogether the lecture was well worth listening to'.[68]

As was typical of other naturalists of the day, McCoy also carried the good fight into the newspapers.[69] He wrote a regular column for the *Australasian* under the pseudonym 'Microzoon'. Essays with titles such as 'Why is Australia Odd' could be expected to touch on the debate over progressive development, but even such innocuous topics as 'Our Colonial Mollusca—No. 1 Oysters' were used to develop the argument that if the theory of progressive development was valid, the simplest invertebrates should appear in the earliest geological formations. 'Microzoon' could categorically state that one of the more advanced groups of invertebrates, the mollusca, were the oldest known fossils.[70]

The Reverend Bromby also lectured in the 1870 series of the Early Closing Association. While continuing to assert that the progressive development or evolution of a species was possible, his lecture 'Creation versus development' suggested that it was just as possible for God to work through evolution as any other means. Bromby was also at pains to point out that the more intelligent natural philosophers espousing evolution (he specifically cited Darwin and Huxley) all repudiated atheism. In a consummate display of tightrope walking, Bromby reasoned that while it might be true that one species developed from another, for example man from monkey, because it occurred over long periods of geological time the event could be regarded as a distinct act of creation.[71] Despite his equivocation, Bromby was immediately castigated by fellow clerics. In a review of Bromby's lecture, published in the *Church of England Messenger*, Charles Perry suggested that Bromby's liberalism had led him astray and perverted his judgement. Nonetheless, he thanked Bromby for 'demolishing the pretentious edifice of Huxley, and practically put[ting] aside the absurd hypothesis of Darwin'.[72]

Gerard Krefft

Before the 1870s, evolutionary theory in Australia drew most of its support from individuals only marginally concerned with natural history. In the next decade the Darwinian hypothesis found a staunch advocate in at least one taxonomist, Gerard Krefft. Possible reasons for Krefft's conversion to the Darwinian cause during the 1870s can be found in Krefft's relationships with some of the central figures in a debate over a quite different issue.

Early in his career as a naturalist, Krefft began a concerted effort to establish ties with a range of prominent naturalists in both Australia (including McCoy, Pittard, Bennett) and in Europe (including Gunther, Gould, Flower, Owen, Gray). These well-placed connections stood Krefft in good stead in his application for the position of assistant curator of the Australian Museum in 1860. McCoy, for instance, provided a testimonial for Krefft by telegraph message.[73] Although Krefft's subsequent work was to prove him well-qualified for his employment as assistant curator, his appointment was the subject of a power struggle between the autocratic governor of New South Wales, William Denison, and the trustees of the Australian Museum.[74]

When Krefft's appointment as assistant curator was mooted, William S. Macleay objected to Denison's usurping the trustees' prerogative and pressed for a competitive selection for the post. Advertisements for the office drew fifty applicants, and Krefft himself admitted that one of the applicants, John MacGillivray, a former naturalist aboard HMS *Rattlesnake*, had superior qualifications to his own. MacGillivray's downfall, Krefft noted, was that the Macleay family disliked him, for he was reputed to be a 'clever man'.[75] However, Denison's choice of Krefft eventually proved acceptable to the Macleays even if he was not their liegeman, and he was appointed assistant curator on 15 June 1860.[76] Just over a year later, Simon Pittard, curator of the Australian Museum, died of tuberculosis, hurried to his grave by the 'mean acting' Macleay clan, as Krefft later bitterly recalled.[77] The trustees of the Australian Museum advertised in Europe and Australia for applicants to fill the position, and Richard Owen and Thomas Huxley were requested to recommend a qualified individual for the post of curator.[78] The applicants varied widely in their credentials. Louis Frazer, curator of the museum of the Zoological Society of London, supported his application with recommendations from an impressive list of British naturalists including George Waterhouse, John Gould, Robert Grant, William Flower and Thomas Belt. John MacGillivray, rejected for the position of assistant curator, submitted an application, as did William Jones whose sole qualification seemed limited to: 'these past two years and more I have been perambulating the recesses of the bush contemplating the beauties the wonders and the wisdom of God manifested in the work of his Creation'.[79] Jones had the correct ideology for the trustees but lacked other qualifications. Although not formally appointed until 1864, Krefft won the position of curator.[80] If never the first choice of the Macleay dynasty, Krefft was at least tolerable to them. Without their tacit approval, he would never have been appointed to the Museum.

The seeds of Krefft's dissidence with creationism were sown in the mid- to late 1860s. By the 1840s a group of fossils from Wellington Caves, although virtually ignored in the initial excitement of the discovery of the caves a decade earlier, had been sufficiently supplemented for Richard Owen to describe the new species *Thylacoleo carnifex*. *Thylacoleo*, later to be characterized by Owen as 'one of the fellest and most destructive of predatory beasts', became better known as Australia's marsupial lion.[81] In an 1859 letter to the *Sydney Morning Herald*, William S. Macleay disputed that *Thylacoleo* was a lion, or even a beast of prey,[82] claiming that *Thylacoleo* was a fruit-consuming marsupial.

By the mid-1860s Krefft also had begun to question Owen's description of *Thylacoleo* as a carnivore. Krefft maintained a steady correspondence with Owen, supplemented with specimens, casts of fossils, and photographs. By late 1865 Krefft had indicated to Owen his unease at characterizing *Thylacoleo* as carnivorous.[83] The following year an English journal published Krefft's paper 'On the dentition of the

Thylacoleo carnifex', in which he concluded that the species was no more carnivorous than present-day phalangers, and criticized Frederick McCoy's identification of some supposed *Thylacoleo* fossil teeth.[84] Owen's response was a cordial but firm letter thanking him for specimens and a copy of the paper, but explaining why he did not accept that *Thylacoleo* was herbivorous. Owen indicated that he adhered to the rule of his mentor in palaeontology, Cuvier, which stated that the molars of an animal were the key feature in characterizing the species as either a carnivore or herbivore; *Thylacoleo* was therefore a carnivorous modification of the *Diprotodon*.

As late as 1869 Krefft continued to try to convince Owen of his argument by shipping him large quantities of fossils from Wellington Caves. Owen replied, 'I have to thank you for the pleasure you have given me in your letter of Dec 21 . . . and have fully quoted your excellent Catalogue. Whatever you may publish at any time will have the same attention . . .'.[85] Owen, however, did not change his mind about *Thylacoleo*.[86]

Throughout the years that he questioned Owen's identification of *Thylacoleo* as a carnivore, Krefft chafed under the intransigence of 'the great Richard', but remained determined that '. . . I will never believe the Thylacoleo to be quite as savage as he looks & prove him quite a different sort of animal'.[87] In 1872 Krefft started a public attack on Owen's work and almost simultaneously began to champion the work of Owen's nemesis, Charles Darwin.

Krefft's declaration of war came in an article in the *Sydney Mail*, reviewing Owen's 'A Cuverian Principle in palaeontology, tested by evidence of an extinct Leonine Marsupial (Thylacoleo carnifex)'.[88] Krefft declared that if the Cuverian principle had been found wanting but once, then its validity needed to be questioned thereafter. That it had been found wanting was clearly shown, to Krefft at least, for in the early 1830s Cuvier had characterized the femur of a giant kangaroo obtained from Wellington Caves as that of an elephant. Krefft then proceeded to accuse Owen of wilfully misinterpreting evidence, but what Krefft seems to have meant was that Owen refused to change his mind about *Thylacoleo* despite all Krefft's exhortations. A week later Krefft continued his attack with a popular article on phalangers. The article reiterated his criticisms of Owen and included illustrations of a skull of *Thylacoleo*.[89] Subsequently Krefft dispatched copies of his review to various people in England, Owen included, and had the review re-published in the *Annals and Magazine of Natural History*.[90] On receipt of a copy of the review, Owen wrote back thanking Krefft for the paper, sent him two scientific papers, and chided Krefft over the article 'in which I made the discovery of motives of some of my remarks that I was quite unaware of, but, as the old Philosopher said, to "know oneself" is the last & highest wisdom'.[91] Not all the recipients of the copies of the *Sydney Mail* article received it with such equanimity. William Flower, successor to Owen as Hunterian Professor of comparative anatomy and zoology at the College of Surgeons, but an ally of Krefft in the vegetarian *Thylacoleo* controversy, replied indicating complete agreement with Krefft's criticisms of Owen, and accusing Owen of 'special pleading, dust throwing and misrepresentation and deprecation of others'. Flower did not doubt that any real anatomist would agree with Krefft's characterization of *Thylacoleo*.[92] J. E. Gray at the British Museum, in an almost incoherent letter, adopted the same attitude, urging Krefft to 'work on never mind his [Owen's] mistakes'.[93] A third undated letter, from British naturalist Henry Woodward, also sided with Krefft against Owen.[94] The British naturalists' support of Krefft had more to do with the isolated position of Owen among the scientific community in Britain than the intrinsic merits of Krefft's case. Owen had become increasingly conservative as he grew older, but even as early as 1851 Thomas Huxley wrote to W. S. Macleay about the intense dislike in which Owen was held by his peers.[95]

A letter to Krefft from William Stephens perhaps supplies the rationale for Krefft's conversion to evolutionary ideas. Stephens sympathized 'I know you had some right to feel savage at your work being so disregarded by the ancient Owen'.[96] After years of unsuccessfully trying to convince Owen that he was wrong about *Thylacoleo*, Krefft rejected Owen, Owen's extensions of Cuvier's theories, and Owen's brand of successive and continuous creation. From his own use of the methodology of Cuvier and Owen, Krefft switched his allegiance to Darwin; from an early non-partisan stand, Krefft became the Australian champion of progressive development.

At much the same time Krefft commenced his correspondence with the great man himself, Charles Darwin.[97] In addition to a letter in which Krefft solicited Darwin's opinion of the controversy, Darwin received a copy of the critical *Sydney Mail* review.[98] In his reply, Darwin hedged in support of *Thylacoleo* as a herbivore, pleading lack of knowledge, but Owen again came in for a thrashing.

> It is lamentable that Prof. Owen shd shew so little consideration for the judgement of other naturalists and shd adhere in so bigotted a manner to whatever he said. This is a great evil, as it makes one doubtful on other points about which he has written.[99]

In later letters Krefft informed Darwin that he had undertaken to champion his cause in the antipodes.

> The ignorance of even well-educated people is dreadful and the Bishop of Melbourne and Professor McCoy of Melbourne have a 'go in' now and then at the 'Darwinian Theories' so I . . . give them my version that is explaining some of your ideas in a popular manner . . . I did not mention your name in my first paper, it was only a feeder and the believers in a 'happy life hereafter' *do not like you*, but you will see that i gave you full credit for your kindness of heart in paper no. 2 and now the ice is broken I shall begin to make your works known and show them who enlightened us.[100]

Krefft was somewhat surprised that 'the rather religious' newspaper printed his articles; apparently his surprise was justified for he added a postscript noting that much of one article was edited out, 'as the owner of the paper objects to my remarks regarding your work'. The paper in question was the *Sydney Mail* whose owner, John Fairfax, Krefft thought a 'thorough believer in revealed religion'.[101]

At the time Krefft was alienating many in Sydney with his advocacy of Darwinism, his own position came under attack by the Macleay-led trustees of the Australian Museum. Krefft resisted the entrenched power structure of the colony which he later characterized as '. . . antiquated squatters, lawyers, or general business men . . . ever ready to patronize what they do not understand . . .', and so suffered its wrath.[102] By late 1873 Krefft's problems with the trustees had crept into his letters to Darwin:

> the vanity of our men of science—or better 'collectors of specimens' and accumulators of hard names—is great in proportion as their pursuit is useless . . . they are mere collectors and are the greatest drawback to the success of this Institution [the Australian Museum] because by their constant interference and insatiable desire to possess everything themselves they would have long ago disgusted a less stouter heart than mine.[103]

In 1874 Krefft was dismissed from his position as curator and physically removed

from the Australian Museum.[104] George Bennett, Richard Owen's collector and correspondent in Australia and former secretary of the Museum, reacted quickly to
Krefft's dismissal and wrote to Owen

> There has been great confusion in the Museum and Krefft has been acting injudiciously
> . . . It would be difficult to find a curator to work like Krefft; he has made our Museum
> the admiration of scientific visitors. Both Clarke and myself resigned [as trustees]
> yesterday as you will see from enclosed paragraph.[105]

Krefft appreciated Bennett's stand and later wrote to ichthyologist Albert Gunther
'Dr Bennett acted like a true friend . . . I have made a vow never to say another word
against Prof. Owen again. He is Bennett's friend . . .'.[106]

Late that same year Krefft wrote to Darwin of his removal from the Museum by the
trustees. Appealing to Darwin for help, Krefft closed,

> Had I been an Englishman by birth, had humbugged people, attended church and
> spread knowledge on the principle that the God of Moses and the Prophets made 'little
> green apples' I would have gained the day but a true believer in the theory of devel-
> opment I am hunted down in this Paradise of Bushrangers, of rogues, cheats and
> vagabonds.[107]

Darwin replied sympathetically, but noted that he could do little to help Krefft.[108]

Krefft thought his adoption of evolutionary theory had soured his already deterio-
rating relationship with the trustees of the Museum. He described Captain Arthur
Onslow, trustee, grandson of Alexander Macleay, and one of his bitterest opponents,
as 'a firm adherent of the ancient doctrine of the "creation according to Moses", a man
who detests Darwin, Huxley and Haeckel and who abhors me more still because I
have tried to make people understand what the meaning of evolution is . . .'.

Krefft also wrote to Albert Gunther of the British Museum, 'I sent Mr Darwin some
worm castings found in my garden and fault was found with me (by the trustees) for
that and I was desired not to do so again. Can you believe this!!'.[109] Similarly, Krefft
noted 'I suppose I shall be reprimanded for furnishing Mr Darwin with pictures of
nude men and women'.[110] Over the next seven years, despite his appeals to scientists
and politicians, Krefft was to gain little satisfaction in his battle with the trustees for
reinstatement. He died in 1881, bitter and impoverished.

Apart from Krefft, few individuals of the natural history community of Australia
were converted to a belief in evolutionary theory. McCoy, Mueller and Halford in
Melbourne, John Smith, the Macleays and W. J. Stephens in Sydney, all held fast to
creationism. The Reverend Julian Tenison Woods in South Australia could find no
evidence for evolution in the geological record.[111] Yet, throughout the 1870s, evolutionary theory continued to gain ground in the Australian colonies. Those not as
intimately connected with the established order of natural history were more open to
evolutionary theory. Alfred Howitt, later to become one of Australia's first anthro-
pologists, found *Origin* sufficiently attractive to write to his sister, 'I don't know if you
trouble yourself about such theories, but I take a very great interest in them and feel
satisfied of the main truth of the evolutionary hypothesis'.[112] The French consul-
general in Victoria, F. de Castelnau, in a remarkably free-ranging essay, given its title
'Notes on the edible fishes in Victoria', adopted a quasi-evolutionary stance.[113]
Dr William Thompson defended Darwinism before the Medical Society of Victoria.
The geologist–administrator Robert Brough Smyth corresponded with Darwin and
collected Australian responses to Darwin's anthropological questionnaire on

'Expressions'. Brough Smyth also supported evolutionary theory in a popular lecture before a workingmen's club.[114]

Robert D. Fitzgerald, deputy surveyor-general of New South Wales and an early and continual correspondent of Ferdinand Mueller, also gave public support to Darwin's theories.[115] The premier issue of Fitzgerald's serial publication, *Australian Orchids*, explained that Fitzgerald's interest in undertaking the work had been sparked by Darwin's *The Fertilization of Orchids*.[116] Fitzgerald found that his studies did not altogether support Darwin's contention that the structure of orchids was designed entirely for cross fertilization, but this criticism aside, Fitzgerald came out solidly on the side of the progressive development of species. Orchids were particularly significant to evolutionary theory, for until Darwin's *The Fertilization of Orchids*, extravagant flowers with no obvious utility or advantage were a bastion of the Paleyite design argument. Orchids had been portrayed as floral art created for man's delight. Fitzgerald dispatched the first part of *Australian Orchids* to Darwin and in turn received a courteous, if somewhat patronizing, reply.[117] Fitzgerald continued to send the serial parts of his work to Darwin as they were published, and in exchange was favoured with a copy of the second edition of *The Fertilization of Orchids*. In 1881 Fitzgerald sought and received permission from Darwin to dedicate the seventh part of the work to Darwin, a dedication that was to be posthumous by the time it appeared in October 1882.

The latter part of the 1870s and the 1880s saw an influx of academic naturalists into Australia who had been educated in evolutionary theory. Ralph Tate, professor of natural science at the University of Adelaide; P. H. MacGillivray of the Bendigo School of Mines; Daniel McAlpine of Ormond College, University of Melbourne; and Baldwin Spencer, foundation professor of biology at the University of Melbourne, were among those who sought to inculcate a new generation of students in evolutionary thought.

Even the various philosophical and royal societies, which had shown little support for evolution in the 1860s and 1870s, relented. The Royal Society of New South Wales elected avowed evolutionists Darwin, Huxley and Bentham as honorary members in 1879 (Owen was also elected an honorary member), and awarded its Clarke Medal to Bentham in 1879 and to Huxley in 1880 (Owen was honoured with the medal in 1878, McCoy in 1881, and Mueller in 1883).

In April 1882 news of the death of Charles Darwin reached Australia. Both Melbourne newspapers counted him pre-eminent among naturalists. The *Age*, in praising this Newton of zoology, stressed that Darwin never sought to attack religion, denied that Darwin attempted to link man with ape, and suggested that even should Darwin's theory be disproved, he would still retain his place as a scientific thinker.[118] The *Argus* had no such reservations. The theory of evolution had brought a revolution to science. It was, quite simply, 'the most fruitful idea of the present century'.[119]

CHAPTER EIGHT

natural history in schools and clubs

INTERCOLONIAL, 1850–1900

Until late in the nineteenth century natural history was generally regarded as a diversion for idle hours, not a school subject to be taught alongside the traditional Latin, English grammar, arithmetic and history. For much of the century natural history—out of doors, unstructured, and whimsical in what specimens might be obtained—epitomized the very opposite of classroom learning. It has been suggested that much of the appeal of early and mid-century natural history was its freedom from the stultifying atmosphere of the classroom.[1] By the end of the nineteenth century, however, natural history or its academic successor, biology (usually in the guise of physiology and botany), had become absorbed into the school curriculum.

Natural history had unobtrusively found its way into schools before the 1880s and it is probable that the wide popularity of natural history in Australia and the establishment of field naturalists' clubs in the 1880s were due to the groundwork laid by schools in previous decades. Natural history gained entrée into schools primarily through two avenues: the texts set for schools, including the series of readers recommended by the various colonial educational departments, and teacher–naturalists.

State educational systems in Australia were not widely established until the 1850s. Before this, most children received little or no education. A minority found places in private schools, which ranged from the prestigious Church of England grammar schools in Melbourne or Sydney, to the homes of asthmatic or tubercular Englishmen who had moved to the antipodes for reasons of health. The alternative for children of the social élite of the colony, particularly the sons and daughters of squatterdom, was a private tutor. However, natural history found a place in few of these circumstances, and then generally only as an amusement for pupils.

For children afforded some education, or whose parents had the means and literacy, there was a second source of information. Numerous children's books, such as *Sketches from Nature, intended for the use of young persons* (1801), *Geological Sketches and Glimpses of the Ancient Earth* (1832), and any of the prolific Jane Marcet's books (*The Seasons, Stories for very young children*, 4th edition, 1844; *Conversations on Vegetable Physiology*, 3rd edition, 1839, etc.) were available.

These volumes often provided a pedantic and strained introduction to natural history. The most obvious characteristic of the genre was the catechetic style, the question-and-answer technique so beloved of the authors of children's books.[2] The stylized format adhered to the accepted literary tradition of the eighteenth and nineteenth centuries for imparting knowledge to children. Moreover, the inherent artificiality of the device was seldom ameliorated by the literary skills of the author. An example is the Australian-written *A Mother's Offering* (1841):

> Clara: What were the other causes of strange sounds, Mamma? [A reference to unexplained noises heard by explorers of the interior of Australia.]
> Mrs S.: Sir John Herschel (who has studied the subject) considers where extensive caverns exist which communicate with each other, or with the atmosphere by means of small openings, considerable differences of temperature may occasion currents of air to pass through these openings, with sufficient rapidity to produce loud vibrations . . .[3]

At the other end of the spectrum Jane Marcet's volumes, notably *Conversations on Vegetable Physiology*, were little more than tedious slabs of factual information with few concessions made to the conversational style. In spite of the turgid prose Marcet's books sold well in Britain and America, indicating both a market for such literature and a lack of alternatives.

The conversational strategy broke up large blocks of unpalatable information into bite-sized mouthfuls suitable for children. This also allowed introduction of the second characteristic of the books, explicit moral lessons. Scientific texts allow little of this social propaganda, but the conversational style permitted the child protagonists or the parental figures (almost always 'Mamma') of the books the chance for social commentary. Moralizing ranged from the sanction of rational amusement, 'I will remember this account' said Mary 'and pray Maria let us learn together, the history of Insects, Papa says it is what all girls ought to do for their amusement', to sermons on friendship complete with purported animal examples.[4] The 'facts' presented in these volumes, despite nineteenth century society's faith in their reliability, were often dubiously based.

The books, with all their obvious limitations—the incorrect 'facts', the paternalism, the interwoven theological arguments for design, and their morality—still served their purpose. Through such books children acquired a taste for natural history, if only through emulation of Mrs S., who was fond of rambling in the woods and botanizing, or hearing of Mamma's cabinet of shells.[5] Most of the volumes had little relevance to Australia, with its topsy-turvy seasons and the very different flora and fauna. The exception, the Australian *A Mother's Offering*, was remarkable for the informational content of its simple stories. 'Extraordinary Sounds', the first chapter of the book, dealt with the nature of mysterious sounds, but additionally covered such diverse topics as botany, geology and palaeontology. The slim volume touched on contemporary events in colonial natural history, including the Reverend Charles Wilton's exploration of Mount Wingen (the Burning Mountain); the giant marsupials discovered in Wellington Caves by George Ranken; and petrified wood and fossils in coal seams of the Hunter Valley.

Secular schools

By mid-century the school systems of the senior colonies were becoming increasingly institutionalized. The basis for state or national schools in Victoria, New South Wales and Tasmania was the Irish national system of education. Few state schools, however, provided a path to tertiary studies, for state secondary schools were virtually nonexistent before 1900. The slack was taken up by denominational or private schools. Secondary education generally remained an urban, middle-class prerogative.[6]

During the 1850s education in Victoria came under political control. The newly inaugurated national school system was placed under a board of commissioners of national education which set both the texts used in the state schools and the qualifications of the teachers. To some extent this established a *de facto* standard which was followed by denominational schools. Basing the Victorian educational system on the Irish model resulted in the initial adoption of the *Irish National Readers* which were sanctioned and distributed to schools until the 1870s.[7] The readers contained large amounts of natural philosophy (roughly equivalent to physics), some agricultural and chemical commentary, but limited natural history. Mirroring events in Britain, the institutionalization of the school system afforded an opportunity for the introduction of science into the curriculum. However, the minimum requirements for teaching science in schools included cheap and appropriate lesson books, trained teachers, and specimens and apparatus to demonstrate objects and concepts. Although national schools were supplied with lesson books, the other two conditions were infrequently met.[8]

Denominational schools claimed better success in the teaching of natural science. The 1856–57 *Report of the Denominational School Board* noted that seven per cent of its students were studying natural science. Much of this activity had been stimulated by future stalwarts of the Royal Society of Victoria. Dr John Macadam delivered courses on natural history for teachers in Geelong, Castlemaine and Sandhurst, while the Reverend John Bleasdale undertook a similar lecture series for Roman Catholic school teachers.[9]

The *Report of the Denominational School Board* suggested that utilitarian scientific disciplines—chemistry, botany, geology and the like—should be encouraged, for they would have 'an important bearing on our social well-being'.[10] During the late 1850s, utilitarian arguments for the inclusion of science in schools began to be strongly voiced in Australia. The *Sydney Magazine of Science and Art* suggested that a botanical knowledge of poisonous plants might be more practical for the colonial child than the ability to write Latin hexameters; that the requirements of life in the raw antipodes made such practical scientific attainments of greater value than in Europe. Pressing the utilitarian argument, the article also called for the provision of lecturers in botany, agriculture, geology, mineralogy and mechanics at the University of Sydney.[11] Before it met the fate of other ephemeral colonial journals, the *Magazine* reprinted Michael Faraday's 'Science as a Branch of Education', an essay supporting the proposition that science was an intellectual activity equal to the classical disciplines.[12]

School texts

By the 1870s, the creation of the Education Department in Victoria institutionalized education sufficiently for it to partially break from the acceptance of European school texts. The *Irish National Readers*, despite their merits as cheap non-secular readers, had been under criticism from the time of their adoption.

A. B. Ortebar, Victorian inspector of schools in 1856, noted that the *Irish Readers*, with their constant reference to climatic conditions and plants and animals remote from colonial children's experience, contained material unsuitable for colonial education.[13] Not only was the subject material irrelevant but the choice of readings, he believed, was too complex for the mind of the Australian child. Ortebar considered that readings devised for the slow-witted English would be more suitable than those prepared for the cleverer Irish children. In the early 1870s, the *Irish Readers* gave way to the *Nelson Royal Readers*, and in 1877 the Victorian Education Department sanctioned the latter's use.

The change to the *Royal Readers* was ironic, for not only did they contain as much inapplicable material as their predecessors, but in 1872 publication began of *Irish Readers* specifically adapted for use in the Australian and New Zealand colonies. The *Irish Readers* had been revised to include material written by Archibald Gilchrist, a Victorian inspector of schools. Equivalent Australianized editions of the *Royal Readers* did not appear until 1887 when C. A. Topp supplied the necessary material.

The revised *Irish Readers* not only contained Australian material by the 1870s, but they also included substantial natural history. The Australian edition of the *Fourth Irish Reader* (1876) carried articles on snakes which noted Gerard Krefft's work on reptiles, supplied detailed morphological information on Australian species, and discussed Professor Halford's snake bite remedies.[14] These school readers may have embraced natural history, but the great majority of it had been carried over from the natural history of half a century earlier. Animals were given anthropomorphic characteristics—forethought, solicitude and melancholy. The fox was always crafty and cunning, the bear surly, and the tiger insatiable for blood. Members of the clergy, including the Reverend Paley and Cardinal Wiseman, figured prominently as authors of the natural history excerpts. Evolutionary theory might never have existed for all the indications of it in these readers; the creation of species was still under the firm hand of a beneficent deity. Although the readers were not designed to teach natural history, nevertheless, it was intended that children would understand and assimilate their content. For the majority of several generations of school children, the readers provided their only formal introduction to science.

Evolutionary thought did seep into some children's texts, but only in those few books specifically directed towards natural history. Arabella Buckley's *A Short History of Natural Science; from Greeks to the Present day for use of schools and young persons* accepted the Darwin–Wallace hypothesis, but the book was not representative of school texts. Buckley was Charles Lyell's former secretary, and she received help from Alfred Wallace in writing the book. Despite her acknowledgement of the importance of evolutionary theory, Buckley finished up her book on a theological note. The planets were no less held in God's hand because their movements were governed by the laws of gravity, and the development of every plant and animal species from previously existing species did not reduce God's participation in their creation.

As the century progressed there was a growing trend to bring out texts covering specific subjects. Botany received ample attention. In England, Joseph Hooker published his *Botany* in 1878.[15] The widening battle between observational and experimental science was fought even in this school text. Hooker argued that botany was not merely descriptive but also an experimental science, and he outlined various physiological experiments that might be conducted in the classroom: respiration, transpiration and heliotropism. Commenting on another controversy, Hooker noted that one could either believe the unprovable creationist argument that taught nothing and was 'the despair of inquiring minds', or embrace the explanatory power of evolution. Hooker left little doubt about which side of the debate he chose.

Colonial publishers also brought out botanical texts specifically for children. One of the first to appear was T. S. Ralph's 1862 *Elementary Botany*.[16] Ralph's book was little more than an adaptation of his original English text, extended with a few token Australian plants. In common with the majority of botanical texts, it concentrated on morphology. In 1877 the Victorian Education Department published Ferdinand Mueller's *Introduction to Botanic Teaching at the schools of Victoria*.[17] Mueller's book was designed for use in elementary schools, and he tried to limit the use of scientific terminology, the 'hard' names which had made previous botanical books so grammar-like. Hard names died slowly. In the first of the many plant descriptions in the book, Mueller identified the species by 'sessile' leaves, 'quadrangular' branchlets and 'half connate bracteoles'. At much the same time, Mueller embarked on an ambitious programme of supplying herbaria of dried plants with accompanying notes to mechanics' institutions and free libraries. These herbaria, entitled *Educational Collections*, were to form a reference collection for his *Introduction to Botanic Teaching*.

Within a year of the publication of Mueller's book his successor as director of the Melbourne Botanic Gardens, William Guilfoyle, published *First Book: Australian Botany specially designed for the use of schools*.[18] Guilfoyle also sought to divest his book of the 'nauseous and overwhelming' terminology of botany by explaining each technical term when first used. Mueller's book, Guilfoyle's *Australian Botany*, and Guilfoyle's subsequent effort, *The A.B.C. of Botany* (ostensibly more introductory in nature than *Australian Botany* but extracted almost verbatim from it), all ignored the controversy over evolution.

When Curnow and Morrison published their *Elementary Science; arranged for the use of Primary Schools in New Zealand* in 1879, they noted that all manner of science primers were available by the 1870s.

Despite this appearance of activity, little science was taught. In most schools, state or otherwise, science was an area of studied neglect. The demands of teaching reading, writing and ciphering absorbed the efforts of the majority of teachers. Despite their frustrated hopes, liberal educationalists continued to press for an increase in the scientific content of the curriculum. The Reverend John Bleasdale suggested in 1870 that children should be taught less grammar and more 'Chemistry, natural history, physical geography and health'.[19]

In Tasmania the short-lived journal *The Quadrilateral* (1874) published an article under the title 'The Neglect of Science in School Education in Tasmania', which rehashed most of the arguments in favour of devoting part of the time set aside for classical languages to science.[20] Seven years later the royal commissioner into the state of public education in Victoria, Charles Pearson, also recommended that Greek be dropped from the curriculum and Latin reduced to free up time that could be devoted to science. Justifying this new emphasis, Pearson suggested that the faculty of observation, instead of being strengthened by traditional classical schooling, was weakened. This was not a new argument and echoed Thomas Huxley's widely reported address at the opening of John Hopkins University in 1876.[21] Pearson recommended that children could be taught observational skills through botany, with no equipment other than a cheap microscope. This simple device would enable a student to 'venture with Darwin, taking our common sundew as his example, into the debatable land where vegetable seems to encroach on the animal kingdom'.[22] An added advantage of botany, in Pearson's estimation, was the existence of Australian botanical textbooks, specifically those of Guilfoyle. These references, surfacing in Australia in the 1870s, concerning the status of classics versus science in the school curriculum were the late-arriving echo of the same argument that had occupied educationalists in Europe after the 1850s.

During the 1880s science received official status in the primary school curriculum in Victoria. The *Report of the Minister for Public Instruction* for the years 1880–81 noted that

> In August of 1879 teachers were informed by direction of my predecessor that some elementary teaching of science should ultimately be given in State Schools and in furtherance of this view it was desired that every teacher should endeavour to qualify himself to instruct his pupils in at least one branch of science . . .

The list of approved subjects included: physiology, botany, geology and mineralogy, electricity and magnetism, acoustics and heat and light, mechanics and hydrostatics, chemistry, and metallurgy. Of the 299 teachers who took the voluntary first qualifying science examinations of 1880, ninety-seven passed one or more subjects. When the examination was repeated the following year forty-six qualified out of a total of 127.[23] The *Southern Science Record*, commenting on the first exam of 1880, considered that the botanical paper was perhaps too elementary and regretted the lack of a zoological paper, but looked forward to a time when competence in science would be as necessary for teacher certification as the traditional three Rs.[24] By the end of the decade physiology, hitherto an extra (fee-paying) subject, had been included in the ordinary school curriculum, thirty years after natural philosophy had achieved the same status.

The inclusion of elementary science in the curriculum was not without its problems. The reports of school inspectors during the 1880s highlighted the lack of equipment; and the need for demonstration apparatus for physics and mechanics, and specimens and geological maps for geology and mineralogy. One enterprising teacher partially solved the problem of the lack of equipment by manufacturing a galvanic battery from a copper preserving pan, spouting zinc and milliner's wire.[25] This entrepreneurial approach was the exception rather than the rule, however, and one effect of the scant supply of apparates was that physiology, taught almost exclusively from books, became the favoured science.

A second problem, especially in districts remote from the towns, was the continued lack of trained teachers. Conservative teachers resented the intrusion of scientific subjects into time previously given over to traditional subjects which they were better qualified to teach. Even given willing, trained teachers, there was often little or no demand for science courses.

By the end of the 1880s many of the problems associated with science teaching remained, while much of the initial enthusiasm for the new subjects had been lost. School inspectors no longer reported that 'The teachers of this district [Sandhurst] have taken on the teaching of science con amore'.[26] The inspector's reports for 1889 indicate that the lack of equipment still limited science lessons, and the reports record a re-evaluation of the extent to which science should be included in the curriculum.[27]

Not all was gloom, however. W. Hamilton was hopeful that elementary science teaching would soon achieve its potential and described an exemplary small country school where the teacher filled the walls with sketches of scientific specimens, set up cabinets laden with a wide range of specimens (including 130 types of birds' eggs), constructed apparates to illustrate mechanics, and purchased scientific equipment at his own expense.[28]

One focal point of education in the 1880s was the object lesson, a concept developed in England in the early part of the century by Elizabeth and Charles Mayo. The Mayos evolved the thesis that lessons could, and should, be centred around actual physical objects. Botany, mineralogy and zoology readily lent themselves to the thesis. Other sciences, particularly physics and chemistry, depended on diagrams or demonstration experiments performed by the teacher, and were less effective as object lessons. These lessons were never meant to train children to be botanists or zoologists, but to exercise and invigorate their faculty of observation.

Object lessons were employed widely in primary schools in Australia during the 1880s. The portion of the school day set aside for general lessons was often devoted to object lessons, and various publications appeared to cater to the object lesson format. Some, such as the Melbourne pamphlets *Questions in Science, General Lessons, History, etc with answers for State School Scholars* or *Objects and General Lessons for Victorian State Schools*, were devised for the students themselves, while others were aimed at providing teachers with suitable object lessons for classroom use.[29]

Physiology tended to dominate the scientific subjects taught in Victorian schools and this was strongly reflected in the number of state school teachers qualifying in the subject. Between 1880 and 1889, 228 teachers passed the qualification examinations to teach physiology, forty qualified in botany, and twenty-one in geology and mineralogy. By comparison, mechanics and hydrostatics, the most popular physical science, had eighty qualifiers.[30] The proportion of women qualifying in physiology, botany, or geology and mineralogy was always less than twenty per cent of the total, and in the physical sciences rarely topped five per cent (some distortions exist in the statistics for years when less than five teachers qualified in any discipline). The same emphasis was evident at the Victorian Teacher Training Institution where trainee teachers were required to qualify in one scientific subject to gain their trained teacher's certificate. Physiology attracted the most attention from the elective list of physiology, botany, physics and chemistry. The popularity of physiology among both pupils and teachers may be partially attributable to the reputation of other subjects' difficulty: natural philosophy was the domain of arcane formulae and required an above-average competence in mathematics; chemistry suffered from the same problems; botany, despite the best efforts of Mueller and Guilfoyle, was still a science of difficult names; and geology, although still a descriptive science, was not as frequently offered as other subjects.[31]

Ballarat

Although science in the schools was tentative and fitful in much of Victoria during the 1880s, some pockets of strength appeared. The gold mining town of Ballarat was one of these and here much of the success of science in the curriculum was attributable to the establishment of the School of Mines, Ballarat. In 1881, with an annual subsidy from the Education Department, the School of Mines instituted state school science classes. Instruction covered the educational gamut, from training sessions provided for state school teachers (average weekly attendance in 1883, nine), to a junior school division limited during the first years to elementary chemistry, and a senior school division which offered physics, health chemistry, electricity and magnetism, inorganic chemistry, chemistry, and agricultural chemistry. The weekly lectures of the latter two divisions were initially open only to students selected by teachers at state schools, and weekly attendance averaged about 160 pupils in total.[32] The classes were soon expanded to draw pupils from most of the local state schools and by the end of the decade the council of the School of Mines had seconded a lecturer to deliver elementary chemistry lectures at nine of the larger schools.[33] Somewhat surprisingly in a town preoccupied with its mineral wealth, chemistry, rather than mineralogy, was by far the most popular subject for both teachers and students.[34]

The School of Mines also instituted the practice of awarding prizes and scholarships to the School to those students who did well in the senior division. In 1884, girls took eight out of the fifteen prizes awarded in elementary chemistry, and chemistry. They also took three of the six in astronomy but secured none of the five awarded in electricity and magnetism. Five years later, in 1889, of the 665 candidates for the exams, 147 students passed and at least two of the six scholarships awarded went to girls.[35]

The constant pressure, first to include natural history in the school curriculum, then for its continued development, derived much of its impetus from the interest that prominent individuals in the community took in the subject. This lobbying included both individual efforts (John Bleasdale, for example, was a strong advocate of science from the 1850s to the 1870s) and collective action. During the 1880s scientific societies, particularly field naturalists' clubs, encouraged the popularization of science in schools.[36]

Curriculum reappraisal

Having gained a foothold for science in the curriculum, advocates of science sought to gain even greater ground. Officers of the Australasian Association for the Advancement of Science (AAAS) called for more than the token science they saw taught in the schools. Archibald Liversidge tallied the defects of science as then taught in elementary schools. His experience as an examiner had shown him that most candidates at matriculation or public examinations had not only never performed the most elementary scientific experiments, but had neither seen them performed nor ever been shown the necessary apparates. It was not an unusual occurrence for an examination candidate to parrot back a textbook description of a common mineral, but then to be unable to recognize that same mineral when it was placed before him or her. This failure to translate theory into practice Liversidge saw as the result of deficiencies in teachers rather than in students. Until science education was upgraded to include a minimum number of compulsory experiments, there could be little hope of progress.[37] In common with other advocates of science in the school curriculum, Liversidge, quoting that man for all scientific seasons, Thomas Huxley, asserted that science merited equal footing with all other subjects. Science could claim at least as much intellectual rigour as literature, and it was the literary and scientific education that was a 'really liberal one', rather than a classics–mathematics based education.[38] A. Thomas reiterated many of the same concerns in his 'Presidential Address' to Section D (Biology) at the AAAS meeting in 1890, placing much of the blame on untrained teachers, but also lambasting vested interests and stubborn tradition.

Despite the lobbying of AAAS and other organizations, the educational curriculum changed very little before 1900. The idea that education should be based primarily on the classical languages and mathematics remained at the core of the educational process. Intrusion of subjects to the detriment of Latin and Greek met with limited success. The introduction of science was one of those successes, but the victory was hard won. Many schoolmasters remained unconvinced that science lessons helped to develop the mind. Admittedly science seemed to impart convincingly large quantities of information, but there was concern that this was all that science achieved. Arguments for the inclusion of science in the curriculum attempted to show that science trained the intellect as successfully as the classics purportedly did, through observation and inductive logic. However, the amount of descriptive material in science, especially in geology, botany and physiology, remained a cause of concern for those who saw education's role as developing the intellect. Even more troubling, by the 1890s most matriculation candidates sitting a science subject chose one of the descriptive sciences.

For those individuals with a utilitarian bent, the contention that science imparted nothing but masses of information caused few problems. Participants in society did not need the ability to conjugate irregular Latin verbs, but practical knowledge, they argued. Schools should supply information which would allow students both to comprehend the world around them and to become more productive workers: chemistry should be taught to supply the industrial need for analytic technicians; factory workers would become more efficient if they understood the mechanical principles upon which their equipment was based; and the productivity of agricultural workers would increase with some knowledge of agricultural chemistry. Educational and economic objectives were conflated in the developing capitalistic society of Australia. The cry went up that, 'The present age is essentially a practical one'. Everything was to be put to the question 'What is it worth?'. Attempts were made to define a practical value for physiology.[39] It was characteristic of the age that the human body was seen as analogous to a complex machine. As with any machine, it must be kept in good repair to make a profit. An understanding of the principles of physiology was necessary to maintain health, so the body could yield a profit through work.

Throughout the 1890s science consolidated its place in the school curriculum. Education departments encouraged teachers to attend lectures on science and required those attending teacher training institutions to qualify in at least one science. Despite the emphasis on elementary science (which generally meant physics and chemistry), most teachers continued to qualify in physiology. Publications appeared to cater for the various disciplines, ranging from Charles Long's popular *Science Work Simplified*, which could boldly state 'That Elementary Science should have a place in the curriculum of every system of primary education needs no argument at the present day', to the Dendy and Lucas volume *An Introduction to the Study of Botany*.[40]

Much of the lead in introducing science into the Victorian school curriculum had been taken up by a group of liberal and influential schoolmasters associated with the council of the University of Melbourne. Notable among them were the Reverend Dr John Bromby, ex-headmaster of Melbourne Grammar School, and Dr Charles Pearson, royal commissioner, former lecturer in history at the University, and headmaster of the Presbyterian Ladies College. The liberal schoolmasters, abetted by some of the University professors who served as matriculation examiners, formed a powerful coterie for the institutionalization of science in the curriculum (this was only part of their liberal programme which also included the matriculation of women at the University of Melbourne). The schoolmaster circle was often more sympathetic to science than were University professors such as Frederick McCoy whose conservatism led him to defend the place of Greek and Latin in the curriculum.

In Sydney, William John Stephens, former headmaster of Sydney Grammar School, founder of The New School, and subsequent to 1882 professor of natural history at the University of Sydney, strongly supported the inclusion of science in the school curriculum. Science subjects were first included in the matriculation examinations held by the University of Sydney in 1876 when elementary chemistry, elementary physics, and geology papers were set. Similarly, in the 1870s, the University of Adelaide commenced matriculation examinations in natural philosophy, chemistry and natural history.

In Victoria before the 1850s (the other colonies were not appreciably different) science, and natural history in particular, was virtually non-existent in the school curriculum. Natural philosophy, and later natural history, gained a foothold in the curriculum in the ensuing decades, and by the 1870s and 1880s students generally received at least limited exposure to these subjects. The rise of field naturalists' clubs in the 1880s was in large measure dependent on the establishment of a substantial middle class receptive to natural history. Until natural history was incorporated into the school curriculum, field naturalists' clubs lacked a potential membership base.

Field naturalists' clubs

During the 1880s dissatisfaction with the ability of traditional colonial royal societies to serve particular interests resulted in the appearance of new scientific organizations. That the royal societies were beset with problems no one doubted. Archibald Liversidge, in his 1886 'President's Address' to the Royal Society of New South Wales, noted with concern that although the Society was numerically strong, only thirty-five of the almost 800 members contributed papers, and the great majority of these articles came from the pens of seven or eight individuals.[41]

Daily newspapers also drew attention to the decline of the royal societies. In 1880 the *Sydney Morning Herald* claimed 'Scientific societies are not very popular, nor have they been at all successful as a rule! The slow lingering infancy of our own Royal Society of New South Wales is a case in point', although the *Herald* was quick to emphasize that societies in other colonies were even worse off. In 1882 the *Herald* returned to the same theme when it remarked on the fluctuating fortunes and unpopularity of the Royal Society of Victoria, although there may have been an element of intercolonial rivalry in this.[42] This stagnation of the royal societies throughout the 1880s gave rise to new types of scientific societies: field naturalists' clubs at one end of the spectrum and the Australasian Association for the Advancement of Science at the other. These changed circumstances were noted by the *Herald* while discussing the declining fortunes of royal societies: 'In natural history at least the work will soon fall into other hands', probably referring to the Linnean Society of New South Wales.[43] With the exception of the Australasian Association for the Advancement of Science the new groups tended to be much more narrowly based, concentrating on both a limited geographic locality (usually a single colony) and a single scientific discipline.

Previous attempts to found single-discipline societies, as evidenced by the brief existence of the Geological Society of Victoria in the 1850s, failed in part from their small membership.

By the 1880s two circumstances allowed specialized scientific groups to flourish: the increased population base of the colonies and perhaps more importantly, the growing enthusiasm of the Australian public for natural history. The *Sydney Morning Herald* in 1880 noted, 'the popularity which everything connected with natural history enjoys in the present day. Botany, geology, and zoology are eminently popular sciences. Few, it is true, go deeply into them, but everyone likes to know something about them'.[44] A generation which had grown up under the blandishments of rational amusement and had been exposed to natural science in schools found an outlet in the activities of local field naturalists' clubs.

Field Naturalist's Club of Victoria

The first of these to be established in Australia, the Field Naturalist's Club of Victoria, was founded in 1880. It was the onset of a veritable flood of similar organizations. Much as the mechanics' institutes had sprung up mushroom-like in the 1840s and 1850s, field naturalists' clubs burst into existence in the 1880s. During the last two decades of the century, a significant portion of the population saw these clubs as both the ideal of natural history, and a working programme. This ideal was, however, to become increasingly isolated from the ethos pursued by professional science and what was becoming known as biology. Rather than a wan shadow of professional science, field naturalists' clubs formed an alternative, based on the rational amusement ideology of the eighteenth and nineteenth centuries rather than the positivist–experimentalist ideas that flourished in the mid- to late nineteenth century.

Southern Science Record

In December 1880 a new journal, the *Southern Science Record*, was published in Melbourne. The distinction of the *Southern Science Record* was its intimate association with amateur science and those naturalists whose work was euphemistically styled as 'a labour of love', particularly members of the Field Naturalist's Club of Victoria (FNCV).[45] The journal pledged to report the proceedings of scientific societies throughout Australia, but those printed in the first issue of the journal reflected both a local and amateur bias; of the four, three upheld the amateur ethos: the Microscopical Society of Victoria, the Field Naturalist's Club of Victoria and the Geelong Field Naturalist's Club. Both of the original papers printed in the initial issue of the journal had been read before the FNCV.

The *Southern Science Record*, published by J. Wing, a founding member of the FNCV and a member of its council, had a formal relationship with the Club. In return for devoting three pages of each issue to the Club's transactions and a Club advertisement, the *Southern Science Record* received an annual subsidy of £12 from the FNCV.[46] An additional understanding concerning the publication of papers read before the FNCV appears to have been in effect, for in 1883 the Club formed a committee to enquire into delays in publication of the journal. When the committee approached Wing he assured them that the tardiness would be rectified no later than the end of the year. By November, however, this seemed unlikely and a motion was passed by the committee that no further papers were to be forwarded to the journal.[47] At a subsequent meeting on 3 December 1883 the committee decided to discontinue its subsidy to the *Southern Science Record* and to publish its own journal.

Given the *Southern Science Record*'s association with amateur science, its stance towards the evolutionary debate is of interest. The first issue of the journal featured an article entitled 'Evolution', which supported the evolutionary thesis, 'If the doctrine of evolution is founded on sound principles, as we have every reason to believe it is . . .'. The same issued carried a brief commendatory review of a zoological textbook, noting that the book's introduction reviewed the principles of zoology, including 'the Cell, Protoplasm, theory of Descent, Classification &c'.[48]

The advocacy of evolution in the *Southern Science Record* is probably attributable to Wing, but the FNCV was far from uniform on the issue of evolution. Moyal, in her *Scientists in Nineteenth Century Australia*, concludes that Darwinism was not generally accepted in Australia until the late 1890s.[49] While this may be true of individuals occupying established positions in natural history, notably McCoy and Mueller, as the previous chapter has indicated, Darwin was widely read and many in the colonies readily acceded to his hypothesis. As Michael Evans has documented, there was certainly a portion of the FNCV membership which was anti-evolution, but the Club also contained members who accepted the evidence for evolution.[50] From 1880 to 1883 the *de facto Transactions* of the FNCV, the *Southern Science Record*, continued to support evolution in its pages. Similarly, in 1880 the FNCV heard a paper bearing the seemingly innocuous title 'Longicorn Beetles of Victoria' in which D. Best 'expressed the opinion that possibly new species were being produced by evolution'.[51] The minutes of that meeting reveal that Best's views were 'strongly combated by several members and altogether the meeting was opposed to such a belief'. A report in a newspaper indicates just who led the resistance to evolutionary thought: 'Both papers were very attentively listened to, and an animated discussion followed, in which Baron Von Mueller took an important part'.[52] The much-esteemed and anti-evolutionist Mueller swept all advocacy of progressive development from his path.

The dominion that Mueller and his zoological counterpart, Frederick McCoy, exercised over the FNCV is readily apparent. McCoy, who seldom bothered attending meetings or excursions of the Club, was elected its initial president in 1880 and continued to serve until 1883. His major contribution to the FNCV was the delivery of the Club's 'Annual Address'. In 1883, in order to allow McCoy to prepare his annual address, the committee of the FNCV felt it necessary to send McCoy a synopsis of the club's activities.[53] Mueller played a more active role in the Club than McCoy. Part of his extensive network of collectors and collaborators belonged to it and Mueller published frequently in its journal. This suited both parties; Mueller had an assured outlet for his work, while the Club obtained the prestige of Mueller's name associated with their fledgling journal.[54] The FNCV's attempts to obtain legitimization by wooing McCoy or Mueller were sometimes comical. In 1883, after McCoy refused to continue to serve as president, Mueller was immediately approached but also declined the honour. Further meetings of the committee record a series of renewed approaches to both men, neither of whom could be interested.[55]

Despite Mueller's opposition, evolution continued to crop up in the Club. In 1882, while replying to Alexander Sutherland's materialistically inclined article, 'The vanishing boundary between the animate and the inanimate', a member of the FNCV wrote: 'Is it not universally acknowledged by biologists, and, indeed by the majority of educated people, that all the various forms of animal and vegetable existence which we see around us are the results of gradual development . . .'.[56] The anonymous correspondent, although accepting evolution, still acknowledged an initial supernatural creation of life. Another staunch Darwinian, P. H. MacGillivray of the Bendigo School of Mines, joined the FNCV in February 1885.[57] The species descriptions and accounts of Club outings, the natural history usually carried in the Club's journal, required little or no theoretical framework. That the issue of evolution surfaced at all is indicative of the wide currency the issue had gained in the colonies.

The dissatisfaction of the FNCV with the *Southern Science Record* and its 1883 decision to produce its own journal ended the *Southern Science Record*'s status as the *de facto Transactions*. The *Southern Science Record* struggled on. It commenced a new series in 1885 and expanded its contributor list to be more representative of other colonies (primarily South Australia), but it was to no avail. The journal soon ceased publication.

In January of 1884, A. Lucas of Wesley College, University of Melbourne, became editor of the FNCV's house journal, the *Victorian Naturalist*. It was not long, however, before Lucas ran into trouble. A special council meeting was called in April 1884 to discuss Lucas's decision to abstract some of the papers rather than printing them in full.[58] The annual report of that year indicates that the subsequent requirement that all papers be printed in full had financial consequences for the Club. The *Victorian Naturalist*, with only 250 copies per issue, was running at a loss and members were urged to subscribe.[59] The journal continued to run at a loss for many years.

Much of the time and energy of scientific societies were devoted to establishing a scientific journal as a means of legitimizing their existence. John Herschel, the British astronomer, noted that 'Nothing has exercised so powerful an influence on the progress of modern science as the publication of Scientific Journals . . .'.[60] Whether or not journals exercised this influence is arguable, but they were seen by scientists and scientific societies as an essential part of the infrastructure of science.

Field Naturalist's Club of New South Wales

In Melbourne the Field Naturalist's Club of Victoria was soon well established but similar attempts in Sydney proved less successful. After the announcement of a field naturalists' club in Sydney in 1880, little progress was made until 1887 when the Natural History Association of New South Wales was founded in association with the Sydney Mechanics' School of Arts. Under a by-law of the Natural History Association, members either belonged to the School of Arts or had to be nominated by members of the School.[61] In April 1890 the Natural History Association metamorphosed into the Field Naturalist's Society of New South Wales. Paid-up members of the Association were automatically enrolled in the Field Naturalist's Society.[62]

Like other field naturalists' clubs, the Field Naturalist's Society adopted objectives encouraging 'the study of nature and the collection, preservation, and systematic classification of specimens'. The society initially conducted an active field trip schedule; excursions by tram, steamer and train ventured into local districts: Manly, the Botany Swamps, Shark Island, Parramatta and Kogarah.[63] As in Melbourne the extension of railway lines—and in Sydney the steamers on the harbour—facilitated field excursions for groups, while the bicycle gave much the same mobility to individual naturalists. The field clubs placed emphasis on the social interaction of their members: 'The excursions have been arranged in order to afford members of the opportunities for social intercourse, and the purpose of collecting material for examination and mounting'.[64] David Allen has rightly labelled field naturalists' clubs as masterpieces of social mechanics.[65] After a few years the excursion programme of the Field Naturalist's Society declined and by March 1894 lack of interest caused the Society to wind up its affairs with a debt of £4.[66]

The Field Naturalist's Society displayed the characteristic relationship of field naturalists' clubs to the professionally directed Australasian Association for the

Advancement of Science. With few exceptions, members of field naturalists' clubs, if they joined AAAS at all, did so only in the year that it met in the capital city of their colony. While a majority of the officials (officers and committee members) of the Sydney-based Natural History Association joined AAAS during its initial meeting in Sydney in 1888, by the time of the Melbourne meeting in 1890 fewer than half the officials of its successor, the Field Naturalist's Society, were members of AAAS. By the 1891 Christchurch meeting almost all had dropped out. Officials were by and large the most active members of field naturalists' clubs.[67]

The Field Naturalist's Club of Victoria, the Field Naturalist's Society of New South Wales, and the natural history section of the Royal Society of South Australia were all examples of field naturalists' clubs in metropolitan areas.[68] Although these organizations have attracted the most attention, in many ways they were hybrid organizations, an amalgam of amateur and professional.

Ballarat Field Club and Science Society

An example of a field naturalists' club established outside the major city of each colony, on the intellectual periphery as it were, was the Ballarat Field Club and Science Society.[69] By the early 1880s the Victorian town of Ballarat, a boom town based on the discovery of gold in the 1850s, had undergone a significant change in character. Ballarat settled down to a virtually constant population of roughly 40,000, only half that of the turbulent 1850s. Gold still dominated the region's economy but the nature of its acquisition had changed. Shallow alluvial workings, accessible to an individual or a small team of men, were replaced in the late 1850s by crushing operations designed to free gold from quartz reefs. Capital, machinery and men were required and the physical infrastructure needed for such long-term operations stabilized the town.

From its rude beginnings Ballarat and its foremost citizens had sought the patina of civilization. The Ballarat Mechanics' Institute had been organized in 1859, and a brick hall built for it in 1860 when much of the population still huddled in canvas tents. Over the next two decades a series of organizations of social importance, but with a partial focus on natural history, were established: the Ballarat Horticultural Society (1859), the Ballarat Agricultural and Pastoral Society (1865) and the Ballarat Acclimatisation Society (1870). These societies were social rather than scientific institutions and their formation is attributable to social legitimization.

The seminal event for natural history in Ballarat was the foundation in 1870 of the School of Mines, Ballarat, although the heyday of natural history in the town did not occur for another decade. During its early years the School provided a resource for naturalists in the community through its museum of geological and palaeontological specimens and the library's collection of publications. In 1877–78 a proposal for the formation of a microscopical society was entertained by the council of the School, but was deferred when it was pointed out that there were few resident in the town with the necessary skills.

In 1881 Ferdinand Moritz Krause, fellow of the Geological Society of London and the Linnean Society of London, and late of the Geological Survey of Victoria, was appointed lecturer at the School of Mines, with responsibility for geology, palaeontology, mineralogy, electricity, magnetism, scientific mining, and surveying, as well as curatorial duties in the School's museum. The following year Alfred Mica Smith, formerly lecturer in metallurgy, assaying and physics at the Bendigo School of Mines, was appointed lecturer at the School. Krause and Smith were soon elevated to the positions of professor of geology and professor of chemistry and metallurgy, respectively. These two men formed both the impetus for the formation of the Ballarat Field Club and Science Society (BFC&SS) on 23 June 1882, and the nucleus of the Club's future activities.[70]

Typical of field clubs, the organization listed its objective as the study of natural and physical science through a programme of meetings, conversaziones and field excursions, and publication of the Club's transactions.[71] The ambitions of the BFC&SS, although outlined briefly, were never fully enunciated.[72] The inaugural addresses of the presidents of the Geelong Field Naturalist's Club and the Bendigo School of Mines Science Society give a better idea of what provincial naturalists' clubs were about.[73] Broadly stated, the aim of each club was seen as the promotion and encouragement of the study of natural history within a local district. The *raisons d'être* of field clubs can be distilled into a few points: the collection of natural history specimens through fieldwork, the classification of specimens, the social interaction of naturalists, and the popularization of natural history.

In a deliberate attempt to encourage the membership of young men, the BFC&SS imposed no entrance fee and limited the annual dues to five shillings. This determination to focus on youth was reiterated a year later when James Oddie, in his first 'Anniversary Address' to the Club, stressed the need to attract young men to the organization.[74] The emphasis on youth is explained by the strong connection between the Society and the School of Mines, made clear by the automatic associate membership of the School's students in the Club, a statement of the Club's activities in the annual reports of the School, and provision by the School of a meeting room. However, an indication that the Society, with its emphasis on natural history, did not entirely serve the needs of the practical and mechanically minded students of the School of Mines is perhaps shown by the establishment of a Students' Scientific Improvement Society in 1883.[75]

Under the presidency of James Oddie, a prominent local citizen and vice-president of the School of Mines, the membership of the Club soon exceeded ninety. Excursions were made throughout the Ballarat district and meetings held to hear papers describing the geography, geology, flora and fauna of the area. Krause, honorary secretary of the Club, generally accompanied the excursions and Smith, superintendent of the School's laboratories, offered his assistance to Club members in the analysis of mineralogical specimens.[76]

Members of the School of Mines played a major role in the Ballarat Field Club and Science Society. In addition to Krause and Mica Smith, George Day, gardener of the School's botanic garden and later instructor in botany, Dr J. F. Usher, lecturer in materia medica, and Henry Sutton, lecturer in applied electricity and magnetism, formed the nucleus of the Club. These individuals delivered ten of the seventeen papers heard by the Club in 1886 and filled several of the offices of the Society.

How did a provincial natural history society carry out its objective of fostering the study of natural and physical science? One of the evening meetings held within six months of the formation of the Club heard W. Chambers deliver 'A talk about insects', accompanied by a sequence of specimens depicting insect metamorphosis; Krause exhibited two nests of Queensland trapdoor spiders; and microscopes were made available for the good turnout of members to view the wonders of nature.[77] At the first annual meeting of the Society, held 27 June 1883, Oddie could proudly

THE GREAT AUSTRALIAN EXPLORATION RACE.

A race ! a race ! so great a one
  The world ne'er saw before ;
A race ! a race ! across this land.
  From south to northern shore !

A race between two colonies !
  Each has a stalwart band
Sent out beyond the settled bounds,
  Into the unknown land.

The one is captain'd by a man
  Already known to fame,
Who with Australian annals has
  For ever linked his name.

The other owns a leader, who
  Has all his bays to earn ;
Let's hope that he, a well-won wreath
  May claim on his return !

The horseman hails from Adelaide,
  The camel rider's ours :—
Now let the steed maintain his speed,
  Against the camel's powers.

No small concealments each from each,
  No shuffling knavish ways,
No petty jealousies and strifes,
  No paltry peddling traits,

Will find a place in such a race,
  But honor, virtue, worth,
And all that can ennoble man
  Will brilliantly shine forth.

A cheer then for each member, and
  A big one for the lot,
For it is known how all have shown
  These virtues.—*Have they not* ?

13 'The Great Australian Exploration Race', *Melbourne Punch* 8 November 1860.

14 'New Illustration of Progressive Development: Respectfully dedicated to the author of Vestiges of Creation', *Melbourne Punch* 3 July 1856.

15 'Squaring Ye Circle', *Melbourne Punch* 5 July 1860.

BEAUTY AND THE BEAST.

BEAUTY : Now you'd have done much better to have taken me to the
Yeomanry Ball than to go making your head ache with geology
and nasty science, at the Philosophical dinner, dear.

BEAST (who knows and cares as much about science as his boots do)
unbuttons his waistcoat, and endeavours to look as if his sufferings
arose exclusively from over mental exertion.

16 'Beauty and the Beast', *Melbourne Punch* 19 February 1857.

PROFESSOR H———D DRESSING FOR
THE BALL.

17 'Professor H–D dressing for the Ball',
Melbourne Punch 13 August 1863.

MAN'S PLACE IN NATURE.

INTELLIGENT LITTLE BOY.—*Mamma, didn't Mr. OPIFER say the other night that he was descended from a Gorilla?*
MAMMA.—*Yes, dear.*
LITTLE BOY.—*Well, and I think he is right, for there's certainly a family likeness.*

18 'Man's place in Nature', *Melbourne Punch* 6 July 1865.

CYNOCEPHALUS PAPIO, OR COMMON BABOON.

19 'Punch's Illustrations of Natural History: Cynocephalus papio, or common baboon', *Melbourne Punch* 4 October 1866.

NOT VENOMOUS.

GREEN TREE SNAKE.
Dendrophis punctulata.

20 'Green Tree Snake: Dendrophis punctulata' by Gerard Krefft, from *The Snakes of Australia*, 1869.

AUSTRALIAN VEGETATION.
FICUS MACROPHYLLA (MORETON BAY FIG) IN FOREGROUND.

21 'Australian Vegetation: Ficus Macrophylla (Moreton Bay Fig) in foreground', the frontispiece of
W. R. Guilfoyle's *Australian Botany: specially designed for the use of schools*, second edition, 1884.

THE SOOTY OPOSSUM.
(PHALANGISTA FULIGINOSA.)

22 'The Sooty Opossum' from Gerard Krefft's *The Mammals of Australia*, 1871.

23 'Brush-tailed Phascogale [Tuan] *Phascogale*' by John Cotton.

24 An excursion of the Linnean Society of New South Wales on the Nepean River 29 September 1888. From left to right *standing* Professor J. W. Stephens, Messrs Skuse, Merrick de Merick, J. J. Fletcher MA; *sitting* Messrs Henry Deane FLS, McBetchie, J. H. Maiden FLS, J. Brazier FLS, Dr J. C. Cot FLS, Sir William Macleay FLS. From the John Brazier Papers *by courtesy of the Mitchell Library, State Library of New South Wales.*

announce that the Club had held twenty-six meetings over the year, eighteen of which were evening lectures, the other eight, field excursions. After exhorting his members to greater efforts, even if only in bringing in unknown specimens to meetings for identification, Oddie particularly thanked Krause for his unstinting efforts on behalf of the Club.[78]

Three years later, at the fourth annual meeting of the BFC&SS, James Oddie, still president, again recorded the diversity of the Club's activities. Some of the novelty of the Club had worn off and membership had dropped from ninety to thirty-nine members. Even so, the Club had managed a reduced programme of thirteen meetings over the year, but significantly for a field club only two were field excursions. The evening soirées, held at the School of Mines, had entertained a range of talks including 'Spectroscopy' and 'Vortex Motion' from Mica Smith, 'Microphotography' and 'Insect Anatomy and Physiology' from local polymath Henry Sutton, botanical lectures by George Day and geology from Krause.

Despite its location at the physical and intellectual periphery, various members of the BFC&SS maintained communication with the centres of colonial science. Mica Smith read papers before the Royal Society of Victoria, and Sutton patented inventions and submitted papers to both the Royal Society of Victoria and the Royal Society of London. Oddie, Sutton and the Reverend Williams were country members of the Royal Society of Victoria.[79] Other members, including Krause, Mica Smith and Isaac Jones, joined the AAAS.

Despite these connections of the prime movers of the BFC&SS, the general tenor of the natural history in the Club was of a less lofty character. The Club was intimately tied to other cultural institutions in Ballarat and the majority of its members would have attended the winter series of popular science lectures of 1882. This series of ten talks, given in the lecture hall at the School of Mines, drew an average attendance of 270. Publication of the lectures allows some insight into the approach to science and natural history in Ballarat.[80] The audience heard the Reverend T. E. Ick discuss 'The Wonders of Coral Life' and acknowledge that Darwin's theory of coral reef formation was the only tenable explanation for the construction of coral reefs. However, Ick went on to argue that the gaps found in barrier reefs were surely put there by the 'guiding hand of a wise, beneficent, and Supreme Ruler' to provide entrances for the vessels of man. The design argument of natural theology was still very much alive. Similarly, Dr J. Usher, one of the leading members of the BFC&SS, and a lecturer in materia medica at the School of Mines, while discoursing on 'Human Physiology' found it difficult to comprehend people who, seeing design everywhere, nevertheless rejected it as evidence of a designer. To complete the education of the people of Ballarat, the patriarch of Australian botanical science, Ferdinand Mueller, came up from Melbourne to deliver a lecture on general observations on the Australian flora and to drum home the dogma of the fixity of species created under the watchful eye of a supreme being. The chance and chaos of natural selection were banished from the environs of Ballarat. This was entirely in keeping with the aims of the BFC&SS. A report on the establishment of the Club in the *Ballarat Courier*, written either by a Club member or a sympathizer, noted

> Again what better employment could young men have in their leisure hours than to observe carefully the things around them—to see in every stone, in every blade of grass; in every insect evidence of awful grandeur of design. Studying nature they will learn to know their Creator and reap life-long benefits from their study.

The Ballarat Field Club and Science Society continued to function, albeit at a reduced level from the enthusiasm of its early years, until at least 1893; and then after a considerable lapse it was revived in 1915. As with many of the smaller field naturalists' clubs, its momentum had been lost by the early 1890s.

Difficulties faced by the field naturalists' clubs were formidable. Seldom did local adepts cover the spectrum of natural history and a novice's question 'What is this?' was often left unanswered. Additionally, schooling left an individual with little preparation for natural history or science. Yet this very lack of natural history was also a boon, for competition against and comparison with acknowledged experts would have dissuaded many beginners. The open field before them (both literally and metaphorically) allowed club members to achieve recognition. Many a field naturalists' club's existence was based on the status conferred by such knowledge.

CHAPTER NINE

the rise of biology

INTERCOLONIAL, 1850–1900

During the first half of the nineteenth century a new term appeared in the vocabulary of science: biology. Coined in Europe in 1802, the term had entered English by the 1820s, and two decades later William Whewell defined the 'science of biology' as the science of life itself.[1]

The introduction and subsequent use of the word 'biology' reflected a change of emphasis not only in the type of knowledge sought by scientists, but in the philosophy which justified the pursuit of that knowledge. Over the course of the nineteenth century, ways of doing science were recast but, more radically, scientists' conception of their interaction with nature was modified. The dominance of natural theology as a framework for man's place in the material world during previous centuries had granted him dominion over all creation. Natural theology portrayed an anthropocentric nature, essentially depicting the world as a giant clockwork stage wound up by God to allow humans to play out their part. During the nineteenth century this ideology was turned upside down. Nature could no longer be depicted as a collection of stage props for the human race, for it was recognized that the natural world had an existence independent of mankind. Scientific methodology now encouraged the view that a scientist must, conceptually at least, stand apart from nature, and from this remote vantage point actively question the make-up of the material world. Rather than a cabinet of curiosities or a table of facts, science became an investigative tool to probe the natural world and, specifically, science became synonymous with the methodology and techniques used to achieve this goal. Much of the agenda of the new science was grounded in positivism, and struck right to the heart of natural history. The metaphysics of natural theology and the romanticism that coloured much of natural history were stripped out, leaving only 'objective' statements of fact. Science, its practitioners asserted, was to be based on value-free, unbiased facts.

A further element of the restructuring of natural science was a shift in emphasis from the organism to specific processes. Titles of research articles reflected the change to reductive strategies, 'The natural history of . . .' became 'The effect of . . . on . . .'. By the latter part of the century this laboratory-based, experimental approach had become accepted by the individuals most closely associated with the natural sciences.

Acceptance of this approach in the Australian colonies witnessed a break between natural history, henceforth to be characterized as an amateur pursuit, and biology which was appropriated almost exclusively by professional scientists. This distancing of natural history from biology was evident to late nineteenth century Australian commentators, who were quick to isolate evolutionary theory, and particularly Darwin's contribution, as the cause of the change. In the eyes of these commentators *On the Origin of Species*, by presenting a unifying idea, a conceptual framework which satisfactorily encompassed comparative anatomy, taxonomy, biogeography and palaeontology, transformed knowledge about nature into a science.[2] As evolutionary theory became entrenched in the natural sciences it quickly became an exemplar of what biology (as opposed to natural history) should be. In 1880 Edward Sanger penned an article for the *Victorian Review* entitled 'Modern Biology', which, after reviewing the recent history of natural science, suggested that the publication of Darwin's *Origin* had initiated a new era in biology.[3] Sanger saw Darwin's theory as having 'reduced to a scientific basis the many diversified phenomena of biology . . .'. Implicit in this recognition of post-Darwinian biology as science, was its complement, that pre-Darwinian natural history had lacked a true scientific basis.

This devaluation of natural history, although consistent with the notion preached by the scientific professionals (particularly the university professors and government-employed scientists) of science as a continually progressive institution, offended and isolated many traditional naturalists. The *Australasian Scientific Magazine* of October 1885 carried an article entitled 'Botany—The Old and the New' by 'RL'. Both the initials and the sentiment of the article identify 'RL' as the editor of the magazine, Robert Litton, founder of the Geological Society of Australasia in 1885 as an amateur geological counterpart to the Field Naturalist's Club of Victoria. Predictably, the article was critical of the emerging laboratory-based botany. No longer was it sufficient to observe field and forest. Now, the first step in botany, as in all biology, was dissection and 'if seeds are put to grow, they will perhaps be on a rotating wheel to see if gravitation determines at which end they will sprout . . . Indeed, a man might win renown as a botanist in his own special department without ever having seen a living plant'.[4] Physiology had become dominant over taxonomy. The individual who practised traditional taxonomy was out of date, looked upon 'as a feeble man content to take things as he saw them, and incapable of the effort of following the more abstruse problems modern science has entered upon'.[5]

The experimental stance so regretted by Litton led to the bane of field naturalists' clubs, laboratory science, becoming integral to natural science. If a scientist was to question nature and receive an intelligible answer, the range of possible answers must necessarily be limited. Investigations had to be isolated from the multitude of interactions occurring in the world outside the laboratory. To rephrase this approach in the terms used by Litton, the germination of seeds in a meadow may be influenced by numerous factors, not all of which are evident to the field observer. Germinating these same seeds on a rotating wheel at least attempted to isolate the effect of gravity on plant growth. Experimental scientists therefore moved into the laboratory and derided the uncontrolled variables of field work.

These crude simplifications—amateur equated with natural history, and professional synonymous with science (in this case biology)—were obvious caricatures. Yet these equations found a place in the rhetoric of professional science. Indicative of this attitude towards natural history was William Haswell, professor of biology at the University of Sydney, who in an 1891 address to the Australasian Association for the Advancement of Science dismissed

The naturalist of the old school [who] went plodding along, accumulating his descriptions of species and his records of remarkable and interesting facts without a thought of theoretical explanation. He was content to take 'short views' of things, and found satisfaction in the indulgence of a passion for the piling up of concrete things.[6]

Gone were the days of collecting, preserving, classifying and naming species. The emphasis was now on development, and on modification and variation under natural and artificial conditions. Haswell then went on to emphasize the new programme of biology by discussing 'Recent Biological Theories' and dazzled his audience with talk of recent work in evolution, variation of species, germ plasm continuity, and units of heredity. Freed from the shackles of the design argument of natural theology, the focus of biology had become processes rather than objects.

During the early years of the nineteenth century in Australia any separation of amateur from professional scientist had been based more on social standing than on competence. During the mid- to late 1800s, many who felt themselves to be professional sought to distance themselves from amateurs on the basis of superior knowledge. In Britain this differentiation originated in the first half of the century and was correlated with the emergence of science as a profession. In Australia the division between professional scientists and amateurs, and its consequence, the redefinition of natural science from natural history to biology, began in the period 1850–60 for much the same reason. Crucial to the transformation was the acceleration in the growth of academic- and government-funded scientific positions.

Until the early 1850s natural history in Australia had been almost exclusively the province of either the gentleman–amateur or collectors employed through private patronage. The scant number of continuously funded government positions, limited for the most part to the directors of the various botanical gardens, was too small to form a cohesive group. In the 1850s, however, there was a rash of government appointments in natural history. In Victoria, the establishment of the Geological Survey and the appointment of a government botanist, palaeontologist and zoologist all bore witness to the rise of government-supported science. The men who occupied these posts, in conjunction with a second group, the university scientific professoriate, formed a professional interest pressure group advocating the continuance of financial and institutional support for science. Much of the impetus to separate amateur from professional came from this relatively small group of individuals, who wanted to differentiate themselves from the great mass of amateur naturalists. The local natural history society had legitimized the activities of its members by linking them with a defined body of knowledge. The scientific professoriate and government-employed scientists, in turn, sought to differentiate themselves from this increasingly crowded naturalist peer group by raising their own status to a professional scientific élite which sought to justify governmental funding of their research, and to exercise an influence on science related questions. Professional scientists needed to emphasize the distinction between themselves and the dabblers in natural history in order to secure community support and resources. The dismissive rhetoric used by professional biology to draw this distinction was part of the social justification of science.

The rise of the professional scientist did not result in the demise of the amateur naturalist. Many amateurs were drawn into societies formed in the latter half of the century, and others continued to work in isolation, but an uneasy tension began between the amateur and professional orientation. The amateur generally deferred to the professional who, because he was paid for his work (they were exclusively male), was somehow given added insight into the natural world.[7]

Scientific amateurs are typically represented as suspicious of, and resistant to, theory. Yet this fails to explain the acceptance of evolutionary theory by large numbers of amateurs, often in the face of professional opposition. Perhaps more indicative of amateur status was that amateurs upheld observation of nature as primary, rather than subjecting it to experimentation.[8] The 'Introduction' of the inaugural issue of the *Victorian Naturalist* outlined the objectives of the Field Naturalist's Club of Victoria: 'Field work has been the main object of the Society, and the enlarged cabinets, and the exhibits at meetings testify to the activity of members in this direction, while the number of careful observers of Nature in the colony has been greatly magnified'.[9] The terms 'field work' and 'observer' were key to field naturalists' clubs, and appear time and again in their literature. By retaining this emphasis on observation amateur naturalists, in some cases consciously, in others unconsciously, rejected the criteria stipulated by the professional interest group for 'science'.

A programme of field excursions was the focus of field clubs.[10] While the more investigative naturalists in the field clubs (especially those in the metropolitan organizations) adhered to the standards of systematic investigation laid down by professional scientists, reports of afternoon rambles featured prominently in field club journals and annual reports. They provided evidence of the ideal of romantic observation of nature common to the provincial field clubs. The outing of the field naturalists' section of the Royal Society of South Australia to Horsnell's Gully in October 1891 was typical: 'This picturesque glen lies between Magill and Hortons summit . . . At any time the locality is a pleasing one to the lovers of nature, but at the time of the visit the encircling hills were clad in their greenest hue, and the aspect was particularly charming'. The excursionists collected flowers, butterflies and moths, and 'Altogether a very pleasant afternoon was spent, the delightful weather and charming scenery contributing largely to this result'.[11] Common to these reports were phrases such as 'rambles in the romantic region', an emphasis on traditional natural history disciplines such as botany, entomology, ornithology and geology, and the almost obligatory break for afternoon tea at some local hostelry.[12]

A further characteristic of many of the articles that appeared in the field club journals was an emphasis on the 'wonders of nature' approach. E. Bage's article 'Victorian Pond Life' in the *Southern Science Record* provides a clear example.

> It [*Apus*, a shield shrimp] has in its sixty pairs of branchial feet and other appendages no less than 1,802,604 joints . . . about five hundred times as many joints as there are stars visible in the heavens on a clear night . . . more joints than there are human bone in an army of 100,000 men . . . a single fertilized female of Cyclops quadricornis may in one year have a progeny of 4,442 million young.[13]

The equipment of most naturalists remained rudimentary. The material requirements of an entomologist were typically: a stout pair of boots, a coat with plenty of pockets, a bag to hold collecting jars and chip boxes (mustard tins were ideal for carrying live caterpillars), resilient pants to fend off the bush, and a home-made net constructed of wire and gauze. For those insects that must be despatched immediately, a killing bottle containing potassium cyanide sufficed and the victim would then be pinned up with entomological pins on a cork board. An essential item for any Victorian entomologist was the umbrella. On inclement days it provided protection while on sunny days it would be held under a bush or branch and insects shaken into it. The insect net of the entomologist could be used by the microscopist to collect material from streams or ponds; the ornithologist substituted a gun; the mammalogist, traps or snares; the geologist, a hammer; and the botanist, a vasculum. For many naturalists a microscope was a much-sought-after item, and microscopical societies were often second only in popularity to field naturalists' clubs. As its equipment and techniques became less cumbersome, photography began to take its place in the arsenal of the naturalist.[14]

Despite the elementary equipment of the naturalist, much of the purported distinction between amateur natural history and professional science was more rhetorical than real. With few exceptions, the techniques and methodology of both groups remained similar throughout the century. By the last quarter of the nineteenth century a biologist could subject organisms to a variety of experimental tests: measurements of animal heat production through the ice calorimeter, respiratory physiology via gas analysis, or analysis of tissue either by chemical means or the recently invented spectroscope. In Australia facilities for this type of experimentation began to become available in the late 1880s. A chemical laboratory proposed for the University of Sydney was to contain a room for gas analysis, spectroscopy and polariscopy, and a spectroscope was in use in the chemistry laboratory of the University of Melbourne by 1890.[15] Despite the adoption of this type of equipment in the biological laboratories of Europe, little use was made of it in Australia before the turn of the century. Sophisticated equipment may have been available but its utilization was limited to chemistry. For the most part research carried out by the European-trained biologists who arrived in the mid- and late 1880s still required little more than the traditional microscope.

It could be argued that the theory underpinning much biology, and the acknowledgement of such a theoretical basis, differed significantly between amateur and professional. Research by individuals such as Spencer or Haswell was distinguished from the natural history tradition by its emphasis on processes rather than objects. Thus Haswell might work on the muscle fibre of *Peripatus* using a light microscope, but he placed it in the context of the evolution of striated muscle.[16] Spencer and his Australian-trained colleague, Arthur Dendy, engaged in taxonomic studies, but related them to biogeography.[17]

Nevertheless, there was no clear-cut division between the work of the professional biologist and the traditional naturalist. Many of the articles printed in the *Victorian Naturalist* would have been appropriate for the *Transactions* of the Linnean Society or the *Reports* of the AAAS.[18] Two arenas where those with a professional orientation met those with an amateur bias were the metropolitan field naturalists' clubs and the Australasian Association for the Advancement of Science (now the Australian and New Zealand Association for the Advancement of Science). In Melbourne the Field Naturalist's Club of Victoria formed an intermediary between more provincial field naturalists' clubs (such as the Ballarat Field Club and Science Society) and professional science. The FNCV included both traditional amateur naturalists and those who either had already been accepted into the professional scientific élite or were later to be so legitimized. Many of the papers read before the Club, and printed in the *Southern Science Record* or the *Victorian Naturalist* followed the methodology and terminology used in more established journals and accepted by professional science.

In Sydney the Natural History Association of New South Wales (1887) and its successor, the Natural History Society of New South Wales (1890) was also a forum for interaction between amateur naturalists and professional scientists. Official positions in the Natural History Society of New South Wales were held by individuals associated with the Australian Museum, the Technological Museum, and various government departments. This seemingly brought the Natural History Society of New South Wales within the ambit of professional science, but was only an intermediate step. Museums were increasingly seen by university biologists as retrograde institutions. With their emphasis on classification, museums were born, and continued in the tradition, of natural history. In the late nineteenth century professional biologists, usually working within universities and emphasizing physiology over taxonomy and anatomy, often looked at their museum colleagues somewhat askance. Physiology had become the jewel in the biological crown but museums dealt in objects instead of processes. At the 1890 AAAS meeting Professor A. Thomas typified the academic view in dealing trenchantly with the issue.

> The second reason why museums fail to effect their purpose [the first was that they assume too much zoological knowledge] is that they do not present a true picture of nature or of the working of natural laws . . . The animal is a living being, influenced at every moment by other living beings around it; by its food supply; by climate and all other external conditions . . . What is the real interest attached to an animal? Is it so many square inches of brown fur? Is it not rather its life? One would think that the 'Origin of Species' had never entered the doors of a museum.[19]

The identification of field naturalists' clubs with museums improved the clubs' legitimacy, but was not always beneficial for the museums. The disengagement of university with museum science did, however, highlight the changes biology was undergoing and the public's perception of science. Science had become increasingly less accessible to the general populace while museums, with their natural history focus, remained exceedingly popular especially after the question of entry to museums as a right or privilege was resolved in favour of a right.

Australasian Association for the Advancement of Science

A second organization in which amateur met professional was the Australasian Association for the Advancement of Science. Too much can be made of a comparison between the British Association (BA) and the AAAS, for they were founded over fifty years apart in dissimilar circumstances. The BA, for instance, originated from Edinburgh and provincial philosophical societies (notably the Yorkshire Philosophical Society), in opposition to London metropolitan science, although it quickly co-opted the latter.[20] AAAS, on the other hand, was organized from and derivative of the twin colonial metropolises of Sydney and Melbourne. Nevertheless, there were considerable similarities between the BA and AAAS. As with the BA, AAAS was a complex mix of diverse and occasionally antipathetical interests. This mix included both amateur and professional, private ambition and public goals, prestige and patronage.

The impulse for the formation of AAAS occurred in 1878 when Archibald Liversidge, professor of geology and mineralogy at the University of Sydney, attended the International Congress of Geologists in Paris.[21] Liversidge, a vice-president of the congress, was appointed convenor for Australasia with the task of organizing discussion among Australian geologists on various propositions addressed by the meeting. In communicating the proceedings of the conference to the Royal Society of New South Wales, Liversidge regretted that in his opinion attendance by too few geologists would preclude any local geological symposium, but suggested mounting a meeting of the Royal Society of New South Wales and other scientific societies at the International Exhibition planned for Sydney in 1879. He also raised the possibility of modelling an Australian scientific association on the highly successful British Association for the Advancement of Science.[22] Despite his personal enthusiasm for the proposal, it elicited only a limited response and the idea lapsed.

Liversidge's conception of the federation of the scientific societies of Australia, Tasmania and New Zealand into the Australasian Association for the Advancement of Science lay dormant during the early 1880s, but in 1884 impetus for establishing a scientific umbrella association was regained, primarily to lay the groundwork for a meeting of the BA in Australia.[23] The possibility of such a meeting was mooted at the 1884 Montreal meeting of the BA, in part from the enthusiasm for things Australian generated when William Caldwell's startling telegram confirming monotreme oviparity was read to that meeting.[24]

In 1886 Liversidge was ready to give his initiatives for an Australian scientific association a more concrete substance. A council meeting of the Royal Society of New South Wales (28 July 1886) passed Liversidge's motion that steps be taken to form such an organization, and within three days Liversidge had despatched a circular to the councils of various societies proposing they hold a joint meeting in Sydney during 1888 as part of the centenary of the founding of the Australian colonies.[25] An advertisement containing similar information was placed in most of the major newspapers of the Australian colonies and New Zealand. The circular generated a more enthusiastic response than had occurred in 1879 and a preliminary meeting, convened in November 1886, agreed to the formation of the Australasian Association for the Advancement of Science, and set the date of the inaugural meeting as late August and early September of 1888.

In March 1888 a further organizational meeting elected officers for the inaugural meeting of AAAS. Five of the seven individuals present either became officers or council members. Henry Russell, director of the Sydney Observatory, was elected president of the 1888 meeting, and in a melding of the traditional naturalist and professional orientations, George Bennett and Archibald Liversidge became honorary secretaries.[26]

The winter months of 1888 were spent planning the coming meeting: progress reports were read, papers accepted, membership solicited, and problems solved (the date of the initial meeting had to be changed to accommodate the schedules of the universities of Melbourne and Adelaide).

The ostensible reason for the creation of AAAS, laying the groundwork for a BA meeting in Australia (which did not eventuate until 1914), obscured other motives. The Association was a complex amalgamation of motivations and ambitions, and various interest groups held differing agendas for the organization. One group wanted the colonies to have their own version of British institutions. Others sought to emphasize the federalist spirit, then gaining currency throughout the colonies, by creating an Australia-wide organization. The *Mercury* described the Hobart 1892 meeting of AAAS: 'these unions . . . are splendid evidences of the true spirit of Federation. Science can do for itself, can do without much fuss or delay, what politicians are unable to accomplish with infinite talk and labour'.[27] More explicitly, during the Christchurch meeting of the previous year, James Hector had proclaimed AAAS to be the first step towards federation of the Australian colonies.[28]

Less obvious, but perhaps just as important, was the potential of the organization to further the aims of the professional interest group. The motivations of these scientists did not always correspond with those of the amateurs and this tension was evident in the early years of AAAS. The membership policy of AAAS reflected its confusion over exactly what role the Association was to play, whether it was to emphasize its amateur or professional constituency.

Initially, membership in AAAS was to be restricted to members of 'Literary and Philosophical Societies publishing Transactions or Journals in the British Empire', although provision was made for the general committee to waive this requirement. This stipulation would have greatly reduced the potential for members of regional field naturalists' clubs to join AAAS. Under this regulation, members of the Ballarat Field Club and Science Society would have been unable to attend AAAS meetings unless they were also accredited with the Royal Society of Victoria or the Field Naturalist's Club of Victoria. Few local field clubs were ever in a sufficiently strong financial position to even contemplate publishing their own *Transactions*.

In practice and in its constitution, however, the implementation of AAAS membership policy was unrestricted. At the 3 September 1888 council meeting of AAAS, it was moved that anyone paying the annual dues was to be admitted to the Association as a member.[29] This open membership policy eventually came under discussion in the *South Australian Register* during the 1893 Adelaide meeting. The *Register* noted that some objections had been raised to the acquisition of membership in AAAS simply by completing an application and paying the annual fee. The *Register* expressed concern that as social engagements associated with AAAS meetings—garden parties and receptions—became more numerous, membership of AAAS might be sought purely to attend these peripheral events. Despite these reservations the *Register* supported the refusal of AAAS to implement an entry requirement, stating that a love of science should be the sole qualification for membership. To prevent social events from distracting the scientific discussions, the *Register* suggested that they be held in separate weeks.[30] The open membership policy of AAAS continued to unite both amateurs and professionals in the common goal of the advancement of science.

Central to AAAS meetings was the individual scientific paper delivered before an audience. Addresses heard by those who attended the first three AAAS meetings (1888–91) encompassed both the new and the old, but the emphasis was changing from taxonomy to processes. The Geology Section was typical with its focus on processes: the formation of igneous, sedimentary and metamorphic rocks; glacial action; and the formation of strata. Similarly, biology emphasized embryology and plant and animal physiology. Papers a traditional naturalist would have felt at home with (for example, 'On a new Australian mammal', 'New Australian species of a notable genera of Molluscs', 'Acclimatization in Victoria', and 'Notes on the zoology of the Houtman's Abrolhos') were increasingly replaced by papers with a different emphasis: 'On the action of metallic salts on the development of Aspergillus nigrescens', 'Notes on the muscular fibres of Peripatus', and 'Demonstration of light producing bacteria'. This change in emphasis, with natural history increasingly replaced by academic biology, occurred however in fits and starts rather than as a continuous trend.

One of the two central elements of the Association's charter, its commitment to bringing science before the general public, was called into question when this expectation was not met. Before the first congress, the *Sydney Morning Herald* had remarked on the exclusiveness of scientific men.

This is the reason that ground is sometimes afforded for the complaint that the road to knowledge is strewn with thorns instead of flowers for the outside learner, and that scientific persons are exclusive and not liberal in their distribution of the pearls they have gathered.[31]

The *Herald* envisioned that AAAS would tear down the barriers that had restricted the distribution of knowledge to the public. However, after the 1890 AAAS meeting the Melbourne *Argus* regretted that the lectures had drifted into obscure technical points unintelligible to the public. Despite its mandate for the popularization of science, AAAS now seemed unlikely to become a means of disseminating scientific knowledge to all sections of the community.[32] In its initial years AAAS existed for select individuals to co-opt science. The scientific élite of the colonies prescribed the agenda of the organization and dictated its management and direction. As in the BA, control and power in the organization lay in the sectional committees of AAAS, and the committees of investigation. These two sub-groups, the substance of AAAS, were populated almost exclusively by professional scientists. At the inaugural 1888 meeting, for instance, two sections dealt with what had formerly been covered by traditional natural history.[33] The Geology and Palaeontology Section had as its officers: Robert Logan Jack (government geologist, Queensland), T. Edgeworth David (Geological Survey of New South Wales), and Robert Etheridge (government palaeontologist, New South Wales). The officers of the Biology Section were Ralph Tate (professor of natural science, University of Adelaide) and W. Haswell (lecturer in biology, University of Sydney).

At the first general committee meeting of AAAS, a number of committees of investigation were established.[34] As they had for the BA, these committees enshrined AAAS as an organization dominated by the professional interest group. With the possible exception of the Protection of Native Birds and Mammals Committee, the committees were peopled by specialist scientists. The Australasian Geological Record Committee, for instance, was made up of R. Etheridge, W. Hutton, R. Jack, J. Stirling, R. Tate and R. Johnston (the latter was not strictly a geologist but as government statistician of Tasmania had professional status). Similarly, the Australasian Biological Station Committee was heavily influenced by the academic professoriate: A. Dendy, W. Haswell, A. Lucas, P. MacGillivray, Baldwin Spencer and R. Tate. Even the Protection of Native Birds and Mammals Committee, which might have included a sizeable field club or acclimatization society component was composed of Haswell, Spencer, Stephens, Tate and Tyron, all academic or government-employed scientists, and A. Campbell and R. Johnston, who, if not professional scientists were certainly senior civil servant professionals. The same names invariably turn up on all the biologically oriented committees.[35]

Many of the committees were more concerned with the administration of science (a professional preoccupation) than with science itself. The committees, however, did fulfil one of the major aims of AAAS by attracting attention to science and removing obstacles from its path. They accomplished this by arriving at conclusions which were then presented to the public and various offices of the colonial governments as the united opinion of AAAS. AAAS was a pressure group for science, and given the positivist ideas inherent in much of late nineteenth century thought, it formed a lobby backed by the weight of scientific truth.

Russell provided further evidence of the professional interest group's hegemony in the initial formation of AAAS in his inaugural 'Presidential Address'. He stated that of the thirty-eight scientific societies in Australasia known to the officers of AAAS, thirty-four indicated their intention to affiliate with AAAS and twenty-eight sent representatives to preliminary meetings.[36] His list of 'the principal Australasian Societies' ranged from established scientific societies, such as the colonial royal societies, to the Engineering Association of New South Wales, the New South Wales Institute of Surveyors, the Historical Society of Australasia, and the Institute of Architects (Victoria). Australian field naturalists' clubs, with the exception of the Field Naturalist's Club of Victoria, the Natural History Association of New South Wales, and the Natural History Society of Rockhampton (all recognized as scientific societies primarily because they included one or more active and well-known naturalist), were noticeably absent.[37]

Despite the fact that for much of the population field naturalists' clubs were the most relevant science, professional science was generally oblivious to them. The organizers of AAAS, however, did recognize that individuals not belonging to an organization on their list of principal societies might be interested in AAAS, and placed advertisements in newspapers to attract those outside the recognized scientific societies (field club members presumably fell into this category).

While AAAS served the professional scientist well, it gave limited support to the other great division of workers in zoological and botanical science, the amateur natural historian. AAAS was directed towards organized and organizational science. The professionally led AAAS had more to do with performing science than doing science. Its role was that of a forum for discussion (the 'parliament of science') and a mechanism for public influence. Field naturalists' clubs, populated predominantly by amateurs and perhaps led by a few professional scientists (or at least teachers), continued to carry out much of the natural history undertaken in Australia, although this work seldom matched the criteria set by professional science and therefore was often ignored.

With natural history and biology metaphorically heading in different directions there was pressure to meld that which Darwin had purportedly rent asunder. Efforts toward a reunification were made by both amateurs and professionals. Field naturalists' clubs tried to close the gap by exhorting members to focus their efforts on gaining expertise in a particular field rather than acquiring a general knowledge of all natural history. Only by acquiring specialist knowledge could a field club member 'hope to be of real service to the advancement of science'.[38] James Oddie, president of the Ballarat Field Club and Science Society, urged his members to greater exertion, regretting that many left the initiative to 'our professional scientists'.[39]

Attempts by professional biologists to bridge the gap between biology and natural history were mostly gambits to appropriate amateurs as unpaid collectors. Amateurs were often seen by professionals as little more than 'busy hands'. An eloquent example was the Adelaide Philosophical Society's *A scheme for the organization and direction of the efforts of amateur collectors*, edited by Ralph Tate and published in 1880. The pamphlet announced that 'The Adelaide Philosophical Society, being desirous of encouraging the study of Natural History, is prepared to direct the efforts of amateur collectors, and to receive from them observations and specimens . . .'.[40] To entice amateurs to participate in the scheme the Society indicated that those who enlisted would be cited as 'Local Correspondents' in the Society's *Transactions*, and that approved communications from them could be published in the *Transactions* under the heading 'Miscellaneous Contributions to the Natural History of South Australia'. In order that correspondents 'should get beyond mere collecting', the Society would suggest books and other reference material for their edification.

The concept was readily acceptable to many. In reporting the scheme, the *Southern Science Record* commended it and suggested that a similar system be implemented in Victoria.[41] Eight years later Henty Russell, president of the inaugural AAAS meeting, reiterated the view that those less than accomplished in science were viewed as 'ready hands': 'I am convinced that there are many such who require no other stimulus than that of being invited to render services of the highest order. They want work, but do not know where to begin; while on the other hand, a crowd of suggestions meet the busy scientific worker at every turn'.[42] There was to be a benevolent dictatorship of professionals directing amateurs. Amateurs, Russell continued, could even aspire to becoming 'professional men' if they chose to do sufficiently difficult work.[43] The pejorative implication was that professional science was somehow more competent, more difficult, and more worthy than the science pursued by the amateur or provincial (in many cases the terms were synonymous). Amateurs could achieve professional status only if they accepted and matched the criteria set by professionals.

The rise of university science

The inclusion of science and natural history in the primary school curriculum had paved the way for field naturalists' clubs. The establishment and development of science in universities over the latter half of the century furthered the acceptance of science as a vocation in Australia. In the early part of the century natural history had been open to all with the required enthusiasm. One of the great lures of natural history had always been that it could be self-taught. Competence, even expertise, could be attained by a combination of diligence, establishing connections with prominent naturalists, and experience.

As the century progressed, the theoretical content of university-driven biology multiplied, and biologists advocated university training for entry into science. Archibald Liversidge, doyen of organizational science in New South Wales in the 1880s, articulated his idealized tripartite view of proper scientific training thus:

> The requirements of the professional scientific man necessitate his passing through three successive educational stages; in the first instance he must possess a good general or liberal education, which should be followed by a course of instruction of a general scientific character to serve as the necessary groundwork or foundation upon which his special professional education can be built; portions of the latter, or third stage of his education can of course, in certain cases, be taken concurrently with his second or general education.[44]

Although self-taught naturalists could still aspire to and achieve scientific excellence, the entry requirements advocated by the scientific élite now made a more rigorous training almost mandatory.

The initial inclusion of the natural sciences in Australian tertiary education saw universities engage professors of natural history or natural science: the University of Melbourne appointed Frederick McCoy as professor of natural science in 1854; the University of Adelaide employed Ralph Tate as professor of natural science in 1875; and in Sydney, William John Stephens became professor of natural history in 1882. Although the University of Melbourne instituted natural science in its curriculum well before the universities of Sydney and Adelaide, the pattern was roughly similar at each. An early University of Melbourne *Calendar* (1858–59) indicates that the programme of study for the Bachelor of Arts degree required a year's study of natural philosophy, and that McCoy offered a first year composite course on botany, chemistry and mineralogy. Second and third year students could elect to undertake comparative anatomy and zoology, or palaeontology and geology. Although this list of natural science courses seems extensive for a university less than five years old, few took up the opportunity. After an initial surge of sixteen matriculants in 1855 (only four eventually presented for the Bachelor of Arts), University of Melbourne student numbers dropped. Seven students entered in 1856, the same number in 1857, and only two in 1858. In 1859 the University enrolment totalled thirteen students.[45] With limited student numbers, McCoy gave few lectures during his first year. In subsequent years his lecture load was light enough for him to supervise both the layout of the University grounds, and the establishment of a systematic botanic garden, yet still throw most of his energy into the development of the University Museum, and later the National Museum.

By the latter half of the 1880s, biology had begun to oust natural history from the curriculum. Leading the reorganization of the curriculum was the introduction of a Bachelor of Science degree, instituted at the University of Melbourne in 1887. It had been some time in coming. The University council approved the degree in 1883, but did not adopt the necessary regulations until 1886. By 1889 a student pursuing a biologically oriented schedule at the University could take:

First Year
   Natural philosophy Part I
   Chemistry
   Biology
   Mathematics
Second Year
   Inductive logic
   Biology Part II
   Physiology
Third Year
   Biology Part III
   Systematic zoology
   Systematic botany

A strong laboratory requirement was requisite in all three years. In sharp contrast to McCoy's tenure, when complaints had arisen over his reliance on lectures rather than laboratory work, a candidate for each of the end-of-year examinations was required to provide evidence of six months of laboratory practice (five hours per week during the first year; ten hours per week, second year; and twenty hours per week, third year).[46]

Much of the impetus for these changes to the curriculum was a result of creating a chair in biology at the University in 1886.[47] It was a triumph for the liberal educationalists, for the University senate approved the chair of biology knowing that the decision necessitated deferring a proposed chair of Greek. The first occupant of the chair, Baldwin Spencer, assumed responsibility for the biology component of the science curriculum. Educated in the experimental tradition and a supporter of evolutionary theory, Spencer dragged biological science at the University of Melbourne out of its natural history den. Spencer found energetic associates in A. Lucas, D. McAlpine, (former lecturer in botany and biology at Heriot-Watt College in Edinburgh), and Arthur Dendy (initially Spencer's assistant lecturer and later professor of biology at Canterbury College, University of New Zealand). These men formed a core of progressive biologists which enabled the University of Melbourne to achieve primacy in biology over the other two Australian universities, Sydney and Adelaide, during the 1880s.

In Sydney the science faculty was not established until 1882, thirty years after the University opened. William John Stephens was appointed foundation professor of natural history, although Stephens had earned his degree in classics. This breadth of knowledge qualified him for secondment as acting professor of classics in 1884–85. Stephens occupied the chair of natural history until his death in 1890, after which the chair was split into the Challis chair of biology and a chair of geology and palaeontology. William Haswell, demonstrator in comparative anatomy, physiology, and histology at the University, was appointed the first occupant of the Challis chair in biology.

By the 1890s biology, not natural history, dominated natural science in Australian universities. Gone were the days when Stephens, without formal credentials in science, could be named to a chair of natural history. The continued growth of the scientific professoriate ensured that the new programme of biology—experimentalist, and holding a steadfast belief in evolutionary theory—was entrenched in the universities. This professional approach was reflected in the inauguration of Bachelor of Science degrees. Science was no longer seen as a component of a liberal education but an education in itself. Chairs in natural science disappeared, to be reborn as separate chairs of biology and geology. The inclusive 'botany, chemistry and mineralogy' taught by McCoy from the late 1850s to the 1880s, and Stephens' 1880s course in natural history, gave way to courses limited to biology or to the even more specific systematic botany or animal physiology.

In one respect the scientific professoriate had more in common with natural history enthusiasts than with the scientists who were increasingly employed by the colonial administrations in health, agriculture and the geological surveys. Natural history had evolved under the private patronage system, and had seldom been subjected to utilitarian constraints. Justification for the increased number of scientists employed by colonial governments (and indeed, of entire government departments such as the geological surveys) was usually provided by emphasizing the utilitarian benefits of science. During the last quarter of the nineteenth century, however, university science set about absolving itself from these considerations. One interest group within AAAS used the organization as an agent of influence to advance the idea of freeing science from utilitarian constraints. This can be seen particularly in the sectional presidential addresses of the Association. At the inaugural meeting of 1888 Russell declared:

> Science stands or falls as a whole; if we limit it to certain purposes or persons it ceases to be science and becomes mere empiricism. This Association stands as a protest against the short-sightedness and utilitarian policy of those who would cultivate only what they characteristically call the bread and butter sciences . . .[48]

Russell sought to distance science from 'the vulgar view, which sees the necessity for cultivating those branches of science that are direct producers of gold and minerals'.[49] Two years later at the following meeting, Professor E. Rennie reiterated the same message.[50] Increasingly the message that AAAS sought to convey was that the object of science should be the pursuit of science for its own sake, and that science was only indirectly for the public good. Professional scientists had begun the task of persuading society that although it was duty-bound to pay for science, interference in scientific affairs by non-scientists was inappropriate.

During the period 1860–90 the division between natural history and biology in Australia was more theoretical than substantive but the distinction was driven by a group of individuals who saw themselves as included in the ambit of professional science. Any disharmony between amateur and professional generally arose from attempts by these professionals to justify their existence. As naturalists they had little call upon the resources of the community; their acceptance as professional biologists meant they could and did make a case for a share of society's assets: funding, positions and status. If the rhetoric employed by professionals was somewhat more strident in the 1860s and 1870s, it was because science as a profession had not yet been established in Australia, and scientific employment, in academia and in government, was not yet secure. The battle had been closed but not yet won. By the 1880s and 1890s scientific employment had become an accepted facet of science, and the vigilance could be relaxed.

Before the 1890s both naturalist and biologist used much the same equipment and methodology and their output was similar. Ironically, after 1890, when the rift between the two began to heal, the methods and concepts began to part. Natural history remained holistic and firmly entrenched in the humanist tradition. Biology became reductive and empirical. Only when conceptual and methodological divisions clearly demarcated amateur from professional could professional biologists become sufficiently confident to allow some measure of identification with amateurs.

GENERAL REFERENCES AND ENDNOTES

GENERAL REFERENCES: CHAPTER ONE

C. Gillespie, *Genesis and Geology: a study in the relations of scientific thought, natural theology, and social opinion in Great Britain, 1790–1850*, New York, 1951.

M. Rudwick, *The Meaning of Fossils: episodes in the history of palaeontology*, New York, 1976.

ENDNOTES: CHAPTER ONE

1. Cited in D. Allen, *The Naturalist in Britain; A Social History*, London, 1976, p. 45.

2. In a previous book, *To Sail Beyond The Sunset; Natural History in Australia, 1699–1829* (Adelaide, 1984), I chronicled this phase of the development of Australian natural history.

3. David Allen makes this same point in relation to the growth of natural history in Britain, which occurred much earlier than in Australia. Allen places it in the seventeenth century. D. Allen, *The Naturalist in Britain; A Social History*.

4. *Sydney Gazette*, 21 May 1829.

5. There is well-established literature on the spread of Western-based science into non-science cultures. G. Basalla, 'The Spread of Western Science', *Science*, Vol. 156 (1967), pp. 611–22. R. MacLeod, 'On Visiting the "Moving Metropolis": Reflections on the Architecture of Imperial Science', *Historical Records of Australian Science*, Vol. 5(3) (1982), pp. 1–16. I. Inkster, 'Scientific enterprise and the Colonial Model Observations on Australian Experience in Historical Context', *Social Studies of Science*, Vol. 15 (1985), pp. 677–704.

6. During the last decade there has been considerable debate over the issue of the professionalization of science, and even whether such professionalization can be said to exist. N. Reingold has rejected the term 'amateur' as pejorative and suggested the substitution of the terms 'cultivators' (individuals who participate in science but for intellectual recreation rather than as a paid vocation), 'practitioners' (scientific journeymen who earn their living in a scientific career), and 'researchers' (the leaders of scientific research). N. Reingold, 'Definitions and Speculations: The Professionalisation of Science in America in the Nineteenth Century', *The Pursuit Of Knowledge in the Early American Republic*, A. Oleson and S. Brown (eds), Baltimore, 1976.

    I have retained the use of 'amateur' and 'professional' as these were terms often used by the individuals involved, and because the division of scientific personnel into 'practitioners' and 'researchers' is just as pejorative.

7. G. Caley to J. Banks, 12 March 1804, as cited in G. Caley, *Reflections on the Colony of New South Wales*, J. Currey (ed.), Melbourne, 1966, p. 71.

8. *Concise Oxford Dictionary of Current English*, 7th edn, Oxford, 1982, p. 726.

9. J. Moore has proposed a revision of this 'warfare' metaphor, suggesting that the 'struggle' is historiographic rather than real. J. Moore, *The Post-Darwinian Controversies: A study of the Protestant struggle to come to terms with Darwin in Great Britain and America 1870–1900*, Cambridge, 1979.

10. W. Paley, *Natural Theology*, 6th edn (1803) p. 12.

11. For instance, John Ray's *The Wisdom of God Manifested in the Works of the Creation*, 1691. An even earlier proponent of this argument was Thomas Aquinas who, as early as the thirteenth century,

postulated the design argument. C. Gillespie, *Genesis and Geology: A study in the relations of scientific thought, natural theology, and social opinion in Great Britain, 1790–1850*, New York, 1951.

[12] C. Wilton, 'On the Connection between Religion and Science', *Australian Quarterly Journal of Theology, Literature and Science*, No. 1 (1828), pp. 1–6.

[13] C. Wilton, 'The Beauty of Order in the Church of England', *Australian Quarterly Journal of Theology, Literature and Science*, No. 1 (1828), pp. 6–19.

[14] J. Hudson, *The History of Adult Education*, pp. 54–5.

[15] *Sydney Gazette*, 1 July 1826.

[16] J. Furneaux 'Short History of the Prahran Mechanics' Institute as disclosed by the Minute Book', La Trobe Library ms 11068. At the public meeting to establish the Institute a resolution called for it to provide 'recreation and instruction after the toils of the day'.

[17] A. de Tocqueville, *Democracy in America*, Vol. II, Chapter X (1835–40), London.

[18] See, for example: J. Lang, *Historical and Statistical Account of New South Wales*, Vol. II (1834), p. 183; J. Lillie, 'Introductory Paper, *Tasmanian Journal of Natural Science*, Vol. I (1842).

[19] *Sydney Morning Herald*, 28 August 1888; see also the *South Australian Register*, 25 September 1893.

[20] J. Moore, *The Post-Darwinian Controversies*, p. 106.

[21] S. Cannon chastises Baconianism advocates, but her disparaging characterization of a collector, 'as one who wanders into a jungle and grabs now this species, now that one, or perhaps just everything in sight' is probably not far from the truth for many colonial collectors. S. Cannon, *Science in Culture; The Early Victorian Period*, New York, 1978, p. 73. Cannon's adoption of the term 'Humboldtian science' to describe the approach to science pursued at this time may be applicable to individuals such as Humboldt himself and Alfred Wallace, 'who thought about what they collected', but is certainly not applicable to early colonial collectors or later members of field naturalists' clubs.

[22] See, for instance: the Whewell–Mill argument on the nature of induction.

[23] C. Wilton, 'On the Connection between Religion and Science', *Australian Quarterly Journal of Theology, Literature, and Science*, No. 1 (1828), pp. 1–6.

[24] *Hobart Town Courier*, 29 May 1830.

[25] J. Lillie, 'Introductory Paper', *Tasmanian Journal of Natural Science*, Vol. 1 (1842), pp. 1–13.

[26] As cited in R. Yeo, 'An Idol of the Market-Place: Baconianism in Nineteenth Century Britain', *History of Science*, 23(3), 1985, pp. 251–98.

[27] *Transactions, Linnean Society of London*, Vol. XIV (1825), pp. 46–68, 395–517; Vol. XV (1827), pp. 63–73.

[28] In December 1823 Vigors read a paper before the Linnean Society of London on 'Observations on the Natural Affinities that connect the Orders and Families of Birds'. *Transactions, Linnean Society of London*, Vol. XIV (1825), pp. 395–517.

[29] Vigors and Horsfield, 'A description of the Australian Birds in the Collection of the Linnean Society; with an Attempt at Arranging them according to their natural affinities', *Transactions, Linnean Society of London*, Vol. XV (1827), pp. 170–331.

[30] See, for example: *Quarterly Review*, Vol. LXXII (1829), pp. 302–27.

[31] 'Perroquet', *Dictionnaire des Sciences Naturelles*, Vol. 39, pp. 20–1.

[32] W. Swainson, 'A Defence of "certain French Naturalists"', *The Magazine of Natural History*, Vol. IV (1831), pp. 97–108. See also pp. 206–7, 316–19, 319–37 and 481–6. Swainson and Vigors also clashed over other issues.

[33] The derivation of Lamarck's advocacy of the transformation thesis has been attributed to a variety of reasons. R. Burkhardt, 'The Inspiration of Lamarck's Belief in Evolution', *Journal of the History of Science*, Vol. 5 (1972).

GENERAL REFERENCES: CHAPTER TWO

M.E. Hoare, 'Science and Scientific Associations in Eastern Australia, 1820–1890', PhD dissertation, Australian National University, 1974.

ENDNOTES: CHAPTER TWO

[1] See C.M. Finney, *To Sail Beyond the Sunset; Natural History in Australia, 1699–1829*, Adelaide, 1984.

[2] Caley to Banks, 7 August 1803, Banks Papers, Vol. 20, Mitchell Library A83.

3 Philip Gidley King to Banks, September 1803, *Historical Records of New South Wales*, Vol. V, p. 229.

4 G. Nadel, *Australia's Colonial Culture; Ideas, Men and Institutions in Mid-Nineteenth Century Eastern Australia*, 1957, pp. 24–5.

5 Philosophical Society of Australasia, Minutebook, 27 June and 4 July 1821, Mitchell Library FM3/99. The minutes for the first two meetings were combined. The minutes have been published in *Journal, Royal Society of New South Wales*, Vol. 55 (1921), Appendix, pp. lxvii–cii.

6 James Bowman, principal surgeon of New South Wales; Henry Douglass, principal assistant surgeon and superintendent of the Female Factory at Parramatta; Frederick Goulburn, colonial secretary and brother of Henry Goulburn, former under-secretary of the Colonial Office; Barron Field, supreme court judge; Francis Irvine, captain, 11th Bengal Native Infantry; John Oxley, surveyor-general of New South Wales; and Edward Wollstonecraft, merchant.

7 Philosophical Society of Australasia, Minutebook, 27 June and 4 July.

8 *The Australian Magazine; or A Compendium of Religious, Literary and Miscellaneous Intelligence*, 1821–22.

9 E. Newland, 'Forgotten Early Australian Journals of Science and Their Editors', *Journal, Royal Australian Historical Society*, Vol. 72(1) (1986), pp. 59–68.

10 The arrival dates of the founding members of the Philosophical Society of Australasia were: Oxley, 1802; Field, February 1817; Wollstonecraft, September 1819; Bowman, September 1819; Irvine, June 1820; Goulburn, December 1820; and Douglass, May 1821.

11 W.B. Clarke called the Philosophical Society a 'Mutual Friendly Association' rather than a formal body. *Transactions, Royal Society of New South Wales*, Vol. 1 (1867), pp. 1–26. The Philosophical Society may have commenced this way, but a lack of friendliness soon characterized most of its members.

12 Philosophical Society, Minutebook, 27 June and 4 July 1821.

13 I. Inkster, 'London and the Seditious Meetings Act of 1817', *British Journal of the History of Science*, Vol. 12 (1919), pp. 192–6.

14 Philosophical Society, Minutebook, 11 July 1821.

15 Philosophical Society, Minutebook, 18 July 1821.

16 Macquarie's Memoranda, 30 November 1821, Mitchell Library CYA772, p. 175.

17 The museum of the Philosophical Society did not form the progenitor of the Australian Museum when the latter was established toward the end of the 1820s. George Bennett's *A Catalogue of the Specimens of Natural History and Miscellaneous Curiosities deposited in the Australian Museum* contains no items from the museum of the Philosophical Society.

18 The papers presented to the Philosophical Society were: 19 December 1821, 'Journal of an expedition from Bathurst to the Pigeon House' by Hamilton Hume; 26 December 1821,'Journal of a tour to Jervis' Bay from the county of Argyle' by Charles Throsby; 2 January 1822, 'Aborigines of New Holland and Van Diemen's Land', Barron Field; 13 February 1822, 'Narrative of a voyage to Jervis' and Bateman's Bays', Alexander Berry; 6 March 1822, 'Geology of the coastland between Newcastle and Bateman's Bay', Alexander Berry; 13 March 1822, 'Astronomical observations in the Southern Hemisphere', Charles Rumker; 2 October 1822, 'On the maritime geography of Australia', Phillip Parker King. The papers by Field, Berry, Rumker and King were published in Barron Field, *Geographical Memoirs of New South Wales*, London, 1825.

19 Bowman consolidated his alliance with the Macarthur family by marrying Mary Macarthur in 1823.

20 Bowman to Douglass, 16 October 1821, James Bowman Letterbook, Mitchell Library A4246.

21 Goulburn to Wollstonecraft, undated but 1821 or 1822, Berry Papers, Vol. 18, Mitchell Library, uncatalogued mss 315.

22 Philosophical Society, Minutebook, 21 November 1821.

23 Brisbane brought a retinue of his own staff to the Philosophical Society, Charles Rumker, the astronomer Brisbane employed to set up an observatory at Parramatta, and Donald Macleod, Brisbane's private physician, were both accepted into membership. Neither was to contribute greatly to the society. Macleod only attended about one quarter of the remaining meetings of the society. Rumker read a paper on astronomical observations in the Southern Hemisphere before it in March 1822, but quarrelled with Brisbane over precedence in the publication of their astronomical work, and left his employ. Brisbane, somewhat pettily, later attempted to revoke a land

grant made to Rumker, justifying his action on the grounds that Rumker had 'frustrated the hopes that had been excited amongst men of Science from his labours'. A contributory factor to Rumker's break with Brisbane was the former's acceptance into the fold of the exclusive faction. Rumker became particularly friendly with Oxley, and also with Field who had become one of the strongest local critics of Brisbane's administration.

24 From 26 December 1821 until 14 July 1822 there were a total of thirty-three meetings of the ten member Society. Of those, nineteen were attended by four or less, and seven meetings consisted of only two members.

25 *Sydney Gazette*, 22 March 1822. The minutebook records this convivial outing as having taken place on 20 March 1821.

26 *Sydney Gazette*, 19 July 1822.

27 W. Clarke, 'Inaugural Address', *Transactions, Royal Society of New South Wales*, Vol. 1 (1867), pp. 1–26. Clarke's view of the Philosophical Society was undoubtedly derived from information given him by his friend Alexander Berry who also attributed many of the problems of the colony in the 1820s to Brisbane's inflation of the value of the pound.

28 B. Field, 'Preface', *Geographical Memoirs*.

29 Brisbane to Bathurst, 6 September 1822, *Historical Records of Australia*, Series I, Vol. X, p. 746.

30 Brisbane to Bathurst, 6 September 1822, *Historical Records of Australia*, Series I, Vol. X, p. 748.

31 Field's *Geographical Memoirs* includes a paper by Phillip Parker King said to have been read before the Society on 2 October 1822.

32 Brisbane to Bruce, 15 February 1823, Brisbane Papers, Mitchell Library FM1627.

33 Brisbane to Bruce, 20 July 1823, 30 January, 17 April 1824, Brisbane Papers, Mitchell Library FM1627.

34 Brisbane to Bruce, 15 February 1823, Brisbane Papers, Mitchell Library FM1627.

35 Scientific–Agricultural Misc. Papers, Vol. 26, Berry Papers, Mitchell Library uncatalogued mss 315. Reviews of Field's *Geographical Memoirs*, both *in toto*, 'the noxious prejudice of the editor . . . a mass of undigested compilation', and individual articles such as 'Field's "Aborigines of New Holland"', described as 'the mere tissue of random hypothesis', indicate a less than reverential attitude to members of the Philosophical Society, especially Field. *South-Asian Register*, 1827–28. See also *Sydney Gazette*, 26 November 1826 and 17 January 1829. The latter ridiculed Field's poetry and called him a meddler in political affairs.

36 Field to Marsden, 28 June 1824, Marsden Papers, Vol. 1, Mitchell Library A1992.

37 Field to Marsden, 21 November 1824, Marsden Papers, Vol. 1, Mitchell Library A1992. Douglass was never out of controversy during his years in the colony of New South Wales. In 1827 he was removed from office and left for England, but he was to be back in Australia in 1848 and two years later helped form the successor to the Philosophical Society of Australasia, the Australian Philosophical Society.

38 C. Lyell, *Principles of Geology*, Vol. II, p. 294.

39 Bigge Report, Evidence of Alexander Berry, 1 February 1820, Mitchell Library, BT Box 5, pp. 2063–73.

40 *Sydney Gazette*, 17 September 1827.

41 *South-Asian Register*, Vol. I, October 1827.

42 A. Berry, 'Description of Broken Bay', 1827, Berry Papers, Vol. 3, Mitchell Library, uncatalogued mss 315.

43 Adherents of phrenology felt that the brain could be physically partitioned into a number of discrete faculties. The potential for any faculty was correlated with its physical size which in turn was reflected by the morphology of the skull. Phrenologists purported to deduce mental faculties, motives and personality by examining the conformation of the skull. Popularized in Europe by F.J. Gall and J.G. Spurzheim in the early 1800s, the idea gained wide currency in Australia through the emigration of scientific gentlemen. The rise in the popularity of phrenology is tied to both political and social theories of early nineteenth century as well as with classification. Just as the de Jussieu and Brown could classify plants on the basis of external morphological characteristics, so too phrenologists sought to classify human beings by the external morphology of the cranium, more colloquially by the 'bumps on the head'.

44 Berry to Knopwood, 19 November 1819, 29 January 1820, Vol. 5, Letters from Berry;

Knopwood to Berry, 17 January 1820, Vol. 14, Miscellaneous letters to Berry, Berry Papers, Mitchell Library, uncatalogued mss 315.

45 Scott returned to New South Wales as archdeacon of the Anglican Church in 1825, a position he occupied until 1828 when he was succeeded by William Broughton.

46 Berry to unknown correspondent, 20 August 1827, Letters from Berry, Berry Papers, Vol. 5, Mitchell Library, uncatalogued mss 315.

47 J. Hay, 'Alexander Berry', Berry Papers, Vol. 20, Mitchell Library, uncatalogued mss 315.

48 Berry to Davidson, 10 January 1823, Letters from Berry, Berry Papers, Vol. 5, Mitchell Library, uncatalogued mss 315.

49 *Sydney Gazette*, 3 September 1829.

50 One society that flourished briefly in 1829 was the Australian Phrenological Society. When its initial lecture was advertised in the *Sydney Gazette*, that newspaper warily distanced itself from the subject, indicating that it did not support phrenology and provided information on the lecture only for education and amusement. On the night advertised, the lecturer stated the case for phrenology in an attempt to place it in the Baconian tradition of inductive science, and therefore to render it immune to criticism. Not everyone in the colony was willing to accept the elevation of phrenology to a science. The pseudonymous 'Habbakuk' objected by way of a letter to the *Gazette* to the moral determinism of the 'incipient bump hunters'. *Sydney Gazette*, 26 March 1829. In Britain, phrenology was closely tied to social reform, particularly penal reform. While there is no indication of such a link for phrenology in the Australian colonies in the 1820s, the arrival in 1837 of Scotsman, Alexander Maconochie in Van Diemen's Land brought a confirmed phrenologist and penal reformer to Australia.

51 The Agricultural Society of New South Wales existed between 5 July 1822 and 22 February 1826. It then became the Agricultural and Horticultural Society of New South Wales (22 February 1826 to 1836), and metamorphosed into the Australian Floral and Horticultural Society (1836–48), the Australasian Botanic and Horticultural Society (20 June 1848 to 8 December 1856), and the Australian Horticultural and Agricultural Society (8 December 1856). Other related colonial societies include the Australian Society to Promote the Growth and Consumption of Colonial Produce and Manufactures (1830–36), and the Horticultural Improvement Society of New South Wales (15 January 1855 to 8 December 1856). J. Maiden, 'A Contribution to a History of the Royal Society of New South Wales', *Journal and Proceedings, Royal Society of New South Wales*, Vol. 52 (1918), pp. 215–361. The Australian Philosophical Society existed between 19 January 1850 and 30 July 1855. It then became successively the Philosophical Society of New South Wales and the Royal Society of New South Wales.

52 Evidence of Archibald Bell, 27 November 1819, Bonwick Transcripts, Bigge Report, Appendix, BT5, p. 2045.

53 *The Evidence of the Bigge Report*, J. Ritchie (ed.), Melbourne, 1971, p. 210.

54 Brisbane to Berry, 9 December 1824, Brisbane Letterbook, Vol. 2, Mitchell Library A1559-2.

55 *Sydney Gazette*, 30 August 1822.

56 *Historical Records of Australia*, Series I, Vol. XI, pp. 520, 613, 937.

57 The defence put forward by McMinn in *Allan Cunningham: Botanist and Explorer* for Cunningham's complaints, that he had been instructed by Banks to report on his relations with the colonial administration, is suspect. Cunningham also included a copy of the problematic letter in a despatch to William Aiton. Cunningham to Aiton, 1 December 1817, Kew Documents, Mitchell Library M730. Under no obligation to report such matters to Aiton, Cunningham apparently did so to impress his nominal employer with the difficulties he faced. Cunningham was to continue to voice complaints throughout his time in Australia.

58 Bonwick Transcripts of the Bigge Report, Mitchell Library, Box 21, p. 3667.

59 One exception seems to have been George Macleay, who in 1832 wrote to Robert Brown: 'Fraser's career and fate, except that in the prime he was sometimes useful to his fellow creatures, was precisely singular . . .'. Macleay to Brown, 22 March 1832, Ida Marriott Transcripts, Cunningham's Letters and Notes, original mss at Kew and South Kensington, Mitchell Library mss 337.

60 Brisbane to Bathurst, 18 March 1823, Transcripts of Missing Despatches, Mitchell Library.

61 Fraser to Wollstonecraft, undated, Mitchell Library Abl92.

62 W. Macarthur to J. Macarthur jnr, 30 January 1824, Macarthur Papers, Vol. 39, pp. 9b-10b, Mitchell Library A2935.

63 C.R. Dawson, *The Present State of Australia*, London, 1830, pp. 397–8.
64 C.W. Macarthur to J. Macarthur jnr, 30 January 1824, Macarthur Papers, Vol. 39, pp. 10b–11b, Mitchell Library A2935.
65 Cunningham to Brisbane, 7 May, 23 July, Colonial Secretary in-letters, New South Wales Archives CS 28/15.
66 Cunningham to Aiton, 20 May 1821, Kew Documents, Mitchell Library M730.
67 Aiton to Cunningham, undated (received 23 July), Kew Documents, Mitchell Library M730.
68 A. Cunningham to R. Cunningham as extracted by R. Cunningham in his 13 February 1825 letter to W. Hooker, Kew Documents, Mitchell Library M732.
69 See the R. Cunningham–W. Hooker Correspondence, Kew Documents, Mitchell Library M732.
70 R. Cunningham to Hooker, 5 February 1825, Kew Documents, Mitchell Library M732.
71 R. Cunningham to Hooker, 6 February 1825, Kew Documents, Mitchell Library M732.
72 R. Cunningham to Hooker, 22 January 1824, Kew Documents, Mitchell Library M732.
73 R. Cunningham to Hooker, 17 May and 5 November 1825, Kew Documents, Mitchell Library M732. Cunningham had two articles in *Geographical Memoirs*, 'Journal of a route from Bathurst to Liverpool Plains', primarily descriptive geography, and 'A specimen of the indigenous botany . . .', the work that Brown attributed to Hooker.
74 *Sydney Gazette*, 25 August 1825.
75 Wentworth to Attorney-General, 7 September 1825, Legal Letterbook of W.C. Wentworth, 1825–26, Mitchell Library A1440.
76 Wentworth to Attorney-General, 8 September 1825, Legal Letterbook of W.C. Wentworth, Mitchell Library A1440.
77 Wentworth to Attorney-General, 14 September 1825, Legal Letterbook of W.C. Wentworth, Mitchell Library A1440. McMinn, in his book *Allan Cunningham: Botanist and Explorer* attempts to make the case that Cunningham 'blundered into this situation, with no apparent knowledge of the motives of the principal parties'. Given the evidence presented in this chapter of Cunningham's close association with the exclusive faction, this seems unlikely. To claim that he was unaware of the principal source of tension in the colony insults Cunningham's intelligence.
78 Brisbane to Bathurst, 21 May 1825, Transcripts of Missing Despatches, Mitchell Library A1267–4.
79 Caley to Suttor, 7 April 1821, Kew Documents, Mitchell Library M730.
80 Brisbane to Bruce, 15 November 1823, Brisbane Papers, Mitchell Library FM1627
81 Brisbane to Bathurst, 23 May 1825, Transcripts of Missing Despatches, Mitchell Library A1267–4. See also *Historical Records of Australia*, Series I, Vol. XI, p. 520.
82 *Sydney Gazette*, 16 January 1826.
83 N. Vigors and T. Horsfield, 'A description of the Australian Birds in the Collection of the Linnean Society; with an Attempt at Arranging them according to their natural affinities', *Transactions, Linnean Society of London*, Vol. XV (1827), pp. 170–331.
84 Allan Cunningham, Journal, 17 July 1826, transcript in Mitchell Library.
85 Lionel Gilbert, 'Botanical Investigation of New South Wales, 1811–1880', PhD dissertation, University of New England, 1971, considers that individual initiative rather than patronage spurred the development of botany. Michael Hoare in his PhD dissertation, 'Science and Scientific Associations in Eastern Australia, 1820–1890' also concludes that science was driven by individual enterprise rather than vice-regal patronage.

GENERAL REFERENCES: CHAPTER THREE

M.E. Hoare, 'Science and Scientific Associations in Eastern Australia, 1820–1890', PhD dissertation, Australian National University, 1974. This thesis extends the material of Hoare's publications 'Dr John Henderson and the Van Diemen's Land Scientific Society', *Records, Australian Academy of Science*, Vol. 1(3) (1968), pp. 7–24; and 'All things queer and opposite; scientific societies in Tasmania in the 1840s', *Isis*, Vol. 60 (1969), pp. 198–209.

T.E. Burns and J.R. Skemp, *Van Diemen's Land Correspondents*, 1827–49, Records of the Queen Victoria Museum, No. 14, n.s., 1961.

S. Murray-Smith, 'A History of Technical Education in Australia; with special reference to the period before 1914', University of Melbourne, PhD thesis, 1966. G. Winter, 'For the Advancement of Science; the Royal Society of Tasmania, 1843–1885', BA (Honours) thesis, University of Tasmania, 1972.

K. Fitzpatrick, *Sir John Franklin in Tasmania, 1837–43*, Melbourne, 1949.

L.L. Robson, *A History of Tasmania; Van Diemen's Land from Earliest Times to 1855*, Volume 1, Melbourne, 1983.

ENDNOTES: CHAPTER THREE

1 *Colonial Times*, 23 March 1827.
2 *Colonial Times*, 16 March 1827.
3 *Colonial Times*, 5 January 1827.
4 *Colonial Times*, 22 June 1827; the *Hobart Town Almanack* of 1828 dropped Burnett from the list of vice-presidents.
5 'Numbskull', *Colonial Times*, 20 July 1827.
6 'Opifex', *Tasmanian*, 26 July 1827.
7 Plomley, *Friendly Mission; The Tasmanian Journals and Papers of George Augustus Robinson, 1829–1834*, p. 35, endnote 14.
8 *Colonial Times*, 22 June 1827.
9 *Hobart Town Courier*, 11 June 1841.
10 *Hobart Guardian*, 16 March 1850. Other meetings were reported in the *Guardian* on 30 March, 11 and 25 May.
11 J. Hudson, *The History of Adult Education*, 1851, Preface.
12 The alienation of mechanics' institutes from the lower classes has also been noted by Australian commentators. See S. Murray-Smith, 'A History of Technical Education in Australia, with special reference to the period before 1914', PhD dissertation, University of Melbourne, 1966; G. Nadel, *Australia's Colonial Culture; ideas, men and institutions in mid-nineteenth century eastern Australia*, Sydney, 1957.
13 The case was made by Shapin and Barnes, 'Science, Nature, and Control; Interpreting Mechanics' Institutes', *Social Studies of Science*, Vol. 7 (1977), pp. 31–74.
14 *Hobart Town Courier*, 17 November 1827.
15 *Hobart Town Courier*, 5 and 26 September 1829.
16 J. Henderson, *Observations on the Colonies of New South Wales and Van Diemen's Land*, 1832.
17 *Hobart Town Courier*, 12 December 1829.
18 The committee included Captain Boyd, James Bryant, A. Crombie, W. Gellibrand, J.T. Gellibrand, W.H. Hamilton, Samuel Hill, Joseph Hone, P.A. Mulgrave, James Ross, John Russell and James Thompson. *Hobart Town Courier*, 19 December 1829. It is worth noting that the officers of the Van Diemen's Land Society and the Mechanics' Institute were often the same individuals; the Van Diemen's Land Society claimed Arthur as patron, Pedder and Burnett as vice-patrons, Henderson as president, surveyor-general George Frankland and Captain Swanston as vice-presidents, and Adam Turnbull as secretary and treasurer. The duplication was essentially due to the fact that there were only a limited number of powerful men in the colony. Michael Hoare in his thesis, 'Science and Scientific Associations in Eastern Australia, 1820–1890', identifies the James Thompson involved in the Van Diemen's Land Society as the convict engineer, but in light of events discussed below, it seems certain that he was the master of the Hobart Town academy of the same name.
19 *Colonial Times*, 1 January 1830.
20 *Hobart Town Courier*, 16 and 23 January 1830.
21 Henderson, *Observations*, p. v. Henderson's system was apparently stimulated by the success of the abbreviated symbols introduced into chemistry late in the previous century. He sought to replace arbitrary and obscure names in natural history with letter codes which could be amalgamated into names diagnostic of the organism. Henderson did not subject his audience to the entire dissertation which can be found in full in his *Observations*. M.E. Hoare's thesis contains a discussion of the proposed revision, pp. 68–70.
22 Henderson chose the Institute of France in preference to the Royal Society on the grounds that the latter institution was too conservative and resistant to the revolutionary change that he proposed.
23 *Tasmanian*, 29 January 1830. Those members present were G. Stephen, Ensign Betts, Assistant Surgeon Russell, Captain Swanston, Dr Henderson, J Hone, Captain Wood, G. Frankland, A. Crombie, James Thompson, John Thompson and A. Turnbull.

[24] *Tasmanian*, 12 February 1830.

[25] *Tasmanian*, 22 January 1830.

[26] The advertisement for the special meeting appeared in the *Hobart Town Courier* of 6 February 1830. A copy of Burnett's circular is included in the *Tasmanian* of 12 February 1830.

[27] *Tasmanian*, 22 and 29 January 1830.

[28] *Tasmanian*, 12 February 1830.

[29] Swanston remained a member of the Society, attending a meeting in March 1830. *Hobart Town Courier*, 27 March 1830.

[30] In his amendment Stephen noted that he strongly disapproved of the rejection of Dunn and Bilton and suggested that because the Van Diemen's Land Society had public objectives, anyone of good moral character should be eligible for membership. However, in a classic exposition of exclusivism, he stated that there were many individuals eligible for membership in such societies that neither he, nor his friends, would be inclined to sit down to dinner with. Thus Stephen indirectly posed the question of whether the Van Diemen's Land Society was to be a social club or a scientific society.

[31] *Tasmanian*, 19 February 1830. The anti-blackball faction consisted of Burnett, Bohan, Bryant, Bisdee, Butler, Cartwright, Fenton, Kerr, Dr Ross, H. Ross, Turnbull, James Thompson, Westbrook and Young. The pro-blackballers were Charles Arthur, Adey, Bedford jnr, Betts, Brock, Frankland, Henderson, Mulgrave, Stephen, Stephen jnr, John Thompson, H. Thompson and Thornloe.

[32] *Hobart Town Courier*, 29 May 1830.

[33] *Hobart Town Courier*, 18 August 1830.

[34] *Colonial Times*, 4 June 1830; *Tasmanian*, 21 May 1830.

[35] I. Inkster regards the growth of an infrastructure as the key event in the success of colonial science. I. Inkster, 'Scientific Enterprise and the Colonial 'Model'; Observations on Australian Experience in Historical Context', *Social Studies of Science*, Vol. 15 (1985), pp. 677–704. While true to an extent, it is dependent on a more basic premise. Early in the history of most colonies, the social, cultural and intellectual élite tend to be the politically powerful. It is not until the cultural and intellectual élite of a colony have gained some measure of autonomy from the politically powerful that a scientific or literary tradition can survive and grow.

[36] *Hobart Town Courier*, 1 May 1830.

[37] *Hobart Town Almanack*, 1834.

[38] *Hobart Town Courier*, 2 May 1834.

[39] Lempriere's interest during the period from 1834 to 1836 was portrait and landscape painting, although he did correspond with William Swainson and send him entomological and ornithological specimens. T.J. Lempriere Papers, 23 March 1834, Mitchell Library A3343; G. Whitley, 'T.J. Lempriere, An Early Tasmanian Naturalist', *Australian Zoologist*, Vol. XIII (1966), pp. 350–5.

[40] Bothwell Literary Society, Tasmanian Archives NP75.

[41] T.E. Burns and J.R. Skemp, *Van Diemen's Land Correspondents, 1827–1849*, Records of the Queen Victoria Museum, No. 14, n.s., 1961.

[42] Extracts of the diary of R. Lawrence, *VDL Correspondents*, T.E. Burns and J.R. Skemp, Records of the Queen Victoria Museum, No. 14, n.s., 1961, pp. 5–11.

[43] Lawrence to Hooker, 1 June 1830, *VDL Correspondents*.

[44] Lawrence to Hooker, 2 April 1832, *VDL Correspondents*.

[45] There is a wealth of primary material on Ronald Gunn. Burns and Skemp's *Van Diemen's Land Correspondents* contains transcripts of letters from T. Scott, R. Lawrence, R. Gunn and J. Milligan, mostly directed to William Hooker. This material in large part derived from the records of Kew Gardens. A much more extensive body of correspondence, primarily letters written to Gunn, is held in Mitchell Library mss A316, A246–53.

[46] Gunn to Hooker, 1 July 1833, *VDL Correspondents*.

[47] 'Some Remarks on the Roots and other Indigenous Esculents of Van Diemen's Land', *Hobart Town Almanack*, 1834, pp. 129–34; 'Index Plantarum', *Hobart Town Almanack*, 1835, pp. 61–114.

[48] Gunn to Hooker, 30 March 1835, *VDL Correspondents*; Hooker to Gunn, 8 January 1836, Gunn Papers, Mitchell Library A253.

[49] Gunn to Hooker, 29 June 1835, *VDL Correspondents*.

50 In 1835 Gunn wrote to Hooker asking him to ignore any requests for money from Gunn's wife, then in Dublin, for 'she has unfortunately acquired a habit of extra-indulgence in drinking.' Hooker replied that her affliction was the hardest of all maladies to cure. Two years later Gunn wrote to tell Hooker that his wife had died in Dublin. Gunn to Hooker, 25 September 1835; 31 March 1837, *VDL Correspondents*; Hooker to Gunn, 24 June 1836, Gunn Papers, Mitchell Library A253.

51 Hooker to Gunn, 8 January 1836, Gunn Papers, Mitchell Library A253. Gunn often had others prepare his specimens but this does not detract from the overall praise.

52 Lindley to Gunn, 8 April 1834; 15 December 1835, Gunn Papers, Mitchell Library A251; Gunn to Hooker, 2 September 1836, 21 April 1838, *VDL Correspondents*.

53 J. Hooker to Gunn, October 1844, Gunn Papers, Mitchell Library A253.

54 Gunn to Hooker, 6 December 1843, *VDL Correspondents*. Gray was particularly obstinate about sending Gunn any return. Repeated attempts by Joseph Hooker to induce Gray to show Gunn some recompense for his specimens went unrewarded. In 1844 Hooker, acting as Gunn's champion, copied extracts of Gray's letters to Gunn promising a return. Gray remained obdurate. J. Hooker to Gunn, October 1844, Gunn Papers, Mitchell Library A253. Despite this, Gunn continued to send specimens to the British Museum throughout the 1840s and 1850s. Gunn Papers, Mitchell Library A250.

55 J. Hooker to Gunn, October 1844, Gunn Papers, Mitchell Library A253.

56 Gunn to Hooker, 14 September 1834, *VDL Correspondents*.

57 Gunn to Hooker, 30 March 1835; 16 November 1836, *VDL Correspondents*. Gunn attempted to reciprocate by sending Hooker books printed in Australia, including Ross's *Hobart Town Almanack*, Lhotsky's *A Journey from Sydney to the Australian Alps*, and later, duplicates of books that Gunn had acquired. The latter, Hooker suggested with characteristic generosity, should be kept by Gunn, 'for you must be laying the foundation of a good Library, for so young a colony'. Hooker to Gunn, 7 April 1845, Gunn Papers, Mitchell Library A253.

58 R.W. Lawrence, 'Notes on an excursion up the western mountains of Van Diemen's Land', *Journal of Botany*, Vol. 1 (1834), pp. 235–41.

59 'Contributions toward a flora of Van Diemen's Land from collections sent by R.W. Lawrence, and Ronald Gunn, Esqrs, and Dr Scott', *Journal of Botany*, Vol. 1 (1834), pp. 241–58. Mitchell Library has the original of one of Gunn's reports, written in December 1843, concerning an excursion undertaken in January 1833. Mitchell Library mss A316. Gunn prefaced his report with 'It is only a hope that you may glean something for your Miscellany that I am induced to attempt the present scroll . . .'. The report describes an excursion from Launceston to his brother's property near Deloraine.

60 See for instance 'Remarks on the Natural History of some of the Australasiatic Animals', *The Van Diemen's Land Monthly Magazine*, September, October, November and December 1837.

61 *Sydney Monitor*, 26 November 1834.

62 *Tasmanian*, 21 October 1836.

63 See his 'Tasmanian Sketches', *Hobart Town Courier*, 21 October and 28 October 1837. Lhotsky's first lectures on natural philosophy were announced in the *Tasmanian* on 2 December 1836.

64 L. Paszkowski, 'John Lhotsky as I see him', *Dr John Lhotsky; The Turbulent Australian Writer Naturalist and Explorer*, Melbourne, 1977.

65 Whitley, 'Early naturalists and collectors in Australia', *Royal Australian Historical Society*, Vol. 19 (1933), p. 321.

66 *Australian*, 6 February 1838.

67 For a recent account of Lhotsky see *Dr John Lhotsky, The Turbulent Australian Writer Naturalist and Explorer*. Unsympathetic treatment was given Lhotsky particularly in the *True Colonist*, 26 April and 24 May 1839.

68 Gunn to Hooker, 30 March 1835, *VDL Correspondents*. De Dassel was a German-born physician then working in Van Diemen's Land.

69 In the apologia for Lhotsky *Dr John Lhotsky; The Turbulent Australian Writer Naturalist and Explorer*, L. Paszkowski charges the author of this letter with 'prejudice'. Unfortunately for Paszkowski's argument the author of the letter is clearly Ronald Gunn, not Jorgen Jorgenson as Paszkowski claims.

70 Frankland to Calder, 12 March 1838, Calder Papers, La Trobe Library. The *Hobart Town Courier* of 2 March 1838 agrees with the essential details of Frankland's letter. This newspaper report

considered the devils to be allegorical representations of the evil genius of the *True Colonist* and the *Cornwall Chronicle*, driving away the good which civilization and education might produce. Both of these papers were harsh critics of Lhotsky.

71 Darwin dedicated much of his visit to Hobart to geology, often in the company of Surveyor-General George Frankland. M.R. Banks, 'A Darwin Manuscript on Hobart Town', *Papers and Proceedings, Royal Society of Tasmania*, Vol. 105 (1971), pp. 5–19.

72 Diary of R.C. Gunn, Mitchell Library B122. The diary also contains entries for Gunn's subsequent visit to Port Phillip and Western Port, a voyage during which Gunn spent most of the time suffering from seasickness.

73 That the 'Journal' was never meant for a wider audience is indicated by the playful 'editorial' in the first issue, and species descriptions such as 'Psittacus terrestris. Ground Parrot. The one dissected by you'. Grant replied in a light-hearted vein, hoping that his contributions would not be rejected by the editor. Although interrupted by such remarks, the 'Journal' by Gunn and 'Contributions' by Grant contained detailed species descriptions. The Circular Head Scientific Journal, Vol 1, No.1 and Supplement dated 21 June 1836, contributions by Grant variously dated July to October 1836.

GENERAL REFERENCES: CHAPTER FOUR

[as for Chapter Three]

ENDNOTES: CHAPTER FOUR

1 Hooker to Gunn, 24 June 1836, Gunn Papers, Mitchell Library A253. The reference to Gunn's possible departure from Van Diemen's Land was occasioned by Gunn's consideration of settling in Port Phillip.

2 Gunn to Burnett, 10 May 1834; Gunn to Hooker, 16 November 1836, *VDL Correspondents*.

3 Gunn to Hooker, 31 March 1836, *VDL Correspondents*.

4 Gunn Papers, November 1839, Mitchell Library A252.

5 Jane Franklin to John Franklin, 20 June 1839, Copy of Franklin's Correspondence, Royal Society of Tasmania Archives RS 16/6(1). Hobson, who had studied medicine in Europe in the mid-1830s, apparently applied to the Colonial Office for a position as colonial naturalist in 1838 but was rebuffed. Unknown correspondent to Hobson, 28 September 1838, Hobson Papers, La Trobe Library Box 865/1 A-C.

6 Gunn to Hooker, 15 February 1838, *VDL Correspondents*.

7 Gould to Gunn, 11 December 1846, 16 October 1850, 2 March 1852, Gunn Papers, Mitchell Library A250. Those who took copies of Gould's *Birds of Australia* in 1846 were Bedford, Bicheno, Breton, Dry, the Franklin Museum, Gunn and Maclean. Joseph Hooker, with a touch of youthful exaggeration and prurient indignation wrote in 1841, 'Three hundred copies of Gould's most extravagant book are purchased by these colonists solely for the pleasure of seeing the show of it on their tables'. *Life and Letters of Sir Joseph Dalton Hooker*, L. Huxley, London, 1918, p. 107. In 1859 Gould's son Charles was appointed geological surveyor of Tasmania and John Gould asked Gunn to give him the benefit of his assistance and advice. Gould to Gunn, 14 April 1859, Gunn Papers, Mitchell Library A251.

8 *Hobart Town Courier*, 14 April 1837.

9 Jane Franklin to John Franklin, 20 June 1839, Royal Society of Tasmania Archives, RS 16/6(1).

10 J. Lillie, 'Lecture upon the Advantages of Science', 1839.

11 The lectures for 1839 totalled twenty-eight and were devoted to agriculture (4), botany (2), chemistry (3), education (4), entomology (1), evidences of Christianity (1), eye-structure (1), geology (1), geographical discoveries (2), history (1) moral philosophy (1), mathematics as connected with mechanics (1), painting (3), phrenology (1), the steam engine (1), the wisdom displayed in the structure of the universe (1), plus an opening and a closing lecture.

12 John Franklin to Jane Franklin, 17 May 1839, *Some Private Correspondence of Sir John and Lady Jane Franklin*, G. Mackaness (ed.), Australian Historical Monographs, Vol. XVIII, n.s.

13 The *Hobart Town Courier* of 6 April 1838 published a request from the British Museum, transmitted to Franklin through the office of Glenelg, for natural history specimens from Van Diemen's Land. In the following weeks (13 and 20 April) the *Courier* published instructions for collecting botanical, zoological and geological specimens.

14 Gell to Lillie, 18 October 1843 (misdated); Lillie to Gell, 17 October 1843, Crowther Collection, State Library of Tasmania, No. C3645.

15 The paper, 'Notes on dissections performed at Hobart Town', is in a collection of papers most of which seem to have been read before the Tasmanian Society, Gunn Papers, Mitchell Library A248.

16 Tasmanian Society, Minutes, 17 October 1839, Gunn Papers, Mitchell Library A246. Much of the paperwork relevant to the Tasmanian Society is located in the Gunn Papers housed in Mitchell Library. Gunn was both the initial and final secretary of the Society.

17 Minutes, Tasmanian Society, 5 November 1839, Gunn Papers, Mitchell Library A246. Hobson's paper, 'Observations on the Blood of the Ornithorhynchus paradoxus' was later published in the *Tasmanian Journal of Natural Science, Agriculture, Statistics, &c.*, Vol. I (1842), pp. 94–8.

18 Minutes, Tasmanian Society, 18 November 1839, Gunn Papers, Mitchell Library A246. A manuscript copy of this paper exists at A246.

19 Letters acknowledging the honour done both men are located in the Gunn Papers, Mitchell Library A246.

20 Gunn to Hooker, 18 February 1840, *VDL Correspondents*.

21 Minutes, Tasmanian Society, 30 December 1839. Gunn Papers, Mitchell Library A246, A252. The Gunn Papers often contain two copies of the minutes of the Tasmanian Society which differ slightly from each other. All the minutes cited are in Volumes A246 and A252.

22 Minutes, Tasmanian Society, 13 and 27 January, 10 and 24 February 1840, Gunn Papers, Mitchell Library A246, A252.

23 Published in the *Tasmanian Journal*, Vol I. (1842) 'On the habits of Alectura Lathami', pp. 21–4.

24 Minutes, Tasmanian Society, 18 May 1840, Gunn Papers, Mitchell Library A252.

25 Minutes, Tasmanian Society, 1 June 1840, Gunn Papers, Mitchell Library A246. Lillie read the second section of the 'Essay' at the 13 July meeting. Gunn Papers, Mitchell Library A252.

26 Minutes, Tasmanian Society, August and September 1840, Gunn Papers, Mitchell Library A246.

27 Diary of G.W.T. Boyes, as cited in K. Fitzpatrick, *Sir John Franklin in Tasmania, 1837–1843*, Melbourne, 1949, p. 247.

28 Hooker to Gunn, 16 September 1839, Gunn Papers, Mitchell Library A253.

29 McCormick published two papers in Volume I of the *Tasmanian Journal*, 'Geological Remarks on Kerguelen's Land', pp. 27–34, and 'A Sketch of the Antarctic Regions, embracing a few passing Remarks, Geological and Ornithological', pp. 241–7.

30 Franklin to Hooker, 6 August 1841, *VDL Correspondents*.

31 J. Hooker to W. Hooker, *Life and Letters of Sir Joseph Dalton Hooker*, L. Huxley, London, 1918.

32 J. Hooker, 'Introductory Essay', *The Botany of the Antarctic voyage of H. M. Discovery ships Erebus and Terror, Flora Tasmaniae*, London, 1860, p. cxxv.

33 Gunn to Hooker, 31 October 1841, *VDL Correspondents*.

34 Some of Joseph Hooker's major publications dealing with Tasmania included *Algae Tasmanicae*, *Florae Tasmaniae Spicilegium*, and *Flora Tasmaniae*.

35 L. Huxley, *Life and Letters of Sir Joseph Dalton Hooker*, p. 172.

36 Jane Franklin to Hobson, 18 February 1841, Hobson Papers, La Trobe Library Box 865/lA-C.

37 Minutes of 'The Society of V. D. Land', Royal Society of Tasmania Archives, RS 147/1.

38 Tasmanian State Archives CSO 8/21 C580. Abbott, in addition to complaining to the colonial secretary, despatched a similar letter to the secretary of state for the colonies on 28 September 1841.

39 Gunn to unknown correspondent, 19 September 1842, Royal Society of Tasmania Archives RS 16/4.

40 Boyes Diary, 4 August 1841, Royal Society of Tasmania Archives, RS 25/2(6–7).

41 Barnard to Gunn, 13 April 1841, Gunn Papers, Mitchell Library A246.

42 M.E. Hoare disagrees, stating that, 'Neither status nor position were automatic passports for election to the Tasmanian Society once Franklin had resolved to put science before political expediency. He drew around him only those with a genuine interest in science . . .'. Hoare, 'Science and Scientific Associations in Eastern Australia, 1820–1890', p. 93.

43 Henslowe to Gunn, 18 February 1847, Gunn Papers, Mitchell Library A247.

44 Gell to Gunn, 20 November 1843, Gunn Papers, Mitchell Library A249.

45 Gell to Gunn, 17 June 1845, Royal Society of Tasmania Archives, RS 17/3.

46 In 1844, Gunn, referring to the Tasmanian Society, wrote '. . . science being republican, we have got rid of all vice presidents, &c., and flourish alike as humble members'. Rather than an accurate

assessment of Gunn's political and social beliefs, this seems to reflect the return of the Tasmanian Society to an exclusive scientific club in contrast to an unwieldy scientific society. *VDL Correspondents*, p. 112.

47 There were other reasons contributing to the non-membership of some of these men. Ross, for instance, had died in 1839.

48 Bothwell Literary Society, Minute Book 1, Tasmanian State Archives, NP 75. A meeting held 26 June 1834 was apparently to formally organize the Society. A name was chosen, rules approved and officers appointed. The Society ruled out only politics and religion as subjects for discussion. At the first meeting discussion, led by the president, the Reverend James Garrett, concerned 'Whether knowledge is conducive to human happiness?'. Given its nature presumably the group answered the question in the affirmative. Tasmanian State Archives, Bothwell Literary Society, NS 429.

49 Bothwell Literary Society, Minute Book 1, 4 May 1836, Tasmanian State Archives NS 429.

50 Mrs Williams' Journal, 28 July 1836, *Clyde Company Papers*, Vol. II (1836–40), p. 11. See also 23 September 1836, 14 July 1837. The *Hobart Town Courier*, 22 September 1837, gave a report on the lecture series of 1836–37.

51 Bothwell Literary Society, Minute Book 1, Annual Report 1836, Tasmanian State Archives NS 429.

52 Bothwell Literary Society, Minute Book 1, 11 March 1837, Tasmanian State Archives NS 429. Franklin accepted the position of patron and also contributed books to the Society. Mrs Williams' Journal, 24 February 1837, *Clyde Company Papers*, Vol. II.

53 Bothwell Literary Society, Minute Book 1, 10 May 1837, Tasmanian State Archives NS 429.

54 Bothwell Literary Society, Minute Book 1, Third Annual Report, Tasmanian State Archives NS 429.

55 *Hobart Town Courier*, 18 November 1836.

56 At the 8 September meeting Allandyne, Garrett, Hall, Macdonald, Redmond, Robinson, Schaw and Wigmore were present. Only Hall and Garrett voted against the motion indicating the exclusivists to be in the majority that night. Royal Society of Tasmania Archives RS 8/2/7.

57 Royal Society of Tasmania Archives, RS 8/2/7. The Minute Book of the Society, Tasmanian Archives NP 75, has had the pages subsequent to the 15 September meeting removed. The next entry is for 15 August 1843.

58 O.W. Reid, 'The Bothwell Literary Society', manuscript based on a report of temporary secretary, J. Garrett, Tasmanian Archives.

59 On 22 October William Clark, a leader of the anti-transportation movement and a member of the Bothwell Literary Society, wrote to William Elliston, editor of the *Hobart Town Courier*, protesting the publication of the 'Vindex' letter. Clark charged that the pseudonymous 'Vindex' was none other than the police clerk at Bothwell, Robinson, acting in concert with Major Schaw to bring the Society into disrepute. Clark made these same charges in a letter of Matthew Forster, the chief police magistrate. In this letter Clark referred to 'the baneful spirit of discord which has so long agitated this unhappy district'. Clark to Elliston, 22 October 1841; Clark to Forster, 28 October 1841, Royal Society of Tasmania Archives, RSA 15.

60 *Hobart Town Courier*, 29 October 1841.

61 Bothwell Literary Society, Minute Book 1, 15 August 1843, Tasmanian State Archives NS 429.

62 This censorship of the minutes caused the removal of the minutes from 15 September 1841 until 15 August 1843. Bothwell Literary Society, Minute Book 1, 20 September, 8 November 1843, Tasmanian State Archives NS 429. Although on the face of it Wigmore was a destructive force within the Bothwell Literary Society, there is evidence that he attempted constructive action. On 10 September 1840 Wigmore wrote to Francis Henslowe, private secretary to John Franklin, 'it is sought by one party to introduce as Members, *Emancipists*, who in all other respects are perfectly unobjectionable characters: another party has taken offense at such an attempt: both are preparing for the Battle'. Wigmore saw clearly that one of his duties as a minister of the gospel was to head off such confrontation and beseeched Franklin, in his capacity of patron, to decide the matter. Wigmore to Henslowe, 10 September 1840. Tasmanian State Archives CSO 19/1/295. Wigmore was later dismissed from his ecclesiastical position by Bishop Nixon who described him as a man with an ungovernable temper.

63 Bothwell Literary Society, Minute Book 1, List of Members, 1 November 1844, Tasmanian State Archives NS 429.

64 Bothwell Literary Society, Minute Book 1, 4 October 1843, Tasmanian State Archives NS 429.

The Bothwell Literary Society existed well into the twentieth century. In this guise it still catered to the natural history student in Bothwell. At the 23 May 1860 meeting, amongst the books ordered was Charles Darwin's *On The Origin of Species*. Bothwell Literary Society, Minute Book 11, 23 May 1860.

65 *Tasmanian Journal of Natural Science*, Vol. I, No. 1., Vol. II, No. 5.

66 Plomley, 'Tasmanian Journal of Natural Science', *Papers and Proceedings of the Royal Society of Tasmania*, Vol. 103 (1969), pp. 13–15. The Royal Society of Tasmania Archives includes a list of those who received copies of the first issue of the *Tasmanian Journal*. It contains slightly over one hundred individuals and institutions. Parts of the *Tasmanian Journal* were distributed through both public and private channels. An example of the former is the use made of the colonial administration to forward copies around Australia. Watson-Parker to Gell, 25 August 1842, Gunn Papers, Mitchell Library A247. In an example of the latter, Jane Franklin despatched copies to her sister Mary Simpkinson in England for dispersal to prominent naturalists, politicians, scientific societies and the publisher John Murray. Jane Franklin to M. Simpkinson, 21 February 1841, *Some Private Correspondence of Sir John and Lady Jane Franklin*. This letter would appear to have been dated incorrectly as the first issue of the *Journal* was not printed until August 1841.

67 There is little doubt that Montagu manipulated the colonial administration by every means possible under the ineffectual Franklin. By the same token Montagu later, 'worked in harmony with four governors' at the Cape of Good Hope. *Australian Dictionary of Biography*, Vol. II, p. 250.

68 Boyes, in his laconic style, noted that 'I have no doubt they made merry with the honour confirmed upon them, as soon as they left us'. Boyes Diary, 2 January 1843, Royal Society of Tasmania Archives. The attitude of Boyes is hard to fathom as he proposed the election of Renaud and Verreaux at the meeting. Minutes of the Tasmanian Society, 2 January 1843, *Tasmanian Journal of Natural Science*, Vol. II (1846). Verreaux left the French ship, settled in Van Diemen's Land, and occasionally attended subsequent meetings of the Society.

69 Boyes' Diary, 6 and 7 July 1843, Royal Society of Tasmania Archives. The published minutes of the Tasmanian Society are curiously silent concerning this episode. *Tasmanian Journal*, Vol. II (1846), p. 156.

70 Royal Society of Tasmania Archives RS 16/11.

71 John Franklin returned to England and sought to clear his name from the injury he felt it had been subjected to, but he received no redress from the Colonial Office. By 1845 Franklin was again before the public eye in the role of Arctic explorer. In May 1845, in a reversal of the roles of 1840, it was Captain James Ross (who declined command of the expedition) who watched Franklin, in command of HMS *Erebus*, and Crozier, in command of HMS *Terror*, set sail to discover the fabled North-west Passage. None of the 135 men ever returned. The fate of the expedition was not conclusively established until the last of a series of search missions returned in 1859.

72 An unsigned, undated manuscript that appears to have been the basis for the Eardley-Wilmot proposal, 'Proposal of the Lieutenant Governor for ceding to the community the present Government Garden' is located in the Tasmanian State Archives, Crowther Collection, C3645. The proposal suggests an amalgamation of the Mechanics' Institute, the Tasmanian Society and the Horticultural Society into a 'Tasmanian Horticultural and Botanic Institution'. Suggestions for the management of the Government Garden, for a paid secretary to be nominated by the governor, and an entrance fee of two guineas indicate that this document was probably the notes that Eardley-Wilmot read to the meeting. The *Launceston Examiner* of 11 October 1843 had already mooted the nominal union of the Mechanics' Institute, the Tasmanian Society and the Horticultural Society, although suggesting that a complete union would be impractical.

73 Cited in E.L. Piesse, 'The Foundation and Early Work of the Society; with some account of earlier institutions in Tasmania', *Papers and Proceedings of the Royal Society of Tasmania*, 1913, pp. 117–66.

74 Lillie to Gell, 17 October 1843, Crowther Collection, Tasmanian State Archives C3645.

75 Joseph Milligan, in reference to the Tasmanian Society, later wrote to Gunn of the 'disguised hostility of one or two of its former supporters, who not satisfied with effecting its downfall want to trample it with bitter animosity'. 13 November 1844, Gunn Papers, Mitchell Library A316.

76 Gunn to Hooker, 6 December 1843, *VDL Correspondents*.

77 Gell was most definitely against the proposal. However, as secretary, he was required by the decision of the meeting to communicate the suggestion to the Botanical and Horticultural Society giving rise to Hoare's statement 'An overture from Gell and the Tasmanian Society "proposing a junction" of the two societies . . .'. M.E. Hoare, 'Science and Scientific Associations in Eastern Australia, 1820–1890', p. 110.

78 Gell to Gunn, 26 March 1844, Gunn Papers, Mitchell Library A247.

79 Tasmanian Society, Minutes, 30 April 1844, Gunn Papers, Mitchell Library A247. Those present at this meeting were R.H. Davies, C. Friend, Dr J. Grant, R. Gunn and W.R. Pugh.

80 Gell to Gunn, 21 May 1844, Gunn Papers, Mitchell Library A247.

81 Tasmanian Society, Minutes, 4 June 1844, Gunn Papers Mitchell Library A246. A copy of these minutes was published in the *Tasmanian Journal*, Vol. II (1846), p. 317.

82 There were some curious changes. For instance, Joseph Allport replaced Mrs Allport as a member. *Tasmanian Journal*, Vol. I, II.

83 Gell to Gunn, 20 and 30 November 1844, 24 January 1845, Gunn Papers, Mitchell Library A249.

84 Barnard to Gunn, 14 September 1844, Gunn Papers, Mitchell Library A246.

85 Gunn to Hobson, 12 February 1847, Hobson Papers, La Trobe Library, Box 865/1A-C.

86 Royal Society of Tasmania, Minutes 1845–53, 29 January 1847, Royal Society of Tasmania Archives A1.

87 Lillie to Gunn, 2 February 1847, Gunn Papers, Mitchell Library A247.

88 Valentine to Gunn, 19 February 1847, Gunn Papers, Mitchell Library A247.

89 Henslowe to Gunn, 19 February 1847, Gunn Papers, Mitchell Library A247.

90 Hobson to Gunn, 30 November 1847, Gunn Papers, Mitchell Library A246.

91 Agnew to Gunn, 19 February 1847, Gunn Papers, Mitchell Library A247.

92 As quoted in K. Fitzpatrick, *Sir John Franklin in Tasmania*, pp. 197–8.

93 Henslowe to Gunn, 18 February 1847, Gunn Papers, Mitchell Library A247.

94 Gunn to La Trobe, 17 November 1846, Gunn Papers, Mitchell Library A246; Henslowe to Gunn, 18 February 1847, Valentine to Gunn, 17 February 1847, Gunn Papers, Mitchell Library A247.

95 Bicheno to Gunn, 2 February 1849, Gunn Papers, Mitchell Library A247.

96 Van Diemen's Land Mechanics' Institute, Minutebook, 6 and 10 October, 14 November 1843, Mitchell Library A583-1.

97 Launceston Mechanics' Institute, Minutebook, 6 June 1842. In the 1850s Gunn became a vice-president of the Mechanics' Institute.

98 *Launceston Examiner*, 22 April 1843.

GENERAL REFERENCES: CHAPTER FIVE

John Cotton's Birds of the Port Phillip District of New South Wales, 1843–49, A. McEvey, 1974.

L. Gillbank, 'The Acclimatisation Society of Victoria', *Victorian Historical Journal*, Vol. 51 (1980), pp. 255–70.

M.E. Hoare, '"The half-mad bureaucrat" Robert Brough Smyth (1830–1889)', *Records*, Australian Academy of Science, Vol 2(4) (1974) pp. 25–40.

——'Learned Societies in Australia; The Foundation Years in Victoria, 1850–1860', *Records*, Australian Academy of Science, Vol 1(2) (1967), pp. 7–29.

——'Science and Scientific Associations in Eastern Australia, 1820–1890', PhD dissertation, 1974, Australian National University.

A. Moyal, *Scientists in Nineteenth Century Australia; A Documentary History*, Stanmore, 1976.

R. Pescott, *Collections of a Century; The history of the first hundred years of the National Museum of Victoria*, Melbourne, 1954.

G. Serle, *The Golden Age; A History of the Colony of Victoria, 1851–1861*, Melbourne, 1963.

ENDNOTES: CHAPTER FIVE

1 The *Port Phillip Gazette* Supplement, 28 September 1839, recorded a meeting of mechanics which expressed a desire for a mechanics' institute. On 2 November the *Gazette* advertised the Union Benefit Society meeting of 5 November, and on 6 November it reported on the preliminary meeting.

2 *Port Phillip Gazette*, 12 January 1839.
3 R. Gunn, 'Observations on the Flora of Geelong, Port Phillip', *Tasmanian Journal of Natural Science*, Vol. I (1842), pp. 203–7.
4 Gunn to Hooker, 6 December 1843, 9 May 1844, *Van Diemen's Land Correspondents*.
5 J. Backhouse, *A Narrative of a Visit to the Australian Colonies*, London, 1843, see Chapter XLII.
6 J Stokes, *Discoveries in Australia; with an account of the coasts and rivers reported and surveyed during the voyage of the Beagle*, London, 1846, Vol. II, p. 481.
7 W. Westgarth, *Commercial and Statistical Report on Port Phillip*, Melbourne, 1844.
8 *Port Phillip Gazette*, 13 August 1845.
9 Bunce emigrated to Hobart in 1835 and found employment in a nursery which he subsequently purchased. In October 1839 he sold up and crossed the strait to settle in Port Phillip where he opened another nursery.
10 D. Bunce, *Manual of Practical Gardening*, Hobart, 1837–38. The second edition was retitled *The Australian Manual of Horticulture*, Melbourne, 1850.
11 Bunce described his part in the expedition in D. Bunce, *Australasiatic Reminiscences*. The book was later republished as *Travels with Dr Leichhardt*, Melbourne, 1857.
12 Leichhardt to Macarthur, 25 February 1848. Macarthur Papers, Vol. 96, Mitchell Library A2992.
13 After Bunce's rejection as superintendent of the Melbourne Botanic Gardens he applied for a similar position in Adelaide. He was again unsuccessful. After a varied career he became the director of the Geelong Botanic Gardens in 1858.
14 D. Bunce, *Hortus Victoriensis: A Catalogue of the most generally known Flora of the colony of Victoria with their Linnaean classification and general remarks*, Melbourne, 1851. This catalogue was often bound together with the 1850 edition of his *Australian Manual of Horticulture*.
15 E. Pescott, 'The writings of Daniel Bunce, 1813–1872', Victorian Historical Magazine, Vol. 23(3), pp. 115–25. The criticism comes from a manuscript note attributed to Gunn by Pescott. The original manuscript is located in the Parliamentary Library, Canberra. Part of Gunn's rejection of Bunce's work may be attributable to Bunce's continued use of the Linnaean botanical classification. Gunn preferred natural affinity classifications. Bunce defended his use of the Linnaean system in the *Port Phillip Magazine*, Vol. IV (1843).
16 *Illustrated Australian Magazine*, Vol. II (1851), p. 326.
17 *Port Phillip Gazette*, 12 June 1839.
18 *Port Phillip Gazette*, 18 February 1840.
19 *Port Phillip Gazette*, 20 June 1840.
20 *Port Phillip Gazette*, 27 June 1840.
21 *Port Phillip Gazette*, 4 , 22, 25 July and 2 September 1840.
22 *Port Phillip Gazette*, 12 June 1841.
23 W. Westgarth, *Commercial and Statistical Report on Port Phillip*.
24 *Melbourne Mechanics' Institute and School of Arts, Annual Report for 1844.*
25 Ibid.
26 The Hobson Papers contain a letter from Jameson admitting Hobson to lectures at the University of Edinburgh, and a letter from the Medical Faculty of Berlin to Hobson concerning his enquiry about pursuing a degree there. The latter gives Hobson's address as University College, London. Hobson Papers, La Trobe Library Box 865/1A-C.
27 'Memoir of the late Dr Hobson', *Illustrated Australian Magazine*, 1850, p. 395.
28 E. Hobson, 'Diary of a journey overland from Melbourne to the Hume River with Lady Franklin's party', La Trobe Library Box 25/1 mss 383/09. See also H.B. Parris, 'From Melborne to the Murray in 1839', *Victorian Naturalist*, Vol. 66 (1950), pp. 183–90, 203–10.
29 E. Hobson, 'On the Callorynchus australis', *Tasmanian Journal of Natural Science, Agriculture, Statistics, &c.*, Vol. I (1842), pp. 14–20.
30 E. Hobson, 'Observations on the blood of the Ornithorhynchus paradoxus', *Tasmanian Journal of Natural Science*, Vol. I (1842), pp. 94–8. See also Chapter 3. The popularity of this approach to taxonomy can also be seen in G. Gulliver's 'On the size of red blood corpuscles of the blood in the Verterbrata, with copious tables of measurements', *Proceedings of the Zoological Society of London*, Vol. XIII (1845), pp. 93–102. This article noticed Hobson's work, as did Richard Owen's observations in the same journal, pp. 81–2, and Owen's article on the Monotremata in the *Cyclopedia of Natural History*.

31 A letter from Jane Franklin to Hobson in February 1841 refers to a third paper submitted to the *Tasmanian Journal* which was returned to Hobson for revision. Hobson Papers, La Trobe Library Box 865/1A-C. This letter also indicates the warm relationship Hobson enjoyed with the Franklins.

32 E. Hobson, 'On some fossil bones discovered at Mount Macedon, Port Phillip', Tasmanian Journal of Natural Science, Vol. II (1846), pp. 208–10.

33 For Hobson's unpublished letters to Gunn, see Gunn Papers, Mitchell Library A247.

34 *Tasmanian Journal*, Vol. III (1849), pp. 240–1, 387–9.

35 Gunn to Hobson, 3 July 1847, Hobson Papers, La Trobe Library Box 865/1A-C. The fictitious letter is presumably that referred to by Gunn in *Tasmanian Journal*, Vol. II (1846), p. 242.

36 *Tasmanian Journal*, Vol. III (1849), pp. 406–7.

37 J. Cotton, *The Resident Song Birds of Great Britain*, London, 1835; *The Song Birds of Great Britain*, London, 1836. Cotton completed another book on birds before leaving England, which he refers to in letters. *The Correspondence of John Cotton; Victorian Pioneer, 1842–49*, G. Mackaness (ed.), Sydney, 1953. The manuscript was left with a publisher on the condition that Cotton receive copies of the finished work as payment. Some of the illustrations were transferred to stone before the expense caused the project to be abandoned. Cotton labelled the work a mere compilation and disassociated himself from the manuscript. This manuscript seems to be that eventually published as *Beautiful Birds Described*, edited from the manuscript of John Cotton by the Reverend Robert Tyas, London, 1855. Two features of the book date it prior to Cotton's departure for Port Phillip. First, the book, although dealing with birds of the world, contains very little information on Australian species. Second, the book is based on the Vigors–Swainson quinary classification of birds, or more accurately on Cotton's modifications of the system. While this taxonomic system might still have been used by some English ornithologists in the early 1830s, by the late 1840s the system had well and truly fallen from use.
   Cotton appears to have lost all interest in the fate of *Song Birds of Great Britain* upon setting out for Australia. When questioned by his brother William about copies, John replied that rather than colouring further plates he would prefer to occupy his spare time in painting the birds of his adopted country. *Correspondence of John Cotton*, November 1844. Cotton at one point suggested that he might induce his daughters to colour some of the plates, but only one had any talent for it and he preferred that she draw Australian flowers from nature, rather than colour his sterile etchings. Finally Cotton sent the plates to William, whose wife coloured several sets to be put up for sale. William later informed John that not a single copy had sold.

38 *Correspondence of John Cotton*, 1 August, 20 November 1843, January and April 1844.

39 *Correspondence of John Cotton*, August 1844.

40 *Correspondence of John Cotton*, April 1846. Cotton discussed other books in his letters to Robert Hudson, including Charles Lyell's *Elements of Geology*. John Cotton's Letterbooks, 1848–49. La Trobe Library mss 9095.

41 *Correspondence of John Cotton*, August 1844.

42 Both the original manuscript and a typescript of 'Some Account of the Colony of Port Phillip in Australia Felix in a series of letters to a brother in England by a squatter' are located in the library of the Museum of Victoria, NMV/0 1/2.

43 *Correspondence of John Cotton*, April 1846. Cotton included sketches of various animals with this letter.

44 *Correspondence of John Cotton*, August 1848.

45 *Correspondence of John Cotton*, December 1848.

46 Cotton wrote to Hudson about *Birds of Australia* in June 1841. The first part of the work had been out for six months and Cotton had inspected some of the plates. Despite his financial stability, Cotton claimed that Gould's works were too expensive to purchase, but continued 'I think for the benefit of science the society [Zoological Society of London] should buy up a number of these works and distribute them amongst its members, or those of them who might be inclined to purchase at half price'.

47 Some of John Cotton's ornithological sketches were eventually published, but not until 1974 when A. McEvey wrote *John Cotton's Birds of the Port Phillip District of New South Wales, 1843–49*.

48 *Correspondence of John Cotton*, February and October 1845.

49 W. Cotton to Hudson, 21 August 1849, Cotton Family Letterbook, La Trobe Library mss 9095.

50 Daguerreotype apparatus reached Australia in the early 1840s. An early reference to George Gilbert's attempts with the daguerreotype appeared in the 25 November 1845 *Port Phillip Gazette*.

51 Correspondence of John Cotton, November 1846, February 1847.

52 Gunn to Hooker, 17 March 1849, *Van Diemen's Land Correspondents*. Gunn would have become aware of the daguerreotype process in 1840 when John Franklin received letters describing the technique from John Richardson and William Buckland. *Tasmanian Journal of Natural Science*, Vol. I (1842), pp. 71–2.

53 John Cotton's Diaries 1823–33, 14 February 1832. In the possession of Jane McGowan.

54 J. Cotton, 'A List of Birds which frequent the upper portion of the River Goulburn, in the district of Port Phillip, New South Wales', *Tasmanian Journal of Natural Science*, Vol. III (1849), pp. 361–5. Cotton carried on a correspondence with Gunn subsequent to the publication of his paper, chiefly concerning additions and corrections to the Goulburn checklist. Cotton to Gunn, August 1848, undated, Gunn Papers, Mitchell Library A247. The original manuscript of Cotton's catalogue is also in the Gunn Papers, Mitchell Library A248.

55 In a reflective letter, Cotton wrote of his frustrated aspirations: 'It is probable that had I become a student at the Royal Academy I might have succeeded as a painter as Denning observes. If diligence could overcome poverty of talent and want of confidence I would probably not be in Australia but an aspirant for fame in one of the most elegant branches of the fine arts'. *Correspondnce of John Cotton*, February 1845.

56 W. Irving, *A Tour of the Prairies*, 1835. La Trobe's keen interest in natural history can be seen in the letters he exchanged with Ronald Gunn. *Letters of Charles Joseph La Trobe*, Melbourne 1975.

57 Howitt Family Papers, La Trobe Library Box 10551/3.

58 Westgarth was given shells and fossils for the Mechanics' Institute by the Melbourne social diarist, Georgiana McCrae. *Georgiana's Journal*, 17 August 1844.

59 A. Creelman, *The life of a Dilettante; George Alexander Gilbert*, 1979, La Trobe Library mss 11258. Gilbert presents a fascinating character. He arrived in Port Phillip in November 1841 and promptly threw himself into all manner of activities. He was reputed to have sent 10,000 Australian insect specimens to the London Entomological Society. *Port Phillip Herald*, 23 September 1847. In the early to mid-1840s, Gilbert served as secretary of the Mechanics' Institute and lectured there until 1852 when, along with thousands of other Victorians, he set off for the goldfields.

Gilbert was much taken with current vogues in science including mesmerism, clairvoyance and phrenology. See *Argus*, 1 and 19 August 1850; 22 January 1851; *Illustrated Australian Magazine*, 1850, pp. 166, 177; Hobler Journals, 3, 26, 30 August 1850, 26 November 1851, Mitchell Library. Gilbert furthered more conventional science through his work at the Mechanics' Institute and his association with Ronald Gunn's *Tasmanian Journal of Natural Science*. In 1844, soon after Gunn commenced rejuvenating the *Tasmanian Journal*, Gilbert offered to serve as agent for the journal in Port Phillip. Gilbert to Gunn, 14 October 1844, Gunn Papers, Mitchell Library A246. Gilbert set to work finding new subscribers and also offered to execute lithographs or etchings for the journal without charge. Gilbert to Gunn, 12 December 1844, Gunn Papers, Mitchell Library A246.

60 P. de Serville, *Port Phillip Gentlemen and good society in Melbourne before the gold rushes*, Oxford, 1980.

61 G. Haydon, *Five Years in Australia Felix*, 1846, Vol. I, p. 84.

62 La Trobe to Gunn, 23 January 1847, *Letters of Charles Joseph La Trobe*; La Trobe to Gunn, 8 March 1847, Gunn Papers, Mitchell Library A246.

63 Gilbert to Gunn, 9 May 1847, Gunn Papers, Mitchell Library A246.

64 Gunn to Hobson, 12 February 1847, Hobson Papers, La Trobe Library Box 865/1A-C.

65 R. Gunn, 'On the "Bunyip" of Australia Felix', *Tasmanian Journal of Natural Science*, Vol. III (1849), pp. 147–9.

66 W. Macleay, 'On the skull now exhibited at the Colonial Museum of Sydney, as that of the "Bunyip"', *Tasmanian Journal of Natural Science*, Vol. III (1849), pp. 275–8.

67 Owen to Hobson, December 1847, Gunn Papers, Mitchell Library A246.

68 *Argus*, 26 July 1851.

69 A. Geike, *Life of Sir Frederick I. Murchison*, Vol. II, pp. 131–6, London, 1875; Royal Geographical

Society, Vol. XIV (1844), pp. xciv. Strzelecki may have found gold in Gippsland in 1839–40. *Victorian Yearbook*, 1973.

70 *Progress Report from the Select Committee on the claims of the Reverend W.B. Clarke*, Legislative Assembly, New South Wales, 1861. See also *The Claims of the Rev. W.B. Clarke*, 1860; *Sydney Morning Herald*, 28 September 1847; *Papers relating to Australian Gold presented to Parliament 16 August 1853*.

71 *Progress Report from the Select Committee on the claims of the Reverend W.B. Clarke*, Legislative Assembly, New South Wales, 1861.

72 J. Clutterbuck, *Port Phillip in 1849*, London, 1850, p. 44.

73 La Trobe to Gunn, 2 March 1849, *Letters of Charles Joseph La Trobe*.

74 Selwyn and the Geological Survey remained aloof from much social interaction with Victorian naturalists. This lack of communication contributed to the eventual demise of the Geological Survey. When the Survey came under pressure in the late 1860s, few Victorian naturalists, with the exception of the Reverend John Bleasdale, rallied to its support. Not surprisingly for some-one who later frequently quoted J.B. Jukes to the effect that, 'If the palaeontology does not agree with the stratigraphy, so much the worse for the fossils', Selwyn received little support from McCoy. H. Ami, 'Memorial or Sketch of the life of the late Dr A.R.C. Selwyn', *Transactions, Royal Society of Canada*, Vol. (1904), p. 173.

75 See for instance, F. Mueller, 'An Historical View of the Exploration of Australia', *Transactions, Philosophical Institute of Victoria*, Vol. II (1857), pp. 148–65. The *Transactions* of the Victorian Institute, the Philosophical Society, and their successor, the Philosophical Institute, all contain articles with theoretical content.

76 *Argus*, 9 October 1852, 1 and 26 January, 17–19 August 1853. Gibbons, an analytical chemist, was a member of the subcommittee set up by the gold reward committee to examine gold specimens from Deep Creek. On 4 October 1851 Gibbons delivered a lecture at the Mechanics' Institute on gold mining. W. Stacpoole, 'The man who named Ballarat', La Trobe Library mss 57860.

77 *Argus*, 9 October 1852.

78 *Argus*, 26 January 1853.

79 *Argus*, 4 October 1852.

80 This view of Stephens is partially mitigated by his other activities. In a letter to the editor of the *Argus*, Stephens noted that part of his duties as vice-president of the Geological Society included the diffusion of mineralogical knowledge in the colony. Stephens cautioned miners to avoid wasting time and effort in gathering what they thought to be the metal platina (platinum). The *Australian Gold Diggers Monthly Magazine*, in its December 1852 issue, had reported that platina was frequently met with in Victoria, but Stephens warned that this was improbable. In all instances he was familiar with, the presumed platina turned out to be no more than a micaceous variety of iron. Stephens included in his letter three simple tests which allowed miners to dif-ferentiate platina from iron. *Argus*, 8 January 1853. The *Gold Diggers Magazine*, during its brief run (October 1852 to May 1853), included not only practical mining advice, but discussion of theoretical issues. The Wernerian–Huttonian battle was refought again in its pages.

81 *Argus*, 24 September 1853.

82 Ibid.

83 There was the expectation in Melbourne that Clarke would take a leading role in any scientific society. The 15 June 1854 *Argus* noted that Clarke had played an important part in the Royal Society of Van Diemen's Land while resident in Tasmania and could be expected to do so in any similar Victorian venture.

84 Reprinted in the *Argus*, 3 June 1854.

85 *Argus*, 28 June 1854.

86 *Argus*, 3 June 1854. The committee on natural history, formed to help organize the collections, included: A. Greeves, G. Howitt, F. Mueller, M. Nicholson, J. Palmer, A. Selwyn, C. Pasley, with Redmond Barry as president and Andrew Clarke as honorary secretary.

87 *Official Catalogue of the Melbourne Exhibition*, 1854; *Argus*, 17 October 1854. Just over a week later the *Argus* again praised the Museum exhibit, but complained that the catalogue of the exhibition made it difficult to find the names of many specimens. *Argus*, 29 October 1854.

88 *Argus*, 26 January 1853.

GENERAL REFERENCES: CHAPTER SIX

[see Chapter Five]

ENDNOTES: CHAPTER SIX

[1] *Argus*, 2 and 5 June 1854.

[2] *Argus*, 2 February 1854.

[3] Gibbons had been employed as reporter on the Victorian goldfields for the *Melbourne Daily News* in 1851. The *Daily News* was absorbed by the *Argus*, and Gibbons continued to write for that paper as well as to practise his profession of analytical chemist. William Kerr, publisher of the *Argus* also attended the organizational meetings of the Victorian Institute although his name did not appear on a subsequent membership list. *Transactions, Victorian Institute for the Advancement of Science*, 1854–55.

[4] *Argus*, 31 May 1854.

[5] The Victorian Institute for the Advancement of Science set up sections, but did not exist as an independent body long enough for them to function.

[6] *Argus*, 15 June 1854.

[7] *Argus*, 26 June 1854. The temporary council of the Victorian Institute met in late June and adopted Gibbons' proposed constitution with negligible change.

[8] By the time the *Transactions, Victorian Institute*, 1854–55, was published John Maund had replaced Montefinore as treasurer. Montefinore had left the colony.

[9] *Transactions, Victorian Institute*, 1854–55, 22 September 1854.

[10] Brooke to Gibbons, 5 October 1854, La Trobe Library Box 122/2.

[11] Royal Society of Victoria, Minutebook, 17 June 1854, Vol. I, June 1854 to February 1888, La Trobe Library mss 11663.

[12] Royal Society of Victoria, Minutebook, 24 June, 15 July 1854.

[13] *Argus*, 2, 3, 5 and 7 June 1854.

[14] Royal Society of Victoria, Minutebook, 24 June 1854.

[15] Royal Society of Victoria, Minutebook, 2 August 1854.

[16] Royal Society of Victoria, Minutebook, 19 July 1854.

[17] A. Clarke, 'Inaugural Address', *Transactions, Philosophical Society of Victoria*, Vol. I, pp. 1–5.

[18] Prospectus of the Philosophical Society of Victoria, bound with the *Victorian Institute for the Advancement of Science*, 1854–55.

[19] Special general meeting, 18 September 1854, *Transactions, Philosophical Society of Victoria*, Vol. I.

[20] *Argus*, 18 and 19 September 1854.

[21] Royal Society of Victoria, Minutebook, 6 December 1854.

[22] *Transactions, Philosophical Society of Victoria*, Vol. I, 22 November and 6 December 1854.

[23] *Transactions, Philosophical Society of Victoria*, Vol. I, 9 January 1855. The *Report of the Select Committee on Coalfields*, 1856–57, based on evidence given by Andrew Clarke and McCoy, also suggested that the coalfields at Cape Paterson were extensive. Selwyn, the government geologist, rejected the idea of a large coalfield there, and speaking very much as a professional to amateurs, when pressed by the committee about supposed evidence of a coalfield, replied, 'What amounts to proof in their minds is not proof to me'.

[24] *Transactions, Philosophical Society of Victoria*, Vol. I, 9 January 1855.

[25] *Transactions, Philosophical Society of Victoria*, Vol. I, 8 March 1855

[26] Royal Society of Victoria, Minutebook, 23 June 1855.

[27] *Transactions, Philosophical Society of Victoria*, Vol. I, 27 March 1855.

[28] The Victorian Institute published twenty papers including its inaugural address. The papers were concentrated in the disciplines of engineering and botany. Almost half were given by a small, active group of just four men. The Philosophical Society printed twenty-one papers including its inaugural address. Once again the dominant areas were engineering and botany. The active members of the Philosophical Society (those who published two or more papers) formed a larger group (seven) than in the Victorian Institute, but these individuals contributed all but two of the published papers. Ferdinand Mueller spanned both societies, publishing three papers in each set of *Transactions*. Ironically the Victorian Institute for the Advancement of Science was more catholic than the supposedly wider-based Philosophical Society of Victoria. The former published papers on economics and statistics, while the latter tended to concentrate on science.

29 *Transactions, Victorian Institute*, 1854–55, 8 March 1855.

30 *Transactions, Philosophical Institute*, 1854–55, 7 September 1855.

31 Having been instrumental in forming the Geological Society of Victoria and the Victorian Institute for the Advancement of Science, Gibbons was not content to retire from society life. In 1857, and again in 1858, he attempted to found a corresponding microscopic society. *Journal of Australia*, March and August 1857, January 1858; *Illustrated Melbourne News*, 2 January 1858. In 1872 the Royal Society of Victoria conferred life membership upon Gibbons in recognition of the part he had played in the establishment of the Victorian Institute. Rusden to Gibbons, 6 June 1872, La Trobe Library, uncatalogued.

32 Royal Society of Victoria, Minutebook, 24 June, 5 and 25 July 1856.

33 Royal Society of Victoria, Minutebook, 28 February 1855.

34 *Transactions, Philosophical Institute of Victoria*, Vol. I (1855–56), 13 March 1855.

35 Royal Society of Victoria, Minutebook, 17 October 1855.

36 Royal Society of Victoria, Minutebook, 23 November 1855. The published proceedings put a different face on it, 'he [Hotham] replied in a most courteous manner that in the absence of Capt. Clarke, the Surveyor General, he could not arrive at any decision respecting the museum, but that on that officer's return to Melbourne, would communicate with him on the subject of our letter'. *Transactions, Philosophical Institute of Victoria*, Vol. I (1855–56), 4 February 1856.

37 *Transactions, Philosophical Institute of Victoria*, Vol. I (1855–56), 15 July 1856.

38 There was some precedent for the University of Melbourne's grab for the Museum. In 1852 the University of Sydney unsuccessfully proposed that the Australian Museum be transferred to its custody.

39 McCoy to Mueller, 26 January 1860, Royal Society of Victoria, Correspondence, 1856–88, La Trobe Library mss 2/1.

40 McCoy wrote to J.E. Gray at the British Museum cautioning him that the National Museum should never be referred to as the University Museum as 'it would be cakes and ale to some opponents of the museum here'. McCoy to Gray, 24 October 1860, National Museum Letterbook, 1857–61, Museum of Victoria Library.

41 'A statement to the council of the Philosophical Institute of Victoria in reference to a correspondence between Professor McCoy and the Honorary Secretary of the Institute upon a paper entitled "Museums in Victoria"', August 1857.

42 National Museum Letterbook, 21 May 1857 to 26 September 1861, Museum of Victoria Library.

43 McCoy to Gould, 26 June 1867, National Museum Letterbook 3, Museum of Victoria Library.

44 James to Secretary of the Smithsonian Institution, 28 September 1860, National Museum Letterbook, 1857–61.

45 *Melbourne Punch*, see particularly 27 and 13 March 1856, 19 February, 8 October 1857, 28 April 1859, 23 February, 5 July 1860.

46 *Melbourne Punch*, 7 and 14 August 1856.

47 F. Mueller, 'Account of some New Australian Plants', *Transactions, Philosophical Institute of Victoria*, Vol. II (1857), pp. 62–77.

48 Royal Society of Victoria, Minutebook, 14 October 1856.

49 W. Blandowski, 'Recent Discoveries in Natural History on the Lower Murray', *Transactions, Philosophical Institute of Victoria*, Vol. II (1857), pp. 124–37.

50 Krefft's version of the Lower Murray expedition exists in manuscript form in Krefft Papers, Mitchell Library A267. It was apparently written well after the expedition and is a comic, if biased, tale of disaster rife with implicit and explicit criticism of Blandowski.

51 *Illustrated Melbourne News*, 6 February 1858. It was partly to mitigate this and other disputes that the Victorian government set up its Board of Science in 1858. One of the first claims on the attention of the Board was an investigation of two accusations against the government, one by Blandowski, the other by Henry Stephenson. *Board of Science, Victoria, First Annual Report*, 1858–59.

52 *Transactions, Philosophical Institute Of Victoria*, Vol. II (1857), 21 October 1857; Royal Society of Victoria, Minutebook, 4 November 1857.

53 Royal Society of Victoria, Minutebook, 5 March 1858.

54 Wilson, Bleasdale, Eades, Gillbee, Clarke and Rawlinson voted for the motion, while Wilkie, Acheson, Iffla, MacKenna, Mueller and Macadam voted against it. On major issues before the

council, Wilkie, Acheson, Blandowski and Iffla tended to vote as a block, Wilson, Bleasdale, Rawlinson and Irving voted as a second block, while Hodgkinson, MacKenna, Macadam, Gillbee and Mueller were swinging voters.

55 Royal Society of Victoria, Minutebook, 12 March 1858.

56 This letter appears to be that in the Royal Society of Victoria records, La Trobe Library 35/9, dated 22 March 1858, Bleasdale to Macadam. Bleasdale wrote that he could not 'without forfeiting all claim to the character of a Gentleman, meet Mr Blandowski again at the Council of the Institute'. Bleasdale regretted that the council should retain a member who had insulted and caricatured someone who, because of his ecclesiastical position, could not seek redress. If the council chose to let Blandowski retain his position, then it was unfit to manage a scientific society. A letter dated two days later (24 March) from Bleasdale to Stawell was even more aggrieved. Blandowski's attack was not only unworthy of a gentleman but cowardly. It astonished Bleasdale that anyone with a speck of honour could continue to sit on the council with Blandowski.

57 The committee eventually consisted of R. Knaggs, W. Shultz, Lieutenant H. Amsinck, S. Elliot and J. Millar. It had the power to call for Blandowski's resignation or, under by-law 20, to recommend that the council expel him; by-law 20 dealt with a member bringing the Institute into disrepute.

58 *Transactions, Philosophical Institute of Victoria*, Vol. III (1858), 14 April 1858.

59

60 *Melbourne Punch*, 1 and 8 April 1858.

61 *Victorian Legislative Council Minutes*, 5 February 1856. The alpaca had been considered for introduction to Australia even earlier, *Australian Illustrated Magazine*, Vol. I (1850).

62 *Report from the Select Committee of the Legislative Council on the Alpaca*, 1856.

63 In 1857 Embling, elected to the newly established Legislative Assembly, initiated a committee to consider the introduction of stock into Victoria. Embling expanded the terms of reference to include exotic species and the alpaca featured prominently in the committee's proceedings. A sum of £2,000 was appropriated in 1861 for the introduction of the alpaca to Victoria. L. Gillbank, 'The Acclimatisation Society of Victoria', *Victorian Historical Journal*, Vol. 51 (1980), pp. 255–70.

64 E. Wilson, 'On the Murray River Cod, with particulars of Experiments instituted for introducing this fish into the River Yarra-Yarra', *Transactions, Philosophical Institute of Victoria*, Vol. II (1857), pp. 23–34. Wilson's papers formed a ready target for the *Melbourne Punch* as did the activities of Embling. Acclimatization featured prominently in *Punch* over the next several years. *Melbourne Punch*, 23 April, 21 May, 4 June, 11 June, 2 July 1857, and 27 January, 3 February 1859.

65 F. Mueller, 'On a General Introduction of Useful Plants into Victoria', *Transactions, Philosophical Institute of Victoria*, Vol. II (1857), pp. 93–109.

66 F. Mueller, 'Anniversary Address', *Transactions, Philosophical Institute of Victoria*, Vol. IV (1859), pp. 1–8.

67 P. Nisser, 'On some domesticated animals of South America which would be useful in Victoria', *Transactions, Philosophical Institute of Victoria*, Vol. IV (1859), pp. 65–9.

68 *Argus*, 28 November 1862.

69 Zoological Society, Minutebook, Origin of the Society, Library of the Melbourne Zoological Gardens.

70 *Illustrated Journal of Australia*, Vol. III, November 1857. The *Illustrated Journal*, having previously criticized the lack of Zoological Gardens in Victoria, in an article entitled 'Dull as Ditch-water', found the paltry efforts of the Zoological Society to be a great disappointment. *Illustrated Journal of Australia*, Vol. II, January 1857. The author of this article was probably William Gibbons, editor of the *Journal*.

71 Zoological Society, Minutebook, 11 May 1858.

72 Zoological Society, Minutebook, 29 May 1858.

73 W. Clarke, 'Anniversary Address' 1856, *Transactions, Philosophical Institute of Victoria*, Vol. I (1855–56).

74 *Transactions, Philosophical Institute of Victoria*, Vol. II (1857), 21 October and 11 November 1857.

75 Philosophical Institute of Victoria, Exploration Committee, Minutes, 14 November 1857, La Trobe Library, mss H16254–5 Box 2075/1(a).

76 F. Mueller, 'An Historical Review of the Exploration of Australia' read 25 November 1857. *Transactions, Philosophical Institute of Victoria*, Vol. II (1857), pp. 148–68.

77 Report of the Exploration Committee, *Transactions, Philosophical Institute of Victoria*, Vol. II (1857), pp. xiv–xxiii; A.C. Gregory to Mueller, Royal Society of Victoria Exploration Committee, La Trobe Library, uncatalogued.

78 The records of the Royal Society of Victoria contain an unsigned, undated manuscript which Belt submitted to the Philosophical Institute in either 1857 or 1858. The manuscript outlined the problem of inland exploration as Belt saw it: the over-equipping of expeditions rendering rapid travel impossible. Belt proposed to take six packhorses or mules from north to south via the Albert River, Eyre's Creek, then along Sturt's route to the southern coast.

Belt's proposal to travel alone stemmed from his belief that success would result only from pushing forward under any circumstances. Belt's ideas, although never taken seriously by the Exploration Committee, are worth outlining for his conception of a short sharp dash south towards civilization was viable. After setting out from Melbourne in great numbers and over-burdened with equipment, the eventual dash north from Cooper's Creek by Burke, Wills, King and Gray was of a much reduced size. The four men did accomplish the one-way journey, and it was because they set themselves the return journey that disaster struck. Belt never undertook his lone journey.

On 6 January 1858, and again on 1 March 1860, Belt offered his services to the Royal Society Exploration Committee as leader of the proposed expedition. In mid-March 1860, Belt withdrew his application, for he planned to return to Europe instead. Royal Society of Victoria Exploration Committee, Applications, La Trobe Library ms 9504, 10 March, Thomas Belt.

79 *Argus*, 5 January 1858.

80 The second report of the Exploration Committee claimed that all the resolutions entertained by the meeting were carried unanimously. *Transactions, Philosophical Institute of Victoria*, Vol. III (1858), pp. xxxv–xxxix.

81 One example of a paper read to the Institute was John Cairns' 'On the Weir Mallee (a Water-yielding Tree) the Bulrush, and Porcupine Grass of Australia'. The paper centred around the use of the weir mallee by Aborigines and explorers to obtain water in the desert. *Transactions, Philosophical Institute of Victoria*, Vol. III (1858), pp. 32–5.

82 The anonymous donor was later revealed to be merchant Ambrose Kyle.

83 H. Barkly, 'Inaugural Address', *Transactions, Royal Society of Victoria*, Vol. V (1860), pp. 1–18.

84 Royal Society of Victoria Exploring Expedition, Inward Correspondence, 1858–60. La Trobe Library, Box 2077/5.

85 Ledger to Exploration Committee, 17 June 1859; Mueller to Macadam, 16 July 1860, Royal Society of Victoria Exploration Committee, Inward Correspondence, 1858–60.

86 Macadam to Warburton, 13 February 1860; Warburton to Royal Society of Victoria, 22 February 1860, Royal Society of Victoria, La Trobe Library Box 2079/3.

87 Royal Society of Victoria Exploration Committee Minutes, 1858–60, 25 February, 2 March 1860, La Trobe Library Box 2075/1(c).

88 Royal Society of Victoria Exploration Committee, Minutes, 1858–60, 23 July 1860, La Trobe Library.

89 Royal Society of Victoria Exploration Committee, Minutes, 28 June 1860, La Trobe Library.

90 A 23 July 1860 letter from McCoy to Gerard Krefft, also an applicant for the naturalist position, revealed that McCoy's first choice was Osker Rietmann. National Museum Letterbook, 1857–61. Other applicants included Frederick Waterhouse and R. Kendall. Becker supported his application by petitioning Governor Henry Barkly for the naturalist's position. Becker to Barkly, 4 July 1860, Barkly Correspondence, La Trobe Library, Box 1847/7. Becker was probably chosen on the strength of his long association with the Philosophical Institute. Two days before the departure of the Victorian Exploring Expedition, Becker presented his private museum to the Royal Society. Friends in the Society had raised a sum of over £100 to purchase the museum for this purpose. Becker to Honorary Secretary of the Royal Society, 18 August 1860, Royal Society, Correspondence, 1856–88, La Trobe Library mss 2/1.

91 Royal Society of Victoria Exploration Committee, Minutes, 10 August 1860, La Trobe Library.

92 Royal Society of Victoria Exploration Committee, Minutes, 22 August 1860, La Trobe Library.

93 Royal Society of Victoria Exploration Committee, Minutes, 30 August 1860, La Trobe Library.

94 Royal Society of Victoria Exploration Committee, Minutes, 22 September 1860, La Trobe Library.

GENERAL REFERENCES: CHAPTER SEVEN

B. Butcher, 'Australian Correspondents of Charles Darwin; a Case of Judicious Selection', Paper presented at the International Congress of History of Science, University of California, Berkeley, 1985.

K. Dugan, 'Marsupials and Monotremes in pre-Darwinian theory', PhD dissertation, University of Kansas, 1980.

——'The Zoological Exploration of the Australian Region', *Scientific Colonialism, 1800–1930: A Cross Cultural Comparison*, Melbourne, 1986.

A.M. Moyal, 'Sir Richard Owen and his influence on Australian Zoological and Palaeontological Science', *Records, Australian Academy of Science*, Vol. 3(2), pp. 41–56.

——*Scientists in Nineteenth Century Australia*, Stanmore, 1976.

A. Mozley (Moyal), 'Evolution and the climate of opinion in Australia, 1840–76', *Victorian Studies*, Vol. X (1967), pp. 411–30.

ENDNOTES: CHAPTER SEVEN

1 The 12th edition of *Vestiges*, published in 1884, posthumously acknowledged Robert Chambers, a popular encyclopedist, as the author.

2 (Robert Chambers), *The Vestiges of Creation*, 2nd edition, 1844, p. 322.

3 J. Cotton to W. Cotton, April 1846, *The Correspondence of John Cotton; Victorian Pioneer, 1842–49*, Sydney, 1953.

4 *Life and Letters of The Right Honourable Robert Lowe Viscount Sherbrooke*, London, 1893, Vol. II, p. 205.

5 Anonymous, 'The Natural History of Man', *Australasian*, Vol. I (October 1850), pp. 1–32, reprinted from *Quarterly Review* (December 1849); Anonymous, 'Geology versus Development', *Australasian*, Vol. I (April 1851), pp. 317–38, reprinted from *Fraser's Magazine* (October 1850).

6 Much the same conclusion is arrived at by Barry Butcher in 'Australian Correspondents of Charles Darwin—A Case of Judicious Selection?', Paper presented to the International Congress of History of Science, University of California, Berkeley, 1985.

7 W. Irvine, *Apes, Angels, and Victorians; a joint biography of Darwin and Huxley*, London, 1955, p. 112.

8 Moore's attitude towards evolution, although he was a correspondent of Darwin, is not accurately known. His opinion may have been something less than sympathetic, for in 1880 he was ready to question Darwin's work on insectivorous plants, specifically whether plants derived any benefit from being insectivorous. Moore concluded that Darwin's insectivorous plant theory was plausible, but mistaken. Moore prefaced his remarks with the comment that 'when any man, however great, ascends into the realm of uncertainty for arguments in support of his theory, he cannot be astonished at any effort which may be made to controvert them'. One is left with the impression that the criticism of plants as insectivores was merely a stalking-horse for evolutionary theory. C. Moore, 'Anniversary Address', *Journal and Proceedings, Royal Society of New South Wales*, Vol. 14 (1880), p. 16.

Drummond, another Darwinian correspondent, despite his advanced years, appeared to have been receptive to Darwin's theory. Isolated in Western Australia and dead within three years of *Origin*'s publication, he had little effect on the debate. Ronald Gunn, although not inclined much to theory, may also have accepted the evolutionary thesis. Gunn was enthusiastic about Darwin's *Journal of Researches*, calling it the 'best book of the kind I ever read', and recommending it to his friend Edmund Hobson. Gunn to Hobson, 16 June 1847, Hobson Papers, Box 865/1 A-C, La Trobe Library.

There is also a tantalizing hint that Gunn was open to evolutionary theory in a letter to him from Ferdinand Mueller. Mueller expressed no surprise that Gunn did not share Mueller's view on the fixity of species. Mueller to Gunn, 6/1/65, Gunn Papers A251, Mitchell Library.

9 *Life and Letters of the Right Honourable Robert Lowe Viscount Sherbrooke*, Vol. II, pp. 204–7.

10 Macleay to Clarke, 27 June 1863, Clarke Papers, Mitchell Library mss 139/11.

11 Mueller to Owen, 24 August 1861, Correspondence of Richard Owen, British Museum (NH). As quoted in A. Moyal, *Scientists in Nineteenth Century Australia, A Documentary History*.

12 Ibid.

[13] Darwin to Clarke, 25 October 1862, W.B. Clarke Papers, mss 139/36x (71–2).

[14] F. McCoy, 'On the Ancient and Recent Natural History of Victoria', *Catalogue of the Victorian Exhibition of 1861, with Prefatory Essays*, Melbourne, 1861.

[15] *University of Melbourne, Statutes and Regulations*, General Examination, Palaeontology, Melbourne, W. Fairfax, 1857.

[16] James to Baillieu, 21 December 1861, National Museum Letterbook, Vol. II, Museum of Victoria Library.

[17] National Museum Requisition Book, 17 August 1859 to 1 October 1872, Museum of Victoria Library.

[18] National Museum Letterbook, Vol. I, Museum of Victoria Library.

[19] James to Gerrard, 24 August 1861, National Museum Letterbook, Vol. I, Museum of Victoria Library.

[20] National Museum Letterbooks, 22 February, 24 May, 25 August 1862, and 25 August 1863, and 25 January, 25 March, 24 June, 24 September 1864, Vols I and II, Museum of Victoria Library.

[21] McCoy to Crisp, 25 January, 25 May 1864, National Museum Letterbook, Vol. II, Museum of Victoria Library.

[22] McCoy to Gerrard, 22 February 1865, National Museum Letterbook, Vol. II, Museum of Victoria Library.

[23] McCoy to Halford, 13 and 29 July 1863, National Museum Letterbook, Vol. II, Museum of Victoria Library.

[24] In the 1860s the gorilla was thought to be the primate anatomically most closely allied with man (the chimpanzee is now considered to be more related to *Homo sapiens*). In future years, as the anatomical argument for a clear separation between man and monkey was defeated, the argument changed to the mental and moral gap between humans and primates. Language, the ability to conceptualize, toolmaking, and the concept of a future time, are but some of the more recent attempts to establish a discontinuity between man and the primates.

[25] *Argus*, 17 July 1863.

[26] *Melbourne Punch*, 30 July 1863.

[27] *Melbourne Punch*, 13 July 1863.

[28] *Melbourne Punch*, 'Rather too much monkey', 13 August 1863; 'Groan from Monkeydom', 20 August 1863; 'More of the Gorilla', 5 November 1863.

[29] G. Halford, 'On the skeleton of the Gorilla', *Transactions, Royal Society of Victoria*, Vol. VII (1866), pp. 34–44.

[30] The *Transactions, Royal Society of Victoria* in the Museum of Victoria (successor to the National Museum presided over by McCoy), has disease crossed out and replaced by disuse.

[31] *Transactions, Royal Society of Victoria*, Vol. VII (1866), 24 July 1865, pp. 99–100.

[32] Mueller to Owen, 26 July 1865, Correspondence of Richard Owen, British Museum (NH).

[33] Ibid.

[34] T. Harrison, 'Victoria as a Field for Geologists', *Transactions, Royal Society of Victoria*, Vol. VII (1866), pp. 15–29.

[35] R. Ellery, 'President's Address', *Transactions, Royal Society of Victoria*, Vol. VIII (1867), p. xii.

[36] G. Halford, *Not Like Man, Bimanous and Biped nor yet Ouadrumanous but Cheiropodus*, Melbourne, 1863.

[37] *Australian Medical Journal*, Vol. VIII (1863), pp. 307–12; Vol. IX (1864) pp. 89–92; Vol. X (1865), pp. 215–17; Vol. XIII (1868), pp. 60–1. The *Medical Journal* also defended Halford in 1870 when his treatment of snakebite with ammonia came under attack in the British journal *Lancet*. *Australian Medical Journal*, Vol. XV (1870), pp. 148–9.

[38] G. Halford, *Lines of Demarkation Between Man, Gorilla & Macaque*, Melbourne, 1864.

[39] T. Harrison, 'Notes relative to the respective theories, Creation by Law, and Creation by Fact', *Transactions, Royal Society of Victoria*, Vol. IX (1868), p. 85; *Argus*, 10 August 1868.

[40] W. Clarke, 'Inaugural Address', *Transactions, Royal Society of New South Wales*, Vol. I (1867), pp. 1–27.

[41] *Recent geological discoveries in Australasia*, Sydney, 1861, 2nd edition.

[42] Darwin to Clarke, 25 October 1862, W.B. Clarke Papers, mss 139/36x (71–2), Mitchell Library. In this letter to Clarke, Darwin, replying to Clarke's earlier criticism, noted that he had

conceptually excluded New Zealand from the oceanic islands but should have been more guarded in his writing.

43 Krefft Papers, Mitchell Library A261.
44 H. Barkly, 'Inaugural Address', *Transactions, Royal Society of Victoria*, Vol. V (1860), pp. 1–17. The address was delivered on 10 April 1860.
45 H. Barkly, 'Anniversary Address', *Transactions, Royal Society of Victoria*, Vol. VI (1861), pp. xix–xxxiv, li; Vol. VI (1863), pp. li–lx.
46 W. Denison to Lady Charlotte Denison, 5 November 1860, *Varieties of Vice-Regal Life*, Vol. I, p. 495.
47 King to Darwin, 19 September 1862, Darwin Correspondence, Cambridge University Library, Manuscript Room.
48 W. Hearn, *Plutology, or the Theory of the Efforts to Satisfy Human Wants*, London, 1864.
49 Ibid., pp. 388, 389.
50 J. Tenison Woods, *Geological Observations in South Australia*, London, 1862.
51 R. Hanson, Prefatory Remarks, South Australian Pamphlets, Vol. 6, La Trobe Library.
52 *Sydney Morning Herald*, 26 June 1860.
53 *Sydney Morning Herald*, 12 November 1863. The Abbeville deposits in France, first uncovered in the late 1840s, seemed to establish that man had existed prior to 4,000 BC. Various naturalists such as Lyell and Flower visited the site and agreed that man's antiquity was greater than 6,000 years.
54 *Sydney Morning Herald*, 19 November 1863.
55 For instance, the Melbourne Public Library received a copy of *Origin* between 1861 and 1865, and the Free Public Library (Sydney) by 1872. *Origin* could also be found in the Sydney Mechanics' School of Arts library by 1862, the Parliamentary library of Queensland by 1869, the Richmond (Vic.) Public Library by 1875, the Ballarat Mechanics' Institute Library by 1864, and the Prahran Free Library (Vic.) by 1869. Brian Hubber has pointed out in an analysis of the readership of the Prahran Free Library that throughout the 1870s scientific works became increasingly popular and constituted up to eight per cent of the circulation figures by the mid-1880s. *Books, Libraries & Readers in Colonial Australia*, F. Morrison and M. Talbot (eds), 1985.
56 See for example the *Catalogue of the Ballaarat East Public Library* (1869).
57 Indicated by both institutions' accession lists.
58 Personal communication, Gwen Baker, librarian, Australian Museum.
59 William Archer, *Tourist to the Antipodes, William Archer's Australian Journey, 1876–77*, St Lucia (Qld), 1977.
60 *Melbourne Punch*, 24 June 1869.
61 *Argus*, 1 July 1869.
62 *Age*, 1 July 1869.
63 *Argus* 23 and 24 July, 20 August 1869.
64 F. McCoy, 'The Order & Plan of Creation', *Lectures delivered before the Early Closing Association, 1869–70*, Melbourne, 1870.
65 *Age*, 29 June 1869.
66 J. Bromby, *Pre-historic Man*, 1869.
67 *Argus*, 21 September 1869. Alfred Howitt, a late convert to Darwinian theory in 1874, entertained the visiting Perry in Gippsland in 1873 and noted Perry's aversion to 'modern scientific beliefs'. M. Howitt, *Come wind, come weather; a biography of Alfred Howitt*, Melbourne, 1971, p. 180.
68 *Age*, 5 July 1870.
69 For the origins of McCoy's journalistic career, see McCoy to Hurst, 26 July 1869, La Trobe Library Box 169/1.
70 'Microzoon', 'Why is Australia Odd', 6 August, 17 and 24 September 1870; 'Our Colonial Mollusca—No. 1 Oysters', 2 July 1870, *Australasian*.
71 J. Bromby, 'Creation versus development', *Lectures delivered before the Early Closing Association, 1869–1870*, Melbourne, 1870.
72 C. Perry, 'Creation vs Development', reprinted from the *Church of England Messenger*, 1870, La Trobe Library.
73 Krefft Papers, Mitchell Library A261.
74 Denison was much taken with Krefft and they maintained a correspondence for years (1861–

67). Denison, while governor of Madras, arranged for Indian specimens to be sent to the Australian Museum. In turn, Krefft supplied bird eggs and shells to Denison's son. Denison and Krefft were, given the social distance between the two men, sufficiently friendly for Denison to joke with Krefft about his 'decidedly snaky taste', a reference to Krefft's extensive work on snakes, and to comment to him about Huxley's *Man's Place in Nature*. Denison's derisive views on the latter subject were outlined in a letter to Krefft. Denison to Krefft, 29 November 1862; 7 June 1863; 28 August undated year, Krefft Papers, Mitchell Library A262.

75 Krefft Papers, Mitchell Library A261.

76 Pittard to Krefft, 15 June 1860, Krefft Papers, Mitchell Library A267.

77 Krefft Papers, Mitchell Library A267.

78 Krefft to Colonial Secretary, 5 December 1861, Krefft Papers, Mitchell Library A267.

79 Krefft Papers, Mitchell Library A262.

80 Louis Frazer apparently also fell victim to William J. Macleay. A letter from Macleay to Krefft noted that Frazer seemed fluent in the classification of mammals and birds, but suggested that Frazer's grammar and spelling were insufficient for the office of secretary to the Museum, a position occupied jointly by the person appointed curator. W.J. Macleay to Krefft, 1 January 1862, Mitchell Library mss 956.

81 R. Owen, 'On the fossil mammals of Australia. Part I. Description of a mutilated Skull of the large marsupial carnivore (Thylacoleo carnifex Owen) from a calcareous conglomerate stratum, eighty miles S. W. of Melbourne, Victoria', *Philosophical Transactions, Royal Society*, Vol. CXLIX (1859), pp. 309–22.

82 *Sydney Morning Herald*, 1 January 1859.

83 Owen to Krefft, 5 September 1866, Krefft Correspondence, Mitchell Library mss. 956.

84 G. Krefft, 'On the dentition of the Thylacoleo carnifex', *Annals and Magazine of Natural History*, Vol. XVIII (1866), series 3, pp. 148–9. During 1868 Krefft questioned the expertise of a second University of Melbourne stalwart, George Halford. Krefft, who had considerable expertise in herpetology, suggested Halford's injection of ammonia into veins as a cure for snakebite was much less effective than cutting open the wound, sucking out the poison, and washing the wound in urine. Letter to the editor, *Sydney Morning Herald*, 6 May 1868.

85 *Exploration of the caves and rivers of New South Wales, New South Wales Legislative Assembly, Votes and Proceedings*, Vol. V (1882), pp. 551–602.

86 A. Moyal in *Scientists in Nineteenth Century Australia; A Documentary History* implies that Krefft was correct in his analysis of the feeding habits of *Thylacoleo*. Such partisanship is always dangerous for a historian. T. Flannery of the Australian Museum suggests that scientific opinion has reversed, *Thylacoleo* now is considered to be, as Owen maintained all along, a carnivore. Personal communication, T. Flannery. See also several papers in *Carnivorous Marsupials*, Vol. II, M. Archer (ed.), Mosman (NSW), 1982.

87 Krefft to Clarke, 19 May 1870, W.B. Clarke Papers, mss. 139/48, Mitchell Library.

88 *Sydney Mail*, 18 May 1872.

89 *Sydney Mail*, 25 May 1872.

90 G. Krefft, 'A Cuverian principle in palaeontology, tested by evidence of an extinct leonine marsupial (Thylacoleo carnifex)', *Annals and Magazine of Natural History*, series 4, Vol. X (1872), pp. 169–182.

91 Owen to Krefft, 14 December 1872, Krefft Papers, Mitchell Library A262.

92 Flower to Krefft, 8 August 1872, Krefft Papers, Mitchell Library A262.

93 Gray to Krefft, 16 July 1872, Krefft Papers, Mitchell Library A262. Gray, after reading Krefft's earlier papers in the 1867 *Exhibition Catalogue* had wondered why Krefft adopted Owen's classification of mammals, contending that it was so incorrect and impracticable as to be unworkable. Gray to Krefft, 15 May 1867, Krefft Papers, Mitchell Library A262. In Krefft's 1867 essay 'Australian Vertebrata—Recent and Fossil', Krefft had based his classification on Owen's 'Cerebral System'. G. Krefft, 'Australian Vertebrata—Recent and Fossil', *Catalogue of the Natural and Industrial Products of New South Wales forwarded to the Paris Universal Exhibition of 1867*.

94 Woodward to Krefft, undated, Krefft Papers, Mitchell Library A262.

95 As cited in R. Macleod, 'Evolution and Richard Owen, 1830–1868; An Episode in Darwin's Century', *Isis*, Vol. 65 (1965), pp. 259–80. The two sides were also separated by their acceptance of evolutionary theory. Falconer was a friend of Darwin's and a convert to natural selection after

the publication of *Origin*. Flower was a colleague of Huxley's and helped him with primate dissections. At an 1862 meeting of the British Association, Flower severely criticized Owen.

[96] Stephens to Krefft, 24 June 1874, Krefft Papers, Mitchell Library A262.

[97] Krefft was later to proclaim his fellow countryman, Ernst Haeckel, professor of zoology at Jena, as 'the greatest of living naturalists' for having 'out-darwined Darwin'. Krefft to Parkes, 23 July 1874, Henry Parkes Correspondence, Vol. 20, Mitchell Library A890. Krefft may have been more influenced by Haeckel's advocacy of Darwinian theory than by Darwin himself.

[98] Krefft to Darwin, 15 May 1872, Darwin Correspondence, Cambridge University Library, Manuscript Room.

[99] Darwin to Krefft, 17 July 1872, Darwin Letters, Mitchell Library Ad1.

[100] Krefft to Darwin, undated, Darwin Correspondence, Cambridge University Library.

[101] Krefft to Darwin, 8 July 1873, Darwin Correspondence, Cambridge University Library.

[102] Krefft to R. Lydekker, 18 December 1880, Krefft Papers, Mitchell Library A262.

[103] Krefft to Darwin, 1 November 1873, Darwin Correspondence, Cambridge University Library.

[104] See 'Trustee-Ridden, 1860–1874', *Rare and Curious Specimens; An Illustrated History of the Australian Museum, 1827–1979*, R. Strahan (ed.), Sydney, 1979.

[105] Bennett to Owen, as cited in *Rare and Curious Specimens*, p. 34.

[106] Krefft to Gunther, 20 March 1874, Krefft–Gunther Correspondence, Mitchell Library mss 1937(1).

[107] Krefft to Darwin, October 1874, Darwin Correspondence, Cambridge University Library, Manuscript Room.

[108] Darwin to Krefft, 6 December 1876, Mitchell Library Ad1.

[109] Krefft to Gunther, 17 May 1874, Krefft–Gunther Correspondence, Mitchell Library mss 1937.

[110] One of the charges brought against Krefft by the trustees in ordering his dismissal was that he allowed indecent photographs to be kept and sold on the Museum premises. Some of the photographs referred to were apparently of Aboriginal men and women and were received from R. Daintree before being forwarded to Darwin. R. Daintree to Krefft, 28 June 1871, Krefft Papers, Mitchell Library A262. The committee investigating the charges could not agree that other photographs were classifiable as indecent. At least one of the latter was no more than a photograph of a classical painting. Mitchell Library mss 1937; Henry Parkes Correspondence, Mitchell Library A890, Vol. 20, undated statement of G. Krefft.

[111] J. Tenison Woods, 'History of Australian Tertiary Geology', *Proceedings, Royal Society of Tasmania*, 1876, pp. 76–8.

[112] As cited in M. Walker, *Come wind, come weather; a biography of Alfred Howitt*. The letter was dated 1874.

[113] F. de Castelnau, 'Notes on the edible fishes in Victoria', *London International Exhibition of 1873, Official Record*, Melbourne, 1873.

[114] R. Brough Smyth, 'Notes for Lectures, 1885–86', La Trobe Library mss 8781 Box 1176/4.

[115] For Fitzgerald's correspondence with Mueller, see the Mueller Correspondence, National Herbarium.

[116] R. Fitzgerald, *Australian Orchids*, Sydney, 1875.

[117] Darwin to Fitzgerald, 16 July 1875, Darwin letters to R.D. Fitzgerald, Mitchell Library A2546. Darwin was amazed that such a magnificent work could be printed in Sydney.

[118] *Age*, 22 April 1882.

[119] *Argus*, 22 April 1882.

GENERAL REFERENCES: CHAPTER EIGHT

D. Allen, *The Naturalist in Britain; A Social History*, London, 1976.

D. Layton, *Science for the People; The Origin of the school science curriculum in England*, London, 1973.

ENDNOTES: CHAPTER EIGHT

[1] Lynn Barber, *The Heyday of Natural History*, London, 1980, p. 294.

[2] Many of the books were even called catechisms: for instance, Parkes' *Chemical Catechism* and Johnston's *The Catechism of Agricultural Chemistry and Geology*. Charles Darwin was introduced to chemistry via the first of these. C. Russell, *Science and Social Change, 1700–1900*, p. 153.

3 Anonymous, 'Extraordinary Sounds', *A Mother's Offering to her Children*, Sydney, 1841.

4 'A Short Dissertation on Insects', *Sketches from Nature*; 'Sea Shells', *A Mother's Offering*, pp. 63–4.

5 'The Purple Beetle', p. 92; 'Sea Shells', p. 161, *A Mother's Offering*.

6 Richard Bourke, governor of New South Wales, suggested setting up the New South Wales system of national schools in 1833. Prior to this time Church of England schools dominated primary education in the colony. Bourke's recommendations, bitterly opposed by the Presbyterian firebrand J.D. Lang, and drawing opposition from other quarters, were not implemented until 1848. In Tasmania, John Franklin, although sympathetic to the Anglican claim to primacy in education, also supervised the implementation of the Irish national system.

7 For a list of the recommended books in 1854 see the *Second Report of the Commissioners of National Education*. Copies of this report and most of the others cited below can be found in the Victorian Ministry of Education Library, Melbourne.

8 The texts relevant to science and recommended by the commissioners of national education were: M'Gauley's *Lectures on Natural Philosophy*; Hodge's *Agricultural Chemistry*; Paterson's *First Steps to Zoology*, Part I, Invertebrate animals; Paterson's *First Steps to Zoology*, Part II, Vertebrate animals; Paterson's *Zoology for Schools*, Part I, Invertebrate animals; Paterson's *Zoology for Schools*, Part II, Vertebrate animals; sets of illustrations for Paterson's texts. As a comparison, the British Committee on Education listed eighteen books on geology, twenty-one on botany, thirty-two on zoology, twenty-eight on chemistry and fifty-eight on natural philosophy. Cited in D. Layton, *Science for the People*, p. 111.

    The Reverend James M'Gauley's *Lectures on Natural Philosophy*, in its 5th edition by 1857, was written to teach the teachers. Pupils received the information secondhand via dictation or the blackboard. Part I of the book devoted chapters to mechanics, hydrostatics, pneumatics, optics, electricity, galvanism, magnetism, electro-magnetism, heat and the steamboat. Part II covered chemistry. The book was a mixture of the theoretical and the practical; the chapter on pneumatics treated the theory of sound propagation as well as the design of rooms for lectures. M'Gauley was a former professor of natural philosophy and connected with the Irish National Board of Education. *Second Annual Report of the Commissioners of National Education for the Colony of Victoria*, 1854.

    Robert Paterson's *First Steps in Zoology* (2nd edition, 1850) was written for the English school system and many of the species included were of limited relevance to Australian students. Those Australian peculiarities which found their way into the text, the kangaroo and the platypus, were the subject of European paternalism. The section on marsupials commenced with a quotation from Shakespeare implying that marsupials had been left unfinished by their maker. Much, if not all, of the information on the Australian animals would have already been familiar to Australian children. Despite their faults the Paterson volumes were useful tracts. They avoided the anecdotal style of many contemporary volumes and excluded the romantic anthropomorphism of others. In the struggle between anecdote and fact that characterized many nineteenth century natural history books, facts clearly won here.

9 The education of the children on the goldfields constantly concerned educationalists throughout the 1850s and 1860s. Frank Tate, later to re-organize Victorian education, was a child of this fluctuating environment.

10 *Denominational School Board, Report of Proceedings for 1856–7*.

11 'Education in Science', *Sydney Magazine of Science and Art*, Vol. I (November 1857), pp. 119–20.

12 M. Faraday, 'Science as a Branch of Education', *Sydney Magazine of Science and Art*, Volume II (December 1858), pp. 110–12. Faraday joined a list of English scholars including William Whewell, James Paget, Thomas Huxley, Herbert Spencer, Richard Owen, Joseph Hooker and John Herschel, all of whom advocated the inclusion of science as part of a liberal education.

13 General Report from A.B. Ortebar. *Third report of the Board of Commissioners of National Education*, 1855–56.

14 *Fourth Reading Book of the Commissioners of National Education*, Ireland New Edition, revised and adapted for the use in schools in Australia, Tasmania, and New Zealand, 1876.

15 J. Hooker, *Botany*, London, 1878.

16 T. Ralph, *Elementary Botany for the use of beginners* (Australian edition), Melbourne, 1862. Ralph inserted a note into the book indicating his willingness to form botanical classes in connection with schools.

17 F. Mueller, *Introduction to Botanic Teaching at the schools Of Victoria*, Melbourne, 1877.

18 W. Guilfoyle, *First Book; Australian Botany designed for the use of schools*, Melbourne, 1878.
19 *Vision and Realization*, L.J. Blake (ed.), Melbourne, 1973, p. 141.
20 The *Quadrilateral* for the year 1874, pp. 87–9.
21 T. Huxley, 'Address on University Education', *Science and Education Essays*, London, 1929.
22 C. Pearson, *Report on the State of Public Education in Victoria*, Royal Commission of Enquiry, 1878.
23 *Report of the Minister for Public Education for 1881–2*, p. xv.
24 *Southern Science Record*, February 1871.
25 Report of J. Dennant for 1881, *Report of the Minister for Public Education,* 1881–82, p. 218.
26 Report of R.F. Russell, *Report of the Minister for Public Education*, 1880–81, p. 219.
27 Reports of J Dennant, R.F. Russell, S. Were, J. Liang, and A. Dean, Inspector's Reports for the year 1889, *Report of the Minister for Public Education*, 1889
28 Report of W. Hamilton, Inspector's Reports for the year 1889, *Report of the Minister for Public Education*, 1889.
29 J. Stewart, *Questions in Science, General Lessons, History, etc with answers for State School Scholars*, Melbourne, 1889; W.R. Smith, *Object and General lessons for Victorian State Schools*, Geelong, 1888; for object lesson material designed for use by teachers see L.C. Miall, *Object Lessons from Nature: A First Book of Science*, Part I, London, 1890.
30 From statistics compiled by L. Gillbank from the *Reports of the Minister for Public Education*, 1880–89.
31 The anecdotal approach to natural history was still available for home use. Books on the subject ranged from the English *Peter Paley's Tales about animals*, which had reached its 14th edition by 1875 and included Australian animals (the dingo, platypus and kangaroo), to local publications represented by Louisa Anne Meredith's alliteratively titled *Tasmanian Friends and Foes, Feathered, Furred and Finned*. Meredith's book continued the tradition of conversational texts but the quality of writing was far superior to many previous efforts. Disclaiming any scientific expertise, Meredith nonetheless insisted that all the incidents were true and the anecdotes factual. Scientific names for some of the animals mentioned in the book had been supplied by Frederick McCoy. L. Meredith, *Tasmanian Friends and Foes, Feathered, Furred and Finned: A Family Chronicle of Country Life, Natural History and Veritable Adventure*, Hobart, 1880.
32 *Annual Report*, School of Mines, Ballarat, 1883.
33 *Annual Report*, School of Mines, Ballarat, 1889.
34 In 1885 the average teacher attendance was: chemistry, twenty-four; botany, thirteen; natural philosophy, twelve; physiology, four; geology, two; and mineralogy, two. *Annual Report*, School of Mines, Ballarat, 1885.
35 *Annual Report*, School of Mines, 1885 and 1889.
36 The Field Naturalist's Society of New South Wales gained the approval of the minister for public instruction to distribute a circular which publicized its goals to state schools. The Society provided for junior members (under sixteen) who paid one shilling per annum fee rather than the five shillings of ordinary members. In 1890 the Society contained twenty-four junior members out of a total of 107.

   In Melbourne, the Field Naturalist's Club of Victoria intended offering prizes to state school scholars for the best natural history collections. For some years this FNCV initiative was limited to discussion for the Club lacked sufficient funds and was unable to obtain government finance for the undertaking. The Field Naturalist's Club of Victoria also encouraged young people to attend its elementary meetings where talks were given on collecting and preserving specimens.
37 A. Liversidge, 'President's Address', *Transactions, Royal Society of New South Wales*, Vol. XX (1886), pp. 1–41.
38 In 1888 the Chancellor of the University of Sydney, William Manning, in addressing the first meeting of AAAS had the temerity to suggest that perhaps too great an emphasis on scientific 'ologies' would result in neglect of general education. 'Science and Art', *Echo*, 31 August 1888; *Sydney Morning Herald*, 1 September 1888; *Daily Telegraph*, 5 September 1888, AAAS Newspaper Clipping mss 988/89, Mitchell Library.
39 E. Field, 'The Practical Values of Physiology', *Victorian Review*, Vol. II (1880), pp. 464–77. Field's article was a not very successful attempt to place a utilitarian value on physiology.
40 C. Long, *Science Work Simplified, Lessons on the Physics and Chemistry Subjects in the Programme of Instruction for IV, V, VI Classes in the Victorian State Schools*, 1892. Long also lectured on the subject of teaching science at the teacher training institution. A. Dendy and A.H.S. Lucas, *An Introduction*

to the Study of Botany with a special chapter on some Australian Natural Orders, Melbourne, 1892.

41 A. Liversidge, 'President's Address', *Transactions, Royal Society of New South Wales*, Vol. XX (1886), pp. 14–15.

42 *Sydney Morning Herald*, 18 September 1880; 31 July 1882.

43 *Sydney Morning Herald*, 31 July 1882.

44 *Sydney Morning Herald*, 18 September 1880.

45 The *Southern Science Record* was not the first popular journal devoted to science (as opposed to Royal Society *Transactions*). The *Sydney Magazine of Science and Art* (1857–59), despite the inclusion of 'Art' in its title had little to say on that subject with the exception of an occasional article on architecture. It was primarily devoted to a mixture of the practical technology and science. Representative articles included: 'The Sanitary condition of Sydney', 'The Moon's rotation', 'Chemistry in the wine cellar', and 'On the structure and functions of the venom apparatus of serpents'. The magazine's contributions, some written by Sydney authors, others reprinted from British or American journals, tended to be pitched at a popular level reflecting the journal's use as the proceedings of the Australian Horticultural and Agricultural Society, rather than its similar association with the Philosophical Society of New South Wales. The magazine ceased publication in 1859.

46 FNCV Minutebook, Vol. I, 6 November 1882.

47 FNCV Minutebook, Vol. I, 5 November 1883.

48 *Southern Science Record*, Vol. I (December 1880).

49 A. Moyal, *Scientists in Nineteenth Century Australia; A Documentary History*, Melbourne, 1975, p. 189.

50 M. Evans, 'Taking to the Bush; Australia's Landscape as a condition of practice for the Field Naturalist's Club of Victoria, 1880–1900', Honours thesis, University of Melbourne, 1983, pp. 24–5.

51 FNCV Minutebook, 1 and 9 August 1880; Best's words were recorded in the *Southern Science Record* as 'it is a question of whether new species are not continually being evolved'. Best seems to have credited evolution with an unlikely rate of change. D. Best, 'Longicorn Beetles of Victoria', *Southern Science Record*, Vol. I (1880), p. 6.

52 Newspaper cutting pasted into FNCV Minutebook, Vol. I (1880).

53 FNCV Minutebook, Vol. I, 6 November 1882.

54 In August 1884 the FNCV granted Mueller the privilege of publishing papers not previously read before the Club in their journal in return for Mueller's offer of subsidizing the printing of such papers at five shillings per page. FNCV Minutebook, Vol. II, 4 August 1884. At a subsequent committee meeting this privilege was extended to other contributors to the *Victorian Naturalist*. FNCV Minutebook, Vol. II, 1 September 1884.

55 See for example, FNCV Minutebook, Vol. II, 3 December 1883, 14 January 1884.

56 A. Sutherland, 'The vanishing boundary between the animate and the inanimate', read before the Royal Society of Victoria, 1882, *Southern Science Record*, Vol. II (1882), pp. 119–23; Anon., 'The distinction between the living and the non-living', *Southern Science Record*, pp. 143–48.

57 FNCV Membership Register, 1880–94.

58 FNCV Minutebook, Vol. II, 21 April 1884.

59 4th Annual Meeting, FNCV Minutebook, Vol. II, 12 May 1884.

60 As quoted in 'Preliminary Announcement', *The Australian Journal of Science*, Liversidge Papers, University of Sydney Archives, Box 9.

61 *General Rules*, 1887, Natural History Association of News South Wales, Mitchell Library.

62 Annual Report, Field Naturalist's Society of New South Wales, Mitchell Library. The continued subordination of the Field Naturalist's Society to the Sydney Mechanics' School of Arts was indicated by a rule stipulating that the Society's council was responsible to the committee of the Sydney Mechanics' School of Arts.

63 Field Naturalist's Society Programmes, 1891, Mitchell Library.

64 Ibid.

65 D. Allen, *The Naturalist in Britain; A Social History*, p. 158.

66 Circulars, 23 February, 8 March 1894, Inserted into the Museum of Victoria's copy of the Society's Annual Reports.

67 One exception was Field Naturalist's Society member J.H. Maiden, who was also active in AAAS. A second example of this relationship was the natural history section of the Royal Society

of South Australia. Only one of the twelve men who were to become officers or committee members of the natural history section was a member of AAAS when it met in Sydney in 1888. By 1893, when AAAS met in Adelaide, seven of the twelve officials belonged to AAAS and two, J. Tepper and W. Howchin, gave papers. By the 1895 Brisbane meeting only three, Dixson, Tepper and Howchin, retained their AAAS membership. List of Members, *Report of AAAS*, 1888, 1893, 1895; List of Members, Field Naturalist's Section, *Transactions, Royal Society of South Australia*, 1891–92, 1892–93.

68 In 1885 a further organization, the Geological Society of Australasia, made its appearance in Melbourne under the impetus of R.T. Litton, founding honourary secretary and editor of its *Transactions*. Despite the 'Australasia' in its title, the Geological Society remained Melbourne-bound for most of its existence. The Society initially emphasized the role of the amateur geologist, for Litton saw the Society as the geological counterpart of the Field Naturalist's Club of Victoria. In later years the Society gradually took on a more professional character, geologists such as James Stirling, T. Edgeworth David and F.W. Hutton all held office at times. The emphasis on professionalism became more marked subsequent to Litton's relinquishing a dominant role in the Society.

69 *Ballarat Courier*, 26 June 1882. The Ballarat Field Club and Science Society had a close contemporary in the Bendigo School of Mines Science Society, although the latter had a more tenuous existence than its counterpart. It commenced in 1881 under the dual aegis of Robert Brough Smyth, installed as director of the School of Mines some years after his removal as secretary of mines for Victoria, and P.H. MacGillivray, who became vice-president of the School of Mines. These two men dominated the proceedings of the Society in its early years. The latter half of the 1880s saw the decline of the Bendigo Society but it was re-established in 1888. *Annual Report*, School of Mines, Bendigo, 1889. The Society remained extant until at least 1893. *Annual Report*, School of Mines, Bendigo, 1893.

70 *Ballarat Courier*, 26 June 1882. The extent to which Krause dominated the BFC&SS is evident from newspaper reports on the Club's activities in 1882: 22 July—excursion predominantly geology and mineralogy, 27 July—Krause lectured on geological features, 31 July—Krause led an excursion, 5 October—Krause gave a lecture on a comet, 2 November—excursion limited to botany because Krause absent, *Ballarat Courier*.

71 *Rules of the Ballarat Field Club and Science Society*. Appended to *Annual Report*, School of Mines, Ballarat, 1882.

72 *Annual Report*, School of Mines, Ballarat, 1882.

73 *Southern Science Record*, Vol. I (1880–81), pp. 121–6, 151–6.

74 *Ballarat Courier*, 28 June 1883.

75 *Annual Report*, School of Mines, Ballarat, 1883.

76 *Annual Report*, School of Mines, Ballarat, 1882, pp. 25–6.

77 John Garibaldi Roberts Collection, 22 November 1882, Envelope 14, La Trobe Library ms 8509 Bay 10/2c.

78 *Ballarat Courier*, 28 June 1883.

79 List of Members, *Transactions, Royal Society of Victoria*, Vol. XXIII (1886).

80 Science Lectures, 1882, Ballarat Council of the School of Mines, 1883.

GENERAL REFERENCES: CHAPTER NINE

L. Barber, *The Heyday of Natural History*, London, 1980.
G. Blainey, *A Centenary History of the University of Melbourne*, Melbourne, 1957.
S.F. Cannon, *Science in Culture; the Early Victorian Period*, New York, 1978.
K. Dugan, 'Marsupials and Monotremes in pre-Darwinian Theory', PhD dissertation, University of Kansas, 1980.
——'The Zoological Exploration of the Australian Region and its impact on biological theory', *Scientific Colonialism, 1800–1930: A Cross Cultural Comparison*, Melbourne, 1986.
M.E. Hoare, 'The Intercolonial Science Movement in Australasia, 1870–1890', *Records, Australian Academy of Science*, Vol. 3(2) (1976), pp. 7–28.
D. Layton, *Science for the People; The Origin of the School Science Curriculum in England*, London, 1973.
E. Scott, *A History of the University of Melbourne*, Melbourne, 1936.

ENDNOTES: CHAPTER NINE

1 W. Whewell, *The Philosophy of the Inductive Sciences, founded upon their history*, London, 1840. Whewell emphasized biology as distinct from physiology because he felt the latter was not carefully defined.

2 Evolution and natural selection not so much ended the sterile debate of eighteenth and nineteenth century naturalists over natural or artificial classifications as reduced it to irrelevance. Species were neither eternally fixed natural verities, nor artificial and arbitrary entities.

3 E. Sanger, 'Modern Biology', *Victorian Review*, Vol. II (May to October 1880), pp. 350–8.

4 RL, 'Botany—The Old and the New', *Australasian Scientific Magazine*, 1 October 1885, pp. 96–8.

5 RL, 'Botany—The Old and the New', *Australasian Scientific Magazine*, October 1885.

6 W. Haswell, 'President's Address', *Report of AAAS*, Vol. III (1891), pp. 173–92.

7 This argument was usually based on the assumption that the increasing complexity of science required full-time attention to a specific discipline and was therefore placed beyond the reach of the talented amateur. A typical case cited in early nineteenth century natural history was the replacement of Linnaean botanical taxonomy (its limited number of obvious morphological characteristics made it appropriate to amateur science) by natural classifications (which, because they evaluated a broad range of often obscure characteristics, required the attention of professional scientists). One objection to this concept that science is limited to professionals is the role of creativity. There is no certitude that professional scientists have any greater claim to scientific creativity than do amateurs. In fact, the rigid specialization of most scientists, while helpful for filling in the gaps of scientific theories, may be counterproductive in that it locks them into conceptual straitjackets.

8 Michael Evans has argued that the disparity between amateur natural history as exemplified by the Field Naturalist's Club of Victoria and professional science was a 'basic misreading of the structure of the scientific community'. M. Evans, 'Taking to the Bush; Australian Landscape as a condition of practice for the Field Naturalist's Club of Victoria, 1880–1900', Honours Thesis, University of Melbourne. Evans is undoubtedly correct in seeing field naturalists' clubs as an alternative to professional science, but rather than a misinterpretation of what professional science was about, I feel the explanation lies in the different traditions from which each sprang. Field naturalists' clubs were a continuation of an ideology that had its roots in natural theology and rational amusement, a tradition based on humanism. Professional science was born in the crucible of empiricism and tempered in the forge of positivism.

9 'Introduction', *Victorian Naturalist*, Vol. I (1884), p. 1.

10 A trend common to most field naturalists' clubs was the initial organization of an ambitious and extensive programme of field excursions, after which the clubs slowly evolved more sedentary habits. The number of evening meetings increased while the number of field excursions declined.

11 *Annual Report*, 1891–92, Field Naturalist's Section of the Royal Society of South Australia, 17 October 1891, 'Excursion to Horsnell's Gully. Similar reports can be found in the proceedings of almost all of the field naturalists' clubs. See for instance, Ballarat Field Club and Science Society, *Ballarat Courier*, 22 July 1882; Field Naturalist's Club of Victoria, *Victorian Naturalist*, Vol. I (1884), pp. 83, 98, 110, 112, etc.

12 David Allen has pointed out that natural history was tied to an aesthetic ideal. D. Allen, *The Naturalist in Britain; A Social History*, Chapter Two, 'The Rise to Fashion'.

13 E. Bage, 'Victorian Pond Life', *Southern Science Record*, Vol. I(3) (February 1881), pp. 40–4.

14 See for instance 'The Use of the Camera in Natural History Work', reprinted in the *Wombat*, Vol. I(3) (1895), pp. 54–6, from *Photography*. 'However much the woodcuts of Berwick or the drawings of Joseph Wolfe may be admired, there can be no doubt that the witness of the camera comes first in order of authenticity . . .'; also D. Le Souef, 'The use of photography to a naturalist', *Wombat*, Vol. II(4) (1896), pp. 17–18.

15 *Report of AAAS*, Vol. I (1888), p. 176; *Report of AAAS*, Vol. II (1890), p. 394.

16 W. Haswell, 'Notes on the Muscular Fibres of Peripatus', *Report of AAAS*, Vol. II (1890), pp. 487–8.

17 W.B. Spencer, 'The fauna and zoological relationships of Tasmania', *Report of AAAS*, Vol. IV (1892), pp. 82–124; A. Dendy, 'The Cryptozoic Fauna of Australasia', *Report of AAAS*, Vol. VI (1895), pp. 99–119.

18 Major exceptions to this continued reliance on microscopic biology were papers detailing the

chemical analysis of foodstuffs or items of potential commercial value. J. Maiden, E. Rennie, W. Hamlet and W. Wilkinson all contributed articles of this type to the *Transactions* of the various royal societies and the Linnean Society. Other exceptions were few in number. W. Dixon's papers on the organic constituents of epiphytic ferns and orchids, D. McAlpine's papers on physiology and N. Cobb's 'Two new instruments for biologists', were slight encroachments of instrumental biology on microscopic biology.

[19] A. Thomas, 'Presidential Address', *Report of AAAS*, Vol. II (1890), pp. 100–9.

[20] Recent book length studies on the early history of the BA include: R. MacLeod and P. Collins (eds), *The Parliament of Science; The British Association for the Advancement of Science 1831–1981*, Norwood, 1981; J. Morrell and A. Thackray, *Gentlemen of Science; Early Years of the British Association for the Advancement of Science*, Oxford, 1981; and its companion volume, Morrell and Thackray, *Gentlemen of Science; Early Correspondence of the British Association for the Advancement of Science*, London, 1984.

[21] Liversidge's European tour was a multifaceted affair. Liversidge examined the state of technical education, and scientific and technological museums while in Europe. He also represented New South Wales and New Zealand at the Paris Exhibition of 1878. Liversidge Papers, University of Sydney Archives, Box 9. This grand tour began to establish Liversidge as one of the senior statesmen of Australian science.

[22] A. Liversidge, 'The International Congress of Geologists, Paris, 1878', *Journal and Proceedings, Royal Society of New South Wales*, Vol. XIII (1879), pp. 35–42.

[23] A. Liverside, 'President's Address', *Journal and Proceedings, Royal Society of New South Wales*, Vol. XX (1886), pp. 1–41; see also *Sydney Morning Herald*, 16 September 1884.

[24] In 1884 William Caldwell, a Cambridge zoologist working on the Burnett River in Queensland, acquired a platypus which had just laid one egg and retained another in its body. Caldwell sent a telegram message to Liverside in Sydney requesting him to forward the news to the Montreal meeting of the BA. There the succinct message 'Monotremes oviparious, ovum meroblastic' was read on 2 September, 1884. H. Burrell, *The Platypus: its discovery, zoological position, form and characteristics, habits, life history, etc.*, Sydney, 1927. Ironically the message was then cabled back to Sydney via London and became distorted. The *Sydney Morning Herald* announced to its readers that monotremes were viviparous. K. Dugan, 'The Zoological Exploration of the Australian Region and its impact on biological theory', *Scientific Colonialism, 1800–1930: A Cross Cultural Comparison*, Melbourne,1986. Before returning to Cambridge, Caldwell briefly addressed the Royal Society of New South Wales on his discovery. In a somewhat condescending manner, Caldwell asserted that he only gave facts, it was possible to disbelieve them, but they were not open to argument.

The issue of monotreme reproduction had not disappeared from the minds of Australian naturalists prior to Caldwell's work. George Bennett had anxiously been trying to solve the riddle. P. MacGillivray gave a lecture to the Bendigo School of Mines Science Society on the state of knowledge of platypus reproduction on 15 September 1884, noting that all the relevant knowledge on the subject was attributable to Bennett and Owen. On 17 November MacGillivray again reported on the platypus after having dissected five specimens. At this second lecture MacGillivray noted both Caldwell's announcement of the oviparity of the platypus, as well as an announcement before the Royal Society of South Australia of the observation of an echidna with an egg in its pouch. School of Mines and Industries, Bendigo, *Annual Report*, 1885, pp. 13, 46–7. W. Haake, director of the South Australian Museum, had exhibited the egg in question to the meeting. The relative lack of publicity given to Haake's announcement, as opposed to Caldwell's telegram, is often cited as an example of the British disinclination to accept colonial evidence. K. Dugan, 'The Zoological Exploration of the Australian Region and its impact on biological theory', *Scientific Colonialism, 1800–1930: A Cross Cultural Comparison*, Melbourne, 1986.

[25] Circular, 31 July 1886, AAAS Minutebook 1, Mitchell Library mss 988/1.

[26] M.E. Hoare, 'The Intercolonial Science Movement in Australasia, 1870–1890', *Records, Australian Academy of Science*, Vol. 3(2) (1976), pp. 7–28.

[27] *Mercury*, 6 January 1892.

[28] J. Hector, 'Inaugural Address', *Report of AAAS*, Vol. III (1891), p. 4.

[29] *Report of AAAS*, Vol. I (1888), p. 10.

[30] *South Australian Register*, 2 October 1893.

[31] *Sydney Morning Herald*, 11 August 1888.

[32] *Argus*, 7 and 11 January 1890.

33 The initial ten sectional committees were A—Astronomy, Mathematics, Physics and Mechanics; B—Chemistry and Mineralogy; C—Geology and Palaeontology; D—Biology; E—Geography; F—Economic and Social Science, and Statistics; G—Anthropology; H—Sanitary Science and Hygiene; I—Literature and Fine Arts; J—Architecture and Engineering. *Report of AAAS*, Vol. I (1888), p. xiv.

34 Those of direct interest to natural history included the Australasian Biological Station Committee (proposed by Haswell), the Australasian Biological Biographical Committee (Spencer), the Protection of Native Birds and Mammals Committee (Spencer), the Australasian Mineral Census Committee (Liversidge), the Australasian Glacial Evidence Committee (Liversidge), the Australasian Seismological Committee (Liversidge), the Australasian Antarctic Exploration Committee (Barnard) and the Australasian Geological Record Committee (Jack). AAAS Minutebook, General Meeting, 3 September 1888.

35 *Report of AAAS*, Vol. I (1888), pp. xxxii–xxxiv.

36 H. Russell, 'Presidential Address', *Report of AAAS*, Vol. I (1888), pp. 1–19.

37 *Report of AAAS*, Vol. I (1888), pp. 20–1. Some New Zealand societies such as the Westland Naturalist and Acclimatization Society were included on the list, but this may have reflected the need for AAAS to have a wide geographic spread rather than any perceived merit of the societies.

38 *Annual Report*, Field Naturalist's Society of New South Wales, 1890–91.

39 *Ballarat Courier*, 28 June 1883, report of the Annual Meeting held 27 June, 1883.

40 A scheme for the organization and direction of the efforts of amateur collectors, Adelaide, 1880.

41 *Southern Science Record*, Vol. I (1) (December 1880), p. 16.

42 H. Russell, 'President's Address', *Report of AAAS*, Vol. I (1888), p. 11.

43 Ibid., p. 12.

44 This quotation comes from a report compiled at the request of and submitted to the University of Sydney. A. Liversidge, *Report upon certain museums for technology, science and art, also upon scientific, professional and technical instruction and systems of evening classes in Great Britain and on the continent of Europe*, Sydney, 1880. Liversidge's view paraphrased that of Thomas Huxley on professional education. It is worth noting that neither man had followed this educational route himself.

45 W. Fairfax, *Handbook of Australasia*, Melbourne, 1859.

46 University of Melbourne, *Calendar*, 1889.

47 The establishment of the chair of biology came at the instigation of A. Lucas and Charles Topp. A. Lucas, *A.H.S. Lucas, Scientist, his own story*, Sydney, 1937.

48 H. Russell, 'President's Address', *Report of AAAS*, Vol. I (1888), pp. 1–19.

49 Ibid.

50 E. Rennie, 'Presidential Address', *Report of AAAS*, Vol. II (1890) pp. 55–6. See also R. Hamilton, 'Inaugural Address', *Report of AAAS*, Vol. IV (1892), pp. 1–30. The interests of opposition groups were also aired. In 1891 Reginald Murray's 'President's Address' to Section C (Geology and Mineralogy) suggested that in relatively immature countries, science should be directed towards objectives materially useful to the community. This attitude, however, was not typical, and was perhaps predictable given the title of Murray's talk, 'The Past and Future of Mining in Victoria'. R. Murray, 'President's Address', *Report of AAAS*, Vol. III (1891), pp. 119–27.

INDEX

179